different

Than I Was Yesterday

LEARNING TO GROW IN CHRIST

Michael Govan

LUCIDBOOKS

This book and all that it contains is dedicated to my very best friend and greatest supporter, my dear wife, Linda. Everything that God has allowed me to accomplish since I have known her has always been blessed with her grace, support, and loving encouragement. I see her fingerprint on every part of my life. My "one flesh" is certainly the most amazing gift from God I have ever received. Thank you, Linda.

Your Loving Husband, Mike

Table of Contents

PART 3

PART 4

Special Thanks

I would like to take a moment to thank two very important people in my life of ministry. Pastor Chuck Newell and his loving wife, Dawn, came into our lives at a time when I had no idea what planting a church looked like, even though I was right in the middle of it.

Pastor Chuck, I will forever be thankful for how you taught me to build godly structure in our church and then lead in it. Most of the content in this book came to life after we met, and I can only conclude that you helped me hear the Holy Spirit better, as I watched you seek to hear Him yourself.

I think what inspired me the most was how well you and Dawn complement each other as you serve our Lord: you are truly a beautiful example of one flesh.

Thank you both so much. We love you with grateful hearts.

Foreword

I've known Mike Govan for over a decade, and I've had the privilege to serve with him side by side for the last several years—first in some counseling that we did together and then as part of the same team at Baptist Temple Church in McAllen, Texas. In that time, I've not only seen Mike's integrity, character, and leadership shine but I have witnessed him personally use, apply, and minister the very lessons you'll learn from this powerful book. I have seen Mike counsel people in their lowest depths, and I've seen him encourage them in the greatest moments of their lives. Mike has a calling and gifting from God that is powerful and unique, and in this book, he shares from his knowledge and experience in helping and counseling others from a biblical perspective. The methods and truths that you will gain from this book have been tried and tested over time, and God has blessed them because they are biblically sound and amazingly practical to incorporate in your life or to minister to others. Enjoy this powerful and practical read and let it bless you and be used to bless others.

Loui Canchola,
Pastor of Campus Development BT Church

Several years ago, Mike Govan and I were driving back from a conference in Austin. It had been a good one, and I think we talked the whole time, not turning on the radio at all. At the time, we both lived in McAllen, Texas. We were about an hour from home passing through the small town of Falfurrias. Mike was making a point to me, and as usual, he was backing up what he said with scripture. As you will see in this book, it's something he does consistently. I remember him saying to me, "Don't you see, Tom? This is God's desire for you! He loves you!" I was overwhelmed in the moment with the truth of the scripture he shared and how it applied to my situation. It connected with my heart and gave me the strength to make some much-needed changes in my life.

Mike is not only a very close friend, but at that time in my life, he was my personal counselor. I credit him for giving me so many marriage tools and enabling me to see Christ's call upon my life as a husband and father.

What Mike Govan has written is a guide, if you will, to navigate many of life's stickiest situations. All Mike's applications are backed up with scripture. I look forward to using this book in my own family as well as in my ministry. I wholeheartedly believe that this book will give you the same tools. Enjoy the journey!

Tom Weaver,
Senior Pastor, Mission Church

Preface

This book is designed to challenge you no matter what stage you currently find yourself in your Christian walk. Since God's truth is perfect and undeniable, I am certain that this book can even assist a nonbeliever in finding their way to the cross, because God's love for us is just that magnificent. Wherever His Word goes, its power to change lives is unstoppable.

Each chapter contains a series of questions that you can answer right on the spot; they are intended to challenge you and make you think. Hopefully, the questions will guide you to a better understanding of yourself and of the God who has gone to such great lengths to know you. My prayer is that each reader will have a life-changing experience—in at least one area of their lives, if not many.

Thank you for joining me on this journey, and may our loving God richly bless you.

PART 1

Life with Christ is both the greatest experience of true rest and the greatest adventure of all time. There is no rest like knowing that who you are in Christ is all you ever need to be. There is likewise no adventure like giving Jesus your yes in all areas as you joyfully surrender your will to His. While these two realities seem to be in contradiction to man, in Christ they are the components of life to the fullest.

—Pastor Chris Dupree, BT Church

Chapter 1

Jesus Is Sovereign over All

My friends, the awesome story of Jesus calming the storm at the end of Mark chapter 4 is not just another one of the many miracles of Jesus. It's also one of the events that define the completeness of His sovereign authority over all creation. Throughout His earthly ministry, Jesus constantly expressed His divine nature, whether it be through the miracle of healing or by exposing what the pharisees were thinking.

Unfortunately, in a world that seems more and more out of control every day, this piece of the gospel story is hard for many to believe today. A lot of Christians look at this as something out of Hollywood, and they don't really take it seriously. But throughout all the Gospels, we find Jesus expressing full and total authority over all things and all situations. But we have seen only a snapshot of His power. God's unseen displays of power are just as incredible.

The same Jesus who calms the storms also forms the human heart and causes it to beat for the first time, which is still a mystery to modern science. And He is the same God who stops it when He chooses, too. Simply stated, God is the giver and taker of life (1 Sam. 2:6) and the maker of all things (John 1:3): *"All authority in heaven and earth has been given to me"* (Matt. 28:18).

The same Jesus who rose from the dead on the third day and wields complete control over everything created also stands as our advocate daily before the Father (1 John 2:1, Heb. 8:6). He does not miss one moment to intercede for us. For a Christian to allow themselves to be convinced they often walk alone is to believe one of the greatest lies the devil ever made up. Just look at some of the names He has been given in scripture:

Jehovah Jireh: "God Is My Provider" or "The God Who Sees to It" (Gen. 16:13)

Jehovah Shammah: "God Is My Abiding Presence" or "The Lord Is There" (Ezek. 48:35)

Jehovah Rapha: "The Lord Who Heals You"

Jehovah Rapha is a name that I just have to elaborate on. Since I have been a counselor, "The Lord Who Heals You" has been the most needed—perhaps for a lot of reasons one may not realize. But because God is the only one who can fully heal, Jehovah Rapha is who we call upon often because our God does not turn away and leave us to suffer. Here are some of the ways scripture describes what Jehovah Rapha does:

- Sickness and infirmity: Psalm 41:3
- Healing from mental affliction: Jonah 2:5–7
- Spiritual fatigue: Psalm 23:3
- Emotional suffering: Psalm 147:3
- Anxiety or worry: John 14:27
- General healing: Psalm 103:3

The moonlight will be as bright as the sunlight, and the sunlight will be seven times brighter—like the light of seven days—on the day that the LORD bandages his people's injuries and heals the wounds he inflicted.

—Isa. 30:26 CSB

I set this beautiful verse apart here because I marvel at the love God continues to show for a stiff-necked, rebellious people. I marvel because I include myself in that lot, because my sin isn't any different from the sin of men 100 or even 1,000 years ago, yet God still poured out the same amazing grace. Praise be to His merciful and mighty name.

Let's continue with some more of His names:

Bread of Life: John 6:32–35
Emmanuel, "God is With Us": Isaiah 7:14, Matthew 1:23
The Resurrection and the Life: John 11:25
The Way, the Truth, and the Life: John 14:6
Alpha and Omega: "The Beginning and the End"
The True Vine: John 15:1
Lord of Lords: 1 Timothy 6:15, Revelation 19:16
Lion of the Tribe of Judah: Revelation 5:5

These names are only a few of the many that try to describe the Living God. Each name is given to describe for us various characteristics of His many attributes, to the best of our ability to understand. We must also understand that God cannot be fully defined or fully described, but when we get to heaven, I believe our minds will be brought to full illumination of the depths of who He truly is.

Also keep in mind that the many names we find in scripture for God are meant to help us understand not only His authority but also the ways He chooses to use it. In just the short list of names above, we see the Living God exalted through His names as King, Savior, Healer, Provider, Conqueror, Abiding Presence, Lord and Master of all creation, and God who walks with us, just to mention a few.

I believe that God wants us to know this. So, the next time we feel that we have been abandoned or left alone, we can call out to "The God Who Is My Abiding Presence" (Jehovah Shammah) and know just by simply calling His name, that He is always there, just as He has promised. Isn't it something that, to some extent, we can be brought into the understanding of the hows and whys of God, just through the description of His name. Why does God want us to know how He works? So we can also tell others.

Now let's discuss control for a moment. We just saw a glimpse of what divine control looks like, through the meaning of some of His names. But when I consider my own feeble attempts to control my life, I realize that all I really end up with are a bunch of consequences for my choices. And I am certain that neither my plans nor my choices put one ripple in His Divine

Will or divert any of His plans by a single millimeter. Proverbs 16:9 affirms this: *"In their hearts humans plan their course, but the LORD establishes their steps"* (NIV).

Furthermore, God warns us through Proverbs 14:12 that *"There is a way that seems right to a man, but its end is the way to death,"* so try as we may, God's plan will always win, and it would no doubt be best for us to search them out and make His plans ours. I hope we can take a quick moment here before we look at the Gospel account in Mark 4 to seriously commit to setting aside the desire or the need to be in control. We have to know that this is solely God's department, and He always executes it perfectly.

Let's look at what happened that day on the Sea of Galilee according to Mark 4:35–41:

> *On that day, when evening had come, he said to them, "Let us go across to the other side." And leaving the crowd, they took him with them in the boat, just as he was. And other boats were with him. And a great windstorm arose, and the waves were breaking into the boat, so the boat was already filling. But he was in the stern, asleep on a cushion. And they woke him and said to him, "Teacher, do you not care that we are perishing?" And he awoke and rebuked* [in Greek, "epitimao," to straightly charge, censure severely] *the wind and said to the sea, "Peace! Be still!" And the wind ceased, and there was a great calm. He said to them, "Why are you so afraid? Have you still no faith?" And they were filled with great fear and said to one another, "Who then is this, that even the wind and the sea obey him?"*

Jesus and His disciples were on the western shore where the large cities were located, and they wanted to cross over to the eastern shore where there were fewer people. It seems He needed a break from continuous preaching and healing. Simply put, He was tired.

The Sea of Galilee is like a large lake, and it sits a little less than 700 feet below sea level and is surrounded by hills, which allow the winds to get trapped over the low-lying water.

Jesus Has Full and Complete Authority over All

What does the word *sovereign* mean? As supreme ruler over the universe, God has the right to do whatever He wants, and He has complete control over everything that happens. Jesus is God, so He is sovereign over all.

> *As you do not know the path of the wind, or how the body is formed in the mother's womb, so you cannot understand the work of God, the Maker of all things.*
>
> —Eccles. 11:5 NIV

> *The LORD has made everything for its purpose, even the wicked for the day of trouble.*
>
> —Prov. 16:4

> *See now that I, even I, am He, and there is no god beside me; I kill and I make alive; I wound and I heal; and there is none that can deliver out of my hand.*
>
> —Deut. 32:39

> *He changes times and seasons; he removes kings and sets up kings; he gives wisdom to the wise and knowledge to those who have understanding; he reveals deep and hidden things; he knows what is in the darkness, and the light dwells with him.*
>
> —Dan. 2:21–22

In John 14:6 King Jesus, with complete authority, tells us "I am the way, and the truth, and the life. No one comes to the Father except through me." So, with the facts of John 14:6, it can be affirmed that if Jesus is the truth, then the foundation of our faith is God's truth.

Q: So how does sin so easily get a foothold in us and cloud the truth or make it easy to compromise?

_____

_____

_____

Q: How have you allowed this to happen in your life?

_____

_____

_____

_____

In Romans chapter 1, the Apostle Paul explains that sin occurs when we willfully exchange the truth of God for a lie. It's this exchange combined with our own selfish desires that seems to make it all fall together so quickly and so easily. Knowing this, let's start to make things different by agreeing not to lie to ourselves anymore, by questioning or turning away from the truth. This part is on us, my friends.

In John 8:44 Jesus calls Satan "the father of lies"; Jesus says that Satan was *"a murderer from the beginning, and does not stand in the truth, because there is no truth in him. When he lies, he speaks out of his own character."*

When we choose to exchange the truth for a lie, we are in effect aligning ourselves with the father of lies, and then it becomes easier to decide to choose sin. We must do whatever it takes to remember that choosing sin is in direct opposition to the complete sovereign authority of Christ. Whether we realize it or not, we are pushing directly against God's authority. And at some point, He will push back.

In Isaiah 14:13–14 we can read the exact words Satan spoke when he chose to exchange the truth for a lie and attempt to defy God's authority:

> *You said in your heart, "I will ascend to heaven; above the stars of God. I will set my throne on high; I will sit on the mount of assembly in the far reaches of the north; I will ascend above the heights of the clouds; I will make myself like the Most High."*

These are the very words of the most infamous liar and traitor; these words were also the beginning of his end. This foolish creature challenged the perfect Creator, and it was all over in the blink of an eye, as Jesus testified in Luke 10:18, telling His followers, *"I saw Satan fall like lightning from heaven"* because Jesus was there when Satan was cast out.

Q: Do you realize that choosing sin is directly challenging God's authority? Y/N _____

Q: Do you also realize that in choosing sin, you are threatening His sovereign right to rule over all things? Y/N _____

Now, you may be saying, "Wait a minute, Pastor Mike. How am I threatening God's sovereign right to rule?" I'm glad you asked! By choosing sin, you are doing the same thing Satan did, and everything he did was directly against or in opposition to the authority of God and His right to sovereignly rule over all things. Satan perfected sin—so when we choose sin, are we trying to make our mark like he did?

Understand that it only requires that we nurture the selfishness in us in order to start down this deadly path. And just so we can be reminded how this finishes one day, Revelation 21:8 tells us where Satan and all "the cowardly, the faithless, the detestable, . . . murderers, the sexually immoral, sorcerers, idolaters, and all liars" end up: "*Their portion will be in the lake that burns with fire and sulfur, which is the second death*"; this is the final fate of all those who choose to rebel against God's authority.

Q: What do we actually have authority over?

_____

_____

Areas of Personal Authority

We really truly own only three things: our thoughts, our words, and our actions.

Our Thoughts

> You have heard that it was said to those of old, "You shall not murder; and whoever murders will be liable to judgment." But I say to you that everyone who is angry with his brother will be liable to judgment.
>
> —Matt. 5:21–22

9

*You have heard that it was said, "You shall not commit adultery."
But I say to you that everyone who looks at a woman with lustful
intent has already committed adultery with her in his heart.*

—Matt. 5:27–28

Our Words

*I tell you, on the day of judgment people will give account for
every careless word they speak, for by your words you will be
justified, and by your words you will be condemned.*

—Matt. 12:36–37

What comes out of your mouth is a reflection of what is in your heart.

Q: What's in your heart?

_____

_____

Q: Do you realize that what comes out of your mouth is a direct reflection of
what is in your heart? Y/N _____

Our Actions

*And I saw the dead, great and small, standing before the throne,
and books were opened. Then another book was opened, which
is the book of life. And the dead were judged by what was written
in the books, according to what they had done.*

—Rev. 20:12

These are the fruits that will reflect the genuineness of your faith. If
you continue to try to take control of what does not belong to you, to usurp
God's sovereignty, you are guaranteed to struggle. We primarily do this by
selfishly seeking our own desires and rationalizing what we do by rejecting
God's truth. Most of us do this—we pick and choose which parts of scripture
we will surrender to and accept, and which parts we will dismiss. Let's look
at how we can overcome this tendency.

Faith Is the Key

In Mark 4:40 Jesus asked the disciples, *"Why are you so afraid? Have you still no faith?"* We too often forget who God is when our faith is tested. After all that the disciples had already been through with Jesus, why were they reacting this way? Why were they so afraid?

After all the miracles they had already seen with their own eyes and after hearing all the parables and teaching meant to build and strengthen their faith, what were they thinking? Had they forgotten already?

Q: Considering all that you know about God, why are you so afraid?

_____

_____

_____

It is normal for us to experience natural fear that results from the trials, difficulties, and storms of life, but God does not expect us to linger there. True faith in God will overcome the fear if you have the courage to believe.

Q: How would you describe the condition of your faith right now?

_____

_____

_____

_____

_____

Remember that faith in Jesus—and Jesus alone—is the key! Hebrews 11:6 says, *"And without faith it is impossible to please God, because anyone who comes to him must believe that he exists and that he rewards those who earnestly seek him"* (NIV).

Q: Is Christ truly greater than the trials, difficulties, and storms in your life? Y/N _____

Q: Maybe you would like to use the space below to explain your last answer here.

_____

_____

_____

_____

Mark 4:41 says, *"And they were filled with great fear and said one to another, 'Who then is this, that even the wind and the sea obey Him?'"* It seems like we see the disciples going back and forth between natural fear (from the severity of the storm) and a reverent fear (a feeling of deep respect and awe) for who Jesus is and the power He has over all things, even the wind and the sea. Unfortunately for us, it's not uncommon for us to waver back and forth between the two. But this is where our faith can help us grow past the wavering point because of who God is and the surety of His great promises, and eventually we trust more and fear or doubt less. Reverent fear acknowledges God's awesomeness and draws us back to Him and confirms in us that He is in fact bigger than the storm.

Consider one of God's great promises from James 1:12: *"Blessed is a man who perseveres under trial; for once he has been approved, he will receive the crown of life which the Lord has promised to those who love Him"* (NASB). God loves us so much that He wants to give an extra reward for those who strive to endure. Don't get caught up in the "earn versus effort mentality" here; God simply wants all your effort because that is the beautiful fruit that shows the world that you love Him.

We cannot earn anything from God—what He has to offer is way outside of our pay grade. My friends, He wants to just give it away, but only to the right kind of heart: He wants us to have a heart like His Son.

What does it look like to put our faith into action? James 4:8 explains it this way: *"Draw near to God and he will draw near to you. Cleanse your hands, you sinners, and purify your hearts, you double-minded."* Notice the grammar used here: the word *draw* is a verb, and that means action, so the first thing we must realize is that our faith is not passive. We are not to just sit on our hands and wait for God to pour out the blessings from heaven onto us. OK, now let's get going; we got stuff that we have to do.

God expects you to live your faith out for the entire world to see. He demands we seek Him and His holy ways of living, and that's what cleansing your hands refers to—our external behavior (which must reflect Christ). Purifying your heart refers to the cleansing of the inner man, which are your thoughts, motives, and desires. God demands that the inner man and the outer man match and look alike, seeking every day to live righteously.

Finally, He commands that we are not to live double-minded. Being double-minded means your heart is going in two directions: having a love for the things of the world but only an affection for the things of God. God must be first in all things.

Q: Would you describe yourself as double-minded? Why or why not?

_____

_____

_____

_____

_____

_____

Friends, let me tell you, I'm tired of striving against God. I have already faced some pretty incredible storms in my life, and I know without a doubt that the only way I survived them was by His sovereign and guiding hand protecting me. It was in the midst of those storms and trials that I came to the end of myself very quickly, realizing that I could not overcome them. And only after I submitted to His authority did He really put me to work, filling me with His Holy Spirit through the gift of salvation. I know that there are greater storms coming my way, but I have no fear. In fact, I feel pretty confident that my faith may either put me in prison one day or even require my life, but His will be done because I know I will face nothing alone. So, in closing, my question for you is this:

Q: Is Jesus Lord of all and greater than anything that is against you today? Y/N _____

Q: Are you ready to finally submit to His perfect and complete authority? Y/N _____

I hope so. Remember, He Loves you with an unending love and asks you to *"cast all your cares and anxieties upon Him because He cares for you"* (1 Pet. 5:7).

Q: Do you believe this? Y/N _____

Chapter 2

The Good Soil

Today, we are going to test your soil. We will be looking at Mark 4:1–9, where Jesus tells the beautiful parable of the sower:

> *Again he began to teach beside the sea. And a very large crowd gathered about him, so that he got into a boat and sat in it on the sea, and the whole crowd was beside the sea on the land. And he was teaching them many things in parables, and in his teaching he said to them: "Listen! Behold, a sower went out to sow. And as he sowed, some seed fell along the path, and the birds came and devoured it. Other seed fell on rocky ground, where it did not have much soil, and immediately it sprang up, since it had no depth of soil. And when the sun rose, it was scorched, and since it had no root, it withered away. Other seed fell among thorns, and the thorns grew up and choked it, and it yielded no grain. And other seeds fell into good soil and produced grain, growing up and increasing and yielding thirtyfold and sixtyfold and a hundredfold." And he said, "He who has ears to hear, let him hear."*
>
> —Mark 4:1–9

In this parable, Jesus describes four types of soil. In this section, we will start by breaking down the four types of soil for you. And as we read this, take an honest look at your heart and your life, and examine which one best describes you. As Christ-followers, we must constantly be checking our soil; if we want it to stay healthy, we must do the maintenance to ensure that it does. But some Christians are more concerned with the soil of others, and that usually ends up leading to bitterness and judgment, which is a sin.

The only soil you will be held accountable for when you stand before God is yours; Jesus expects you to be a seed layer (one who shares/spreads the seed, which is the Word of God) and nothing else, because He and He alone is the One who has authority over **all** soil and how it develops.

Is God not the one who brings the sun and the rain and all the nutrients that are needed for all life to be sustained? Simply stated: It is God's responsibility to judge the condition of the soil of every soul, not ours; so, stop worrying about what others are doing or not doing. Focus on your own witness and walk with Christ—simply put, feed and nurture your own soil.

Now, it's not uncommon for our soil to go through "stages." I recall when my own heart was once a very hard and rocky place, and very little of God's Word was able to penetrate my stubborn selfishness. Thankfully, God sent more than one sower into my life. I was then able to begin to see and experience the amazing love that God had for me, a love that He generously poured out on me even when I was at my worst. As a result, I am living proof that it is possible for a human being to love someone else (God) more than I love myself. The love of my life is Jesus and if you will allow Him in, He will transform the soil of your heart into a rich, fertile, and healthy place where you can begin to experience this life the way God meant you to, regardless of what happens.

I believe that it all starts with us taking an honest look at the condition of our soil as it is right now. And that is the purpose of this reading today: to help you to be able to do this. OK, here we go.

Soil Type 1

Mark 4:4 says that "some seed fell along the path, and the birds came and devoured it." This can be represented as hard ground or a person whose heart has been hardened by life and the consequences of sin. When this person hears the Word, he or she doesn't understand it, and Satan seizes the opportunity to snatch the message away, and that person's heart remains hard, preventing the Word from having any effect at all.

Q: Is this you? Y/N _____

Q: How do you respond to God's Word, especially when it convicts you or exposes your sin?

_____

_____

_____

Q: Does your heart stay hard? Do you get angry and ignore or disregard the message? Y/N _____

Listen up! God is trying to talk to you.

Soil Type 2

Mark 4:5–6 says, "*Other seed fell on rocky ground, where it did not have much soil, and immediately it sprang up, since it had no depth of soil. And when the sun rose, it was scorched, and since it had no root, it withered away.*"

The rocky ground represents the man or woman who at first gets excited by the Word, but deep inside, his or her heart is not changed. Because their soil has no depth, the roots of God's Word are never able to get in deep enough. So, when troubles come (as they always do), their so-called faith quickly fades away.

Q: Is this you? Y/N _____

Q: Is all only well with what you believe when things are going your way?

_____

_____

_____

_____

Q: What is keeping the good news of the gospel from taking root in your heart?

_____

_____

_____

Soil Type 3

Mark 4:7 says that "other seed fell among thorns, and the thorns grew up and choked it, and it yielded no grain."

This man or woman at first appears to have received the Word, but the person's heart is full of the desire for the pleasures and comforts of the world. Before too long, he or she becomes distracted by the pursuit of them and loses interest in the Word and ends up having no time for it. Instead, they choose the things of the world over the Holy Word of God.

Q: Is this you? Y/N _____

Q: Right now, what are you valuing more than God?

_____

_____

_____

The only way to know Him is to live in His Word daily. You can answer this question by honestly looking at how and what you spend your time on.

Soil Type 4

Finally, in Mark 4:8–9 we learn that _"other seeds fell into good soil and produced grain, growing up and increasing and yielding thirtyfold and sixtyfold and a hundredfold. And He said, he that has ears to hear, let him hear."_

This is obviously the man or woman who joyfully hears, understands, and receives the Word, and then allows the Word to accomplish its intended purpose in their life. It must be noted that this represents the person who truly knows Christ because one who is truly saved will produce good fruit.

Q: Is this you? Y/N _____

Q: Are you joyfully being led by our gracious and merciful God, while daily desiring to submit to His loving and perfect authority?

_____

_____

_____

Jesus ends the parable by challenging us with a call to be the ones who actually listen, are attentive, and discern what He is saying here. Jesus makes it very clear that even people who have ears to hear will not hear, let alone understand, and that is very sad.

A person's response to God's Word is determined by the condition of their heart. True love for Jesus will always be more than superficial, and the true believer will go to any length to prove it.

Take time to examine the soil of your heart, and if you are in need of some heart surgery, do not be afraid to call upon the Great Physician. As you do this, meditate on Psalm 139:13–14, which is a beautiful reminder of our Loving God and His tremendous care for every single detail in and about our daily lives. He's the author of your story and in one way or another, He will be your destiny—either as a Glorious Savior or as Righteous Judge.

For you created my inmost being; you knit me together in my mother's womb. I praise you because I am fearfully and wonderfully made; your works are wonderful, I know that full well.

—Ps. 139:13–14 NIV

Chapter 3

Finding Joy

Lately, struggling to find joy has been something I have had a hard time with. Those who know me know that I'm a pretty serious, intense person by nature, so it's not my usual method of operation to gravitate toward an attitude of joy; I usually have to search it out.

This is not an "abnormal" mentality, and if you do a little research, you will find that many Christians feel this way. Let's be honest, life is hard, and days can be dark and challenging for many. The struggles we face daily in battle with the enemy and our own sinful nature can become very discouraging. To live much of this life without the joy of the Lord is exactly what the enemy wants. Consider this reflection:

> "How black can get the night?
> When all is unclear, and out of sight?
> No true trail to guide my way,
> No hint of light to signal day.
> Just how black can darkness be?
> Is it truly there, or just inside of me?
> Oh how much I pray for even a shade of grey,
> For anything different that could change my way."

You can tell that the author of this brief poem understands the battle we are examining and definitely longs for "the light." I wrote that short, painful poem years ago when my life appeared to be joyless most of the time. I can tell you that living with that sort of view is unhealthy and scary, but it is not how it has to be at all.

As believers, we know who the true light is—Jesus Christ! Speaking of Jesus, John 1:4–5 says, *"In him was life, and the life was the light of men. The light shines in the darkness, and the darkness has not overcome it."* I have come back to this scripture over and over as I faced difficulties in my life. But we too often forget the power and comfort of scripture when the trials come because this thing called life is not for the faint of heart.

Christians who truly desire to know God and experience His wonderful goodness through a genuine relationship with Him are going to find His perfect joy, and the peace that comes with it, if they seek Him wholeheartedly. The Christian life is full of peaks and valleys, and I am going to challenge you to believe that our Great God allows valleys in our lives to draw us nearer to Him, simply to teach us to fully rely on Him and seek His joy!

The Humanity of the Saints

Thankfully, God has given us plenty of examples of men and women who have had to fight to find joy. Throughout scripture, we find ordinary people who have been called by God and put on mission, yet while in the midst of their calling and trials, their joy was lost and replaced by fear, anxiety, and depression. A lot of great saints even fell into despair; we can read their stories and relate to them, understanding their heartfelt cries and prayers. Their trials have been graciously recorded for us in the Holy Scriptures.

God gave us these beautifully illustrated pictures of His suffering saints for our encouragement. He also uses them to show how He repeatedly and abundantly met their need and continuously overflowed the cups of their heart with His perfect peace and joy. It is through this comfort that we are allowed to experience another facet of His amazing grace.

For example, David constantly communicated with, sought after, and cried out to the Lord. Probably more than anyone else in the scriptures, David searched for the joy of the Lord his entire life. His passion, desperation, desire, and need for communion with God is beautifully expressed in the psalms; his need is so powerful that it is practically palpable—I can feel his pain as much as his joy, and I am so thankful. Read the passage below and ask yourself how many times have you prayed like this.

> *How long O Lord? Will you forget me forever? How long will you hide your face from me? How long must I wrestle with my thoughts and day after day have sorrow in my heart? How long will my enemy triumph over me?*
>
> —Ps. 13:1–2 NIV

In another part of scripture, David prays like this:

> *Be merciful to me, O God, be merciful to me, for in you my soul takes refuge; in the shadow of your wings I will take refuge, till the storms of destruction pass by. I cry out to God Most High, to God who fulfills his purpose for me. He will send from heaven and save me; he will put to shame him who tramples me. Selah. God will send his steadfast love and his faithfulness!*
>
> —Ps. 57:1–3

How beautiful are these prayers from David to our loving and merciful God. Here we can clearly see David being afraid because he feels God had left him (Psalm 13), and he prays for comfort. In Psalm 57, we know he is praying for safety and deliverance from King Saul, who sought to kill him. It isn't hard to see even in these two examples that peace and joy are only found in the Lord!

Exchanging Your Joy for Fear from Satan

The Bible talks about three "exchanges" that are critical for our overall well-being. The first exchange is popularly referred to as "The Great Exchange." This exchange involves our sin for the righteousness of Christ. This is most certainly a Great Exchange.

> *He made the one who did not know sin to be sin for us, so that in him we might become the righteousness of God.*
>
> —2 Cor. 5:21 CSB

We find the second exchange in Romans:

They exchanged the truth of God for a lie, and worshiped and served created things rather than the Creator—who is forever praised. Amen.

—Rom. 1:25 NIV

When we ignore, dismiss, alter, or compromise the Holy Word of God so as to meet our own selfish needs and desires, we exchange the truth of God for a lie. What dwells here in this very dangerous act of self-deception is the very act that gives sin the ability to exist in our lives.

When a man or a woman finds themselves facing the hardships of life and becoming overwhelmed by life's trials and challenges, they are inclined to be afraid. Why does this happen? Because our enemy who is the author of fear is waiting at the doorstep of our heart offering that fear to us. In our fallen state, it is easy for us to give in and accept it. And we'll accept it because it seems "rational" at the time, because the unknown is scary to us.

Trials, struggles, illness, death, financial worries, relationship problems, and addictions invite fear when Christ is not the One we first run to when life gets hard. The Bible clearly tells us where fear comes from:

For God has not given us a spirit of fear, but one of power, love, and sound judgment.

—2 Tim. 1:7 CSB

We know for certain that fear does not come from God because it is written in scripture. However, the acceptance of fear into our lives is how we forfeit the power God gives us. This is what unhinges our sound judgment and freezes our ability to give and receive godly love. Choose today to hold on tightly to the joy, which God provided to you through the precious blood of His Son.

Joy Can Be Forfeited by Sin and Its Consequences

One way we can lose our joy is through choosing sin. Plainly stated, when sin enters our lives, joy leaves; sin is the darkness. There should be no argument that when we choose sin, we should expect consequences and the chastening of the Lord.

I call this "giving our joy away" for the false and temporary pleasures that do not last. Every time I tried things "my way," they always ended horribly for me and for anyone I tried to influence or take care of. I gave away the joy of the Lord, sacrificing it on the altar of Mike Govan's attempt at self-satisfaction.

I will use David as an example again, except this time David is the king of Israel, which means his decisions carried heavier consequences (2 Samuel 11 and 12). The more we know, the more influence we have; the more power we are given, the more we will be able to do—the greater our accountability and consequences will be when we stand before God, whose great justice is equal to His great love.

David, broken by his sin, prays and pleads:

> *Have mercy on me, O God, according to your steadfast love; according to your abundant mercy blot out my transgressions. Wash me thoroughly from my iniquity, and cleanse me from my sin! For I know my transgressions, and my sin is ever before me. Against you, you only, have I sinned and done what is evil in your sight, so that you may be justified in your words and blameless in your judgment.*
>
> —Ps. 51:1–4

My friend, you can know without any doubt that confession and forgiveness will restore a person's joy; we can find what we are looking for through the precious and priceless act of reconciliation through repentance. This is God's mighty grace at work. Look at what King David prays later in the same psalm:

> *Deliver me from bloodguiltiness, O God, O God of salvation, and my tongue will sing aloud of your righteousness. O Lord, open my lips, and my mouth will declare your praise. For you will not delight in sacrifice, or I would give it; you will not be pleased with a burnt offering. The sacrifices of God are a broken spirit; a broken and contrite heart, O God, you will not despise.*
>
> —Ps. 51:14–17

God never turns His back on the broken hearts of His children. Second Corinthians 7:10 affirms that "godly sorrow brings repentance that leads to salvation without regret, but worldly sorrow brings death" (BSB). Once again, we can affirm that our joy can be, and is often, lost due to sin and its consequences, but we can be completely confident that one of the major ways our joy can be restored is through repentance.

- Joy can be found in seeking to truly know God.
- Joy can be found in reading God's Word daily and communing with Him.
- Joy can be found in spending our lives praising Him.
- Joy can be found in living a life of thanksgiving to God.
- Joy can be found in forgiveness.
- Joy can be found in loving and serving others.
- Joy can be found in submission and obedience to the Savior.
- Truth: salvation is accompanied by joy!

It was said a long time ago that we should always give thanks for the time and place: thanksgiving for a time to live, and thanksgiving for a place to die. I find such joy in that simple prayer, because I know without a doubt in my heart that the Sovereign God of all creation has already determined both for you and me.

Let the comfort of His sovereignty, and peace found in His presence, be transformed into joy for you today, and know that in God, His goodness is always found, and His Joy is guaranteed for those whom He loves.

Chapter 4

Do Not Cause Others to Stumble

As a Christian, you should be aware that your life, in one way or another, is constantly under the microscope—this means that people are constantly watching how you live. If you are a parent, you can bet your children are watching. You are being watched at work, at school, and also on social media. You are even being watched in the grocery store and at the gym. For a variety of reasons, people are interested in what we think, say, or do. Therefore, I believe that God gives each believer what I like to call, "spheres of influence." Believe it or not, our sphere of influence in the people groups we are a part of are influential, especially to nonbelievers and baby Christians.

We must make sure that we walk in a manner worthy of the calling we have received and live and act in a way that first and foremost glorifies the Living God. Let's explore this a bit more through scripture. The Apostle Paul discusses this concept in Romans 14:13–23. In verse 13 of that passage, Paul says, *"Therefore, let us no longer judge one another. Instead decide never to put a stumbling block or pitfall in the way of your brother or sister"* (CSB).

We can count verse 13 as a summary verse of the first 12 verses in this passage and as a preview of the coming 11 verses, which means this: Do not allow judging of others to become an issue in your life, and also do not use the freedom God has given you to cause your brothers or sisters to stumble in their Christian walk.

I do want to say this though: the way we look out for each other and hold each other accountable is called "admonishment." Admonishment means "to indicate duties or obligations" and "to express warning or disapproval to someone in a gentle, earnest, or solicitous manner." When we see a brother or sister walking away from clear scriptural principles, we should admonish them accordingly. Notice that in the definition of admonishment the word *gentle* is used. We must admonish gently:

> *Brothers and sisters, if someone is overtaken in any wrongdoing, you who are spiritual, restore such a person with a gentle spirit, watching out for yourselves so that you also won't be tempted. Carry one another's burdens; in this way you will fulfill the law of Christ. For if anyone considers himself to be something when he is nothing, he deceives himself. Let each person examine his own work, and then he can take pride in himself alone, and not compare himself with someone else. For each person will have to carry his own load.*
> —Gal. 6:1–5 CSB

The Apostle Paul is not referring here to a hardened sinner but to someone who has fallen into sin. We are referring to someone being seduced and overtaken by a sin of the flesh (e.g., drunkenness, pornography, etc.). Notice that the command here is to restore this person (with a gentle admonishment). They are not to be ignored, passed judgment on, gossiped about, excused, or destroyed socially. We don't pretend it didn't happen, either.

They are to be restored. Restore here means to put in order, or return to its former condition, like the mending of a basket. A basket is repaired so it can be used again to carry or store things in. God not only wants us to help restore folks back to useful service, but more importantly back to the right relationship with Him.

Next, we are instructed to help bear their burdens—this means that we must assist them in their recovery, to love and serve them. This isn't that hard to do—if you see a burden, you help bear it. Paul is so sure of this that he says that when we do this, we "fulfill the law of Christ." Jesus was the perfect example of a burden-bearer and the restorer of the broken and lost.

I know and am persuaded in the Lord Jesus that nothing is unclean in itself. Still, to someone who considers a thing to be unclean, to that one it is unclean. For if your brother or sister is hurt by what you eat, you are no longer walking according to love. Do not destroy, by what you eat, someone for whom Christ died. Therefore, do not let your good be slandered, for the kingdom of God is not eating and drinking, but righteousness, peace, and joy in the Holy Spirit. Whoever serves Christ in this way is acceptable to God and receives human approval.

—Rom. 14:14–18 CSB

Paul makes sure to remind us that there is nothing unclean of itself. We make things unclean. Remember what Jesus said: *"A man is not defiled by what enters his mouth, but by what comes out of it"* (Matt. 15:11 BSB). In Romans 14:15, Paul says that *"if your brother or sister is hurt by what you eat, you are no longer walking according to love"* (CSB). So, what the Holy Spirit through Paul is saying here is that it's not always about your comfort or convenience, especially if it causes others to struggle in their Christian walk. When we choose to disregard this teaching, we are no longer walking in love toward the ones Jesus died for.

For example, several years ago, when I used to drink, I would look forward to having a beer or two after church at a local restaurant. Now, drinking in and of itself isn't bad, but my position as a pastor has influence. If someone who struggles with drinking sees me drinking, it could give them false encouragement or even "false permission" to indulge in alcohol because they might think, "If the pastor can, I should be able to, also." This would not be loving my brother or sister who struggles with alcohol. Remember, scripture tells us: *"Everything is permissible for me, but not everything is beneficial. Everything is permissible for me, but I will not be mastered by anything"* (1 Cor. 6:12 CSB).

Everything we say or do is also not beneficial to our witness, and therefore can be dangerous to the walk of others. How much do you love God in order to abstain from things that would either have a negative impact on your witness or cause your brother or sister to stumble?

Do you realize that the way you love others reflects how you love God? If Jesus was willing to give up His life for you, do you think you could give up something that causes your brother or sister to struggle in his or her faith? *"So then, let us pursue what promotes peace and what builds up one another"* (Rom. 14:19 CSB). I think these verses are self-explanatory:

> *Do not tear down God's work because of food. Everything is clean, but it is wrong to make someone fall by what he eats. It is a good thing not to eat meat, or drink wine, or do anything that makes your brother or sister stumble.*
>
> —Rom. 14:20–21 CSB

This is also very clear: If eating or drinking something will cause another brother or sister to stumble, then we need to understand that we are not free to do that. This goes for what type of music we listen to or movies we watch around others. When the movie *Deadpool* came out several years ago, I made a point to look up the reviews to understand why a movie based on a Marvel comic character had received an "R" rating. When I read that there was full frontal female nudity, I was shocked and decided I would not see that movie.

A work associate criticized me for saying I wouldn't go see it, and he took his 12-year-old son to see it and regretted it afterward. What would it have done to my witness for Christ if I had gone to that movie? Nothing good, that's for sure. So, for this reason, I chose to exercise my freedom and not watch it, and I am glad that I didn't. All for Christ!

Being able to discern the right thing to do here was very important as Romans 12:2 affirms: *"Do not be conformed to this world, but be transformed by the renewal of your mind, that by testing you may discern what is the will of God, what is good and acceptable and perfect."* This is why we must stay connected to the Holy Spirit and remain immersed in God's Word—so we can know when not to allow our Christian love and kindness to cater to someone else's legalism. There is a big difference between a struggling or stumbling heart and a person's hang-ups due to their legalistic view of things.

Whatever you believe about these things, keep between yourself and God. Blessed [or happy] is the one who does not condemn himself by what he approves.

—Rom. 14:22 CSB

Check your faith right now: If you feel at peace about the things you do partake in, then most certainly give thanks and praise to our great and generous God. Just be sure that what you take liberty in, through the freedom of what was purchased at the cross, is in alignment with God's Word. Then you will not make your brother or sister stumble.

Q: Are we commanded to be happy or find joy in the things God asks us to give up? Y/N _____

The answer is yes. If God has asked you to give something up (whatever the reason), it is most certainly for His glory and ultimately your greater good. Romans 14:23 gives this word of caution: *"But whoever doubts stands condemned if he eats, because his eating is not from faith, and everything that is not from faith is sin"* (CSB).

Q: What happens when God asks us to give something up, but we say no, refusing to let it go for some reason?

_____

_____

_____

_____

_____

I have seen this behavior in believers who struggle with something like smoking, for example—God would never encourage you to smoke and would never lead you to seek pleasure through something like smoking. What the Holy Spirit is saying through Paul is that when we choose to hold on to things that are not in God's will for us, we condemn ourselves. The final part of verse 23 tells us so plainly that what is not from faith, is in fact sin.

Q: Think about the things that you allow in your life: Are you living in a way that would glorify God with the freedom He has purchased for you in His blood? Explain.

_____

_____

_____

_____

_____

_____

_____

_____

_____

_____

_____

_____

Chapter 5

The Art of Betrayal

Sometimes when I'm looking for a different way to decompress, I like to watch television shows that portray real-life events—shows like *Cops*, *Forensic Files*, *The First 48*, and *American Greed*.

American Greed uses the true stories and events about people who, through their incredible pride, selfishness, and greed, successfully pull off huge financial scams or money-making schemes that rob people of their life savings and ruin their lives. The victims are usually good-hearted trusting people, small businesses, retirees, etc. who "trust" a stranger who claims to be some kind of financial wizard with their life savings.

The good people get swindled and ripped off horribly by the bad people, often being conned out of thousands or sometimes millions of dollars. Of course, in the process, the thieves completely destroy the lives of the victims, who usually get very little back after the criminal is caught. Even worse, if/when the thieves are caught, their jail sentence ends up being practically nothing compared to the amount of (often permanent) damage these horrible people cause in the lives of good, trusting folks.

American Greed planted a root in me as I watched; what I saw really began to create frustration. When you see a sweet little old lady getting ripped off by some young arrogant punk who ends up jet-setting around the globe on her nickels and dimes, it can become very unnerving. Isn't it sickening that we could even refer to something evil as an "art"? I suppose that somehow there could be some "beauty" in the intricate, detailed plans of the perfect crime but I don't see it. Yet I am able to see "beauty" in the perfect planning and execution of a well-organized military operation, and that usually ends up with something being destroyed, someone dead, or both.

We human beings are strange creatures indeed.

Since I believe that the Bible is the finest, most accurate, and complete source in defining every word ever communicated, it would once again serve as my guide to help define all that I needed to understand the evil art of betrayal. The word *betrayal* or *betrayed* comes from the Greek word *paradidomi*, with its primary meaning being "to give or to hand over to another." It is found over 120 times in the New Testament, with 44 of its uses connected to Judas Iscariot, the most infamous betrayer of all time.

Betrayal is one of the oldest diseases that abide in the hearts of men; it has been with us as long as sin has, being one of its most practiced attributes. I am sickened by this sin (and even this very word), and even more so when I witness my fellow man slip his silent, razor-sharp blade into the hearts and lives of friends and family, leaving behind destruction equal to that of a tornado or hurricane. Betrayal has become the perfect weapon to use when you want to destroy someone and watch the look on their face as you do it, all the while knowing they never saw it coming.

I still get chills every time I open the Bible and read about Cain, who, after God rejected his offering, gave way to the evil in his heart by inviting his brother Abel out to the field so he could kill him. In an anger-fueled jealous rage Cain betrayed the trust of a little brother and murdered the one he was supposed to always be looking out for. (You can read all about this in Genesis 4:1–20).

> *Even my close friend whom I trusted, who ate my bread, has lifted up his heel against me.*
>
> —Ps. 41:9

> *If an enemy were insulting me, I could endure it; if a foe were rising against me, I could hide. But it is you, a man like myself,*

my companion, my close friend, with whom I once enjoyed sweet
fellowship at the house of God, as we walked about among the
worshipers.

—Ps. 55:12–14 NIV

As I began to process betrayal and all that is required to bring it to life, I concluded that there were three basic components that made up the evil scheme of betrayal.

Disarming the Skepticism

The first part is what I call "disarming the skepticism." To be "skeptical" simply means to "not be easily convinced or having doubts and reservations." In order for the silent assault of betrayal to slip in sight unseen, whatever would allow room for reasonable doubt must be disarmed. This success of this sin is contingent on people being taught to ignore all the signs that scream something is wrong.

Now, I believe God wants us to question things, so we can ultimately prove out their loyalty and purpose. Once again, scripture has the guidance we need: *"The simple believe anything, but the prudent give thoughts to their steps"* (Prov. 14:15 NIV). In fact, both our Lord Jesus and the Apostle Paul expect us to be skeptical, because it can be a truth detector, when deployed properly and with the right intentions. Jesus said, *"Do not believe me unless I do the works of my Father"* (John 10:37 NIV). Paul tells us to *"Test everything. Hold on to what is good"* (1 Thess. 5:21 CSB).

Stealing the Trust

In order to effectively deploy the evil plans of betrayal, any level of trust that exists between the two parties must be stolen away in such a manner that the victim doesn't know it is gone. And the thief, after he or she has stolen the genuine trust that existed in the relationship, will replace it with some form of counterfeit trust, in order to provide a false sense of security.

Trust is so powerful, and it is an essential element to our faith. We know we can fully trust God, but people must prove themselves to be trustworthy.

Trust in the LORD with all your heart, and do not rely on your own understanding; in all your ways know him, and he will make your paths straight.

—Prov. 3:5–6

When we get close to people, we "relax the trust muscles" because we come to believe that people we care for will not violate our trust. Some people intentionally get close to others simply to take advantage once they have earned their trust. Trust is usually the last line of defense we have in relationships. When trust is stolen, most of the time, the victim doesn't know until they have been hurt really bad. My heart breaks every time I read the book of Hosea. It breaks for the pain in Hosea's heart that is revealed when Gomer continues to cheat on Hosea over and over. Each time she comes back, he chooses to accept her, trusting that she will finally be faithful.

Hosea's life is given as an example of the loving trust God regularly gives us, and it is that very trust we steal away, disrespect, and trample on, when we regularly pour out our love and dedication to everyone and everything other than Him. Betrayal or unfaithfulness is a common theme in scripture, which is why we see so many warnings against it.

It is better to trust in the LORD than to put confidence in man. It is better to trust in the LORD than to put confidence in princes.

—Ps. 118:8–9

In Jeremiah 17:5, God states the point even more directly: *"Thus says the LORD: 'Cursed is the man who trusts in man and makes flesh his strength, whose heart departs from the LORD.'"*

Selling the Lie

Finally, we come to the part in this age-old sin that has the most common ongoing cycle: selling the lies so as to keep the deception alive. This is the one part of the game that has to be repeated over and over in order for the art of betrayal to be able to be effective—every form of sin is built on some manner of falsehood, so this makes sense.

Adolph Hitler was once quoted as saying, "If you can come up with a good lie, tell it often enough, it will eventually be believed and accepted."[1]

How sick, sad, and pathetic is the heart of man who practices deception and betrayal; unfortunately, it seems to be a common part of our depraved human nature.

God plainly tells us that *"A lying tongue hates those it hurts, and a flattering mouth works ruin"* (Prov. 26:28 NIV). And, in Jeremiah 9:3–6 (CSB), He describes how completely the leaders of Judah were given over to deception:

> *They bent their tongues like their bows; lies and not faithfulness prevail in the land, for they proceed from one evil to another, and they do not take me into account. This is the LORD's declaration. Everyone has to be on guard against his friend. Don't trust any brother, for every brother will certainly deceive, and every friend spread slander. Each one betrays his friend; no one tells the truth. They have taught their tongues to speak lies; they wear themselves out doing wrong. You live in a world of deception. In their deception they refuse to know me. This is the LORD's declaration.*

How terribly sad these words are. Lying leaders, deceitful friends, false brothers—selling the lie for personal gain has been going on for a very long time.

In Acts chapter 5, we find the story of Ananias and Sapphira, a couple in the early NT church who set their hearts on deceiving the apostles (and ultimately the Holy Spirit) to make themselves look good in the eyes of the church. Their lies cost them their lives, and maybe even their place in eternity. We can plainly see by their example that selling the lie can and often does come from people we least expect—people in church, for example.

How does this happen? How does a man or woman so easily betray another? We know that this can all be traced back to the Garden, the Fall—where sin was born, at least for mankind.

Betrayal is quickly birthed in the hearts of the prideful and selfish, whose lusts, greed, and desires are more important to them than their love for God or anyone else.

The desires I just mentioned are what cause a man or a woman to seek out adulterous relationships, steal their friend's wife or husband, and even be driven to thievery to fulfill the needs of addictions, lusts, pornography, drugs, and alcohol. Betrayal has even destroyed healthy and solid business relationships, crushed the best friendships, and decimated the closest of families. The sad part is that all this continues to be done before the eyes of God Himself, who sees all things, whether it be thoughts, careless words whispered from quiet lips, or the deeds of the hands and use or abuse of the body.

> *Nothing in all creation is hidden from God's sight. Everything is uncovered and laid bare before the eyes of him to whom all must give account.*
>
> —Heb. 4:13 NIV

> *It is He who reveals the profound and hidden things; He knows what is in the darkness. And the light dwells with Him.*
>
> —Dan. 2:22 NASB

I did not enjoy writing this, and let me tell you why:

I have lied and hurt others.
I have stolen others' trust and tricked them into foolishly trusting me.
I have even betrayed people I care about.

I hope this lesson has been helpful and that you will take time to examine your own heart as I have been doing the entire time I was writing this lesson. It is very important that you repent for every act of betrayal. I believe God is waiting to forgive you right now.

I am ashamed of how I have hurt my gracious God and others in my past and will only rest in peace tonight because I know that His love, forgiveness, and mercy have been poured out to me in my repentance, and that in His love, I can endure forever. Amen.

Q: Have you schemed or plotted against someone for personal gain? (Y/N) _____

Q: If yes, how were you able to subdue your conscience in order to do so?

_____

_____

Q: A person's trust is a valuable gift that usually must be earned. Have you ever taken advantage of or abused the trust that someone willingly chose to give you? (Y/N) _____

Q: If yes, what did that betrayal cost you? A friendship? A job? Close or intimate relationship?

_____

_____

_____

Q: We all have lied and probably will do so again at some point. What has your deception cost you? What has it done to others?

_____

_____

_____

_____

_____

_____

_____

_____

_____

_____

Chapter 6

The Call to Faithfulness

Faith is indeed the most precious of God's gifts to believers. It is what connects us to Him and how we are able to know Him, interact with Him, and do His work. As our faith grows and matures, we begin to develop patterns of faithfulness, which not only become the way our lives ultimately glorify God but also produce evidence of who we really are. So, the next questions we should consider are these: What is the call to faithfulness? What does faithfulness mean for us as Christians?

What Is Faith?

We must start by looking at the definition of *faith*. Hebrews 11:1 answers the question this way: *"Now faith is the substance of things hoped for, the evidence of things not seen"* (KJV). The word *hope* or *hoped* is translated in Greek to mean "guarantee."

- Faith is the connecting power, which joins us to God and makes Him become a tangible reality to the senses and perceptions of a person.
- Faith is the assurance that the things revealed and promised in God's Word are true, even though unseen, and gives the believer a conviction that what he expects in faith, will come to pass.

- This conviction then grows into a connection between the believer and the unseen God (this is called a relationship), which when nurtured will grow into unyielding confidence in God and all His amazing promises.
- So, faith is the tangible essence of what is hoped for—so tangible that the faith itself becomes the evidence/reality of those things that are not yet visible. In other words, the faith becomes so tangible that the believer actually possesses it. Faith becomes a reality in both the spiritual and natural realms.
- Faith is the basic ingredient required to begin a relationship with God and to fully know God as much as is humanly possible.

Hebrews 11:6 adds the following: *"And without faith it is impossible to please God, because anyone who comes to him must believe that he exists and that he rewards those who earnestly seek him"* (NIV). Notice here as we proceed in defining faithfulness that trust is a very important ingredient in both our faith and in our ability to be faithful, and for this reason, it is necessary that it be repeated.

What Does Faithfulness Look Like?

Faithfulness can be described as the act whereby a person, through faith, obtains God's resources and strives to be obedient to what He commands while putting aside all self-interest and self-reliance, choosing instead to trust in God completely.

- Godly faithfulness requires complete surrender of a person's entire being in exchange for full dependence upon Him.
- Faithfulness means fully trusting and relying upon God for all things. It is not just a mental surrender to the facts and realities of the truth; there must be a deep inner conviction that moves us.

Trust in the LORD with all your heart and do not lean on your own understanding.
—Prov. 3:5

He that trusts in his own heart is a fool.

—Prov. 28:26 (NASB 1995)

When the Holy Spirit moves in us, He accomplishes a lot in us at once. The supernatural drawing of the sinful heart to repentance and faith is, in effect, the first step in the act of bringing a dead spirit back to life. So, the order of our conversion is very important for us to understand: Repentance and faith come before salvation. Faith and repentance are present simultaneously: They are inseparable in effecting a genuine conversion.

In Acts 20:21; Paul speaks of both *"repentance toward God and of faith in our Lord Jesus Christ."* God-given faith is a critical element in conversion, and it is through God-given faith that the heart of the sinner is called to repentance. Therefore, it is easy to see how these two important elements are joined and are working together. In terms of our salvation, we cannot separate faith and repentance. To be saved, a person must place faith in Christ for the forgiveness of sins.

That decision requires repentance and a change of direction (a turning away) from our old way of life. Both happen at the same time. To attempt to repent of sin and fail to exercise true faith in Jesus for forgiveness and reconciliation through the cross, will result in either a false conversion or a very quick falling away from belief.

What Does It Mean to Be Faithful?

You can never be truly faithful to anyone or anything without having a foundational faith in someone or something that is greater than who you are and what you are capable of doing. Here's an important illustration from the Gospel of Matthew:

> *For it [the Kingdom of God] is just like a man about to go on a journey. He called his own servants and entrusted his possessions to them. To one he gave five talents, to another two talents, and to another one talent, depending on each one's ability.*
>
> —Matt. 25:14–15 CSB

A talent represents a certain weight and measure of either gold or silver. So, five talents of gold would be a significant amount of money.

Then he went on a journey. Immediately the man who had received five talents went, put them to work, and earned five more. In the same way the man with two earned two more. But the man who had received one talent went off, dug a hole in the ground, and hid his master's money. After a long time the master of those servants came and settled accounts with them.

—Matt. 25:15–19 CSB

The master is returning to find out how his servants have handled the investment given to them.

The man who had received five talents approached, presented five more talents, and said, 'Master, you gave me five talents. See, I've earned five more talents.' His master said to him, 'Well done, good and faithful servant! You were faithful over a few things; I will put you in charge of many things. Share your master's joy.' The man with two talents also approached. He said, 'Master, you gave me two talents. See, I've earned two more talents.' His master said to him, 'Well done, good and faithful servant! You were faithful over a few things; I will put you in charge of many things. Share your master's joy.' The man who had received one talent also approached and said, 'Master, I know you. You're a harsh man, reaping where you haven't sown and gathering where you haven't scattered seed. So I was afraid and went off and hid your talent in the ground. See, you have what is yours.' His master replied to him, 'You evil, lazy servant! If you knew that I reap where I haven't sown and gather where I haven't scattered, then you should have deposited my money with the bankers, and I would have received my money back with interest when I returned.

'So take the talent from him and give it to the one who has ten talents. For to everyone who has, more will be given, and he will have more than enough. But from the one who does not have, even what he has will be taken away from him. And throw this good-for-nothing servant into the outer darkness, where there will be weeping and gnashing of teeth'

—Matt. 25:20–30 CSB

Jesus tells this story and uses it to illustrate the tragedy of wasted opportunity. So, what does the story mean? Obviously, the master represents Jesus, and the servants represent professed believers, and the purpose is to give them the opportunity to express faithfulness with the talents (i.e., gifts and responsibilities) they have been given.

What Jesus means to suggest to us here is that all who are faithful with what they are given will be fruitful to some degree, and that's what God wants from us. When we are faithful to Him, we will produce good fruit that glorifies Him, and all who see our fruit will make much of the goodness of God.

But what about the man who got scared and took the money and buried it? Was he really scared or just selfish and lazy? If he really knew how the master was and if he really cared, then He would have been just as diligent as the others were.

"For to everyone who has, more will be given, and he will have more than enough" (Matt. 25:29 CSB): Those who receive the priceless gifts of God such as divine grace, godly favor, and even eternal life (represented here as the talents) will receive more by honoring both the gift and the giver with faithfulness and fruit. But if the gifts are offered and even given but then ignored or disregarded, the person who receives the gift ultimately loses everything because of their selfishness and faithlessness.

Q: How have you been managing what you have been given?

_____

_____

_____

_____

Q: Is your relationship with Christ clearly visible to those whom you are in relationships with at work, at home, or even to strangers?

_____

_____

_____

_____

Many professing Christians regularly put more value on the things of the world than on the things of the Living God, thereby neglecting His goodness. By "burying what God has given them in the ground," they prove that the word *faith* is just another word that starts with "f" in their lives. These people don't realize it, but they are the ones who are in danger of losing everything—not just in this life, but also in the next.

Our faithfulness can be fulfilled and recognized by two important forms of evidence that should be seen in our faithfulness to our basic calling as Christians and in our faithfulness to our responsibilities as men.

Being Faithful to Our Basic Calling as Christians

We have an **internal responsibility** to be faithful:

- Abide: Accepting and committing to the responsibility to remain fully grafted to the True Vine (Christ) and be faithful to Jesus through our thoughts, words, and actions.
- Confess: Accepting and committing to the responsibility to respond to failure in sin with quick and sincere godly sorrow and repentance.
- Commit: Accepting and committing to the call to continue to nurture and grow our personal relationship with Jesus through prayer and personal bible study.

We have an **external responsibility** to be faithful:

- Produce: Committing to the responsibility to seek to produce godly works and to bear godly fruit first and foremost for the glory of God.
- Serve: Being the hands and feet of God—desiring to love and serve others selflessly without any intent for self-elevation or personal gain.
- Teach: Desiring to make disciples and to proclaim the gospel to all people and all nations.

Being Faithful to Our Responsibilities as Men

There must be an unwavering devotion to the call to be the leaders of our family.

- The call to protect:
  - ➤ Accepting the call to be the sheepdog of the family and constantly being on guard against any wolves who desire to physically hurt, separate, or tear the family apart.
  - ➤ Being constantly on guard against all spiritual attacks—all demonic spirits of fear and division, gossip, lust, addictions, and anger—which may come against our loved ones and/or our church.

- The call to provide:
  - ➤ Accepting the call to honor God with our heart and desiring to produce a work ethic that will bless those we provide for and care for.
  - ➤ Being committed to be diligent to do whatever it takes to make sure that our loved ones and our church do not lack in any need or proper provision.

- The call to pastor:
  - ➤ Gladly accepting the call and responsibility to be the spiritual leader of our home.
  - ➤ Leading in the teaching and instruction in the commandments and statutes of the Living God.
  - ➤ Leading in being the living example of Him and all His goodness so that our family sees Jesus first in us and as a result can learn to trust Him as we do.

What Does the Bible Say about God's Faithfulness to Us?

If we confess our sins, he is faithful and just to forgive us our sins and cleanse us from all unrighteousness.

—1 John 1:9

No temptation has overtaken you that is not common to man. God is faithful, and he will not let you be tempted beyond your ability, but with the temptation he will also provide the way of escape, that you may be able to endure it.

—1 Cor. 10:13

God is not a man, that He should lie, nor a son of man, that He should repent. Has He said, and will He not do it? Or has He spoken and will He not make it good and fulfill it?

—Num. 23:19 NASB 1995

I want to close this chapter with a few comments on yet another verse that has had a big impact on my life:

The LORD does not delay His promise, as some understand delay, but is patient with you, not wanting any to perish but all to come to repentance.

—2 Pet. 3:9 CSB

My friends, we need to understand that God's patience is priceless. When I think about how long I made Him wait for me to call Him Lord, I sometimes tremble as I start to consider what would have happened if He had decided not to wait.

But He is just so faithful to the love that He has for us. I'm certain that He would much rather love us through repentance and restoration than have to love us through punishment. But He has had to love me through discipline, because I am His son, and that's what a good father does—He disciplines those He loves.

We have all experienced the faithful patience and love of God through His wonderful discipline. And I say "wonderful discipline" because it was exactly what I needed at the time and know I will need again.

Activity

I ask you to write a prayer of thanksgiving to God today for His incredible patience with you. Stop and take a moment to recall all the times that you have been rock-headed and stubborn; each time He never left you. Thank Him for that today; add His amazing patience to the gifts you thank Him for regularly going forward from today.

Chapter 7

The Art of Making Excuses

We will consider the parable of the large banquet (Luke 14:15–24) as we examine what I like to call "the art of making excuses." In this lesson, I plan to not only define what an excuse is but also explore how and why we feel we need to use so many of them.

We will also touch briefly on how excuses can hurt us and even affect our relationship with God and receiving true forgiveness from Him. As Christian men and women, we have a large inventory of excuses in the problem-solving center of our brain. It seems that in our society, people prefer to quickly offer up an excuse rather than take ownership of something that was said or done. Let me say this right out of the gate: God does not expect or want, nor will He receive or accept any of your excuses, or any of mine.

> *So whoever knows the right thing to do and fails to do it, for him it is sin.*
>
> —James 4:17

I ask you to keep this verse in the back of your mind as we move forward and explore the act of deploying an excuse. We will start by looking at what else scripture has to say about excuse-making.

As stated above, our main text today will come from Luke 14:15–24, but for the sake of context, let's look quickly at what precedes this parable in Luke 14. This chapter begins by telling us that Jesus has been invited to the house of a well-known Pharisee for the Sabbath. Luke tells us that while He was there, they are all watching Him like a hawk—and how does He react? Jesus starts by correcting the Pharisees on their very warped view of what it means to work on the Sabbath. They had previously become angry with Him for healing a man in the temple on the Sabbath, so that's why they were watching Him—and He was about to do it again! You see, by this time, the Pharisees had become so legalistic that they had forgotten that goodness and charity are supposed to be an integral part of everything we do.

Q: Is your heart first drawn to obedience more than it is drawn to love?

_____

_____

_____

Q: We all want to be known as obedient Christians, but what is the motive of our obedience?

_____

_____

_____

Q: Is the purpose of your obedience to gain favor with God, or do you obey simply because of how awesome He is and how much you love Him?

_____

_____

_____

You will never be in a place of real, fruitful obedience in your life unless it is preceded by a heart that is full of love for God first. A heart that has love and obedience in the wrong order will end up producing a multitude of excuses, because we always miss the mark and can never earn His favor. The Pharisees had also forgotten that adhering to the letter of the law was **not** a reason to abandon common sense or ignore doing the right thing in favor of blind legalism.

Jesus heals a man on the Sabbath and then asks them, *"'Which of you whose son or ox falls into a well, will not immediately pull him out on the Sabbath day?' They could find no answer to these things"* (Luke 14:5–6 CSB).

Jesus drops the mic on this topic and then moves right into teaching about humility to a bunch of men who have none. Now remember, He's a guest at the house of a well-known Pharisee—this could not have gone over very well with them!

He told a parable to those who were invited, when He noticed how they would choose the best places for themselves:

> *When you are invited by someone to a wedding banquet, don't recline at the best place, because a more distinguished person than you may have been invited by your host. The one who invited both of you may come and say to you, "Give your place to this man," and then in humiliation, you will proceed to take the lowest place.*
>
> *But when you are invited, go and recline in the lowest place, so that when the one who invited you comes, he will say to you, "Friend, move up higher." You will then be honored in the presence of all the other guests. For everyone who exalts himself will be humbled, and the one who humbles himself will be exalted.*
>
> —Luke 14:8–11 (HCSB)

I'm willing to bet you could have heard a pin drop in the room after He finished telling them this parable.

Q: Where do you think you deserve to be sitting right now?

_____

_____

Q: Has your title or position in life led you to believe that you deserve the best of everything no matter where you go?

_____

_____

I want you to stop and recognize the conflict you have with Christ commanding that you be humble versus your driving desire for entitlement:

Q: What do you see in your hearts, my friends?

_____

_____

> _When one of those who reclined at the table with Him heard these things, he said to Him, "Blessed is the one who will eat bread in the kingdom of God!"_
>
> —Luke 14:15 NIV

> _Then the angel said to me, "Write, 'Blessed are those who are invited to the marriage supper of the Lamb.'" And he said to me [further], "These are the true and exact words of God."_
>
> —Rev. 19:9 AMP

This is the beautiful truth of things to come for the elect of God, and those who are lost don't even have any idea of what they will be missing. I'm willing to bet everything that the man who said this at the banquet had no clue as to the weight of his words.

> _Then He [Jesus] told him: "A man was giving a large banquet and invited many. At the time of the banquet, he sent his servant to tell those who were invited, 'Come, because everything is now ready.' But without exception they all began to make excuses. The first one said to him, 'I have bought a field, and I must go out and see it. I ask you to excuse me.' Another said, 'I have bought five yoke of oxen, and I'm going to try them out. I ask you to excuse me.' And another said, 'I just got married, and therefore I'm unable to come.'_

So the servant came back and reported these things to his master. Then in anger, the master of the house told his servant, 'Go out quickly into the streets and alleys of the city, and bring in here the poor, maimed, blind, and lame.' 'Master,' the servant said, 'what you ordered has been done, and there's still room.' Then the master told the servant, 'Go out into the highways and hedges and make them come in, so that my house may be filled. For I tell you, not one of those people who were invited will enjoy my banquet.'

—Luke 14:16–24

Let's now move into breaking down this very revealing and instructive parable. Let's first define the term *excuse*, so we can understand what we are talking about here. An excuse is an attempt to lessen the blame attached to something (a fault or offense) or seek to defend or justify something.

Luke 14:17 says, *"At the time of the banquet, he sent his servant to tell those who were invited, 'Come, because everything is now ready'"* (HCSB). Allow me to relate this story to you and me in the here and now. Assume that we just received a great invitation to a once-in-a-lifetime banquet:

"Come, because everything is now ready."

And the Host of the banquet has pulled out all the stops for this dinner—in fact, He has spent all that He has to make this meeting perfect and complete, and it's one that no one in their right mind would ever want to miss.

So, the invitations go out, and they require an immediate response.

And then no sooner than the invitations are received, the Host who had exhausted the best of all He has to make this banquet a life-changing event, starts receiving excuses as to why the guests He has gone to such great expense to invite cannot attend!

So, what are these excuses?

"I have bought a field, and I must go out and see it. I ask you to excuse me" (Luke 14:18 HCSB).

Let me ask you this—who buys a piece of land or let's say a house, without first checking it out?

I recall when Linda and I found the house we wanted, we even paid a man to perform a complete inspection on the entire house before we even came close to surrendering one dollar on the mortgage.

"Another said, 'I have bought five yoke of oxen, and I'm going to try them out. I ask you to excuse me'" (Luke 14:19 HCSB). Another guest says, "I'm sorry I can't make it; I just bought a car and I need to go give it a test drive!" Human beings are so shallow that every time we buy something new, we are preoccupied by it!

My brothers, Jesus has been calling you to His banquet table, and His Father has spent everything He had to make this a special event: You see, the payment required to fund this banquet was started and finished at the cross.

Yet, instead of running to Christ screaming at the top of our lungs, "Yes, Lord, I accept Your most gracious invitation," we choose to seek our value and worth through the temporary satisfactions of material things.

We also try to find satisfaction in our jobs—because we need the recognition of success. We chain ourselves to the never-ending pursuit of money, not realizing that it never comes as fast as it goes, and it also never lasts!

We overindulge in our hobbies (e. g., fishing, football, and other distractions) with Jesus, once again, getting your leftovers—if He is lucky. So, through our choices, you and I spit in the face of the Savior of the world and turn our clean, unscarred backs on His mutilated body, which was beaten nearly beyond recognition for our sins.

Serving self is convenient and easy; we can justify it all by telling ourselves that we need these things, and that they are not bad—and they are not, unless they take priority over your devotion and dedication to Jesus. When Christ calls to you, when He offers Himself to you, instead of saying yes, you make excuses.

Do you understand that excuses come easy when there is a lack of desire? Luke 14:20 (HCSB) says: *"And another said, 'I just got married, and therefore I'm unable to come.'"* Do you realize that the entire time Christ has been pursuing you, His powerful hand of protection has been all over you. Yet, just like this guest, you instead choose your family over Him.

You love your spouse more than you love Jesus.

You love your kids more than you love Jesus.

Do you realize that the best thing you can do is show your family that Jesus is your first love?

52

We also slip in and out of our secret sins, never giving one thought to the fact that our constant pursuit of pleasing our flesh continues to separate us from our relationship with the Living God. Sin is convenient because it can quickly meet the temporary need, but in the moment, we either don't realize or just don't care.

We make excuses to God because we don't want what He has to offer as much as we want our selfish comforts and pleasures. We must realize today that making excuses to God will eventually condemn us.

Why do you make excuses? Here are some of the most common reasons for excuses. Please circle and comment on the ones you can identify with:

- Fear—fear of failure, fear of uncertainty, fear of being compared to others, feeling unsafe, or a lack of protection.
- Lacking courage to face a problem or a situation.
- Lack of a plan.
- Having no real goals.
- Being lazy, unmotivated, or being a procrastinator.
- Having no real intention to follow through with a commitment or promise.

Some of the most common excuses are:

- I don't have time.
- I forgot.
- I don't make enough money.
- I can't because of the kids.
- I'm not good enough.
- I don't have enough education.
- I don't know how.
- I can't change; this is just who I am.
- I am destined to fail.
- I'm just bad luck.

Along with making excuses, we love to try to rationalize our way out of a problem.

Rationalization

The term *rationalization* may be defined as a defense mechanism in which controversial behaviors or feelings are justified and explained in a seemingly rational or logical manner in order to avoid the true explanation. These behaviors are then made consciously tolerable—or even viewed as the best, most admirable choice, by a new acceptable means.

When sin becomes habitual, we become professional rationalizers.

Q: When do you feel like you have to justify your words, beliefs, or actions?

_____

_____

Q: If you feel this need, to whom, and why do you feel this way?

_____

_____

Excuses are often seen as required in many situations today as part of our "human accountability system"—people just seem to need a "reason" for things. Friends, we must understand that there is always a reason why we do something, and these are called motives. Motives can be defined as a reason for doing something, especially one that is hidden or not obvious.

Q: At what point should we begin to question our own motives?

_____

_____

Q: How have corrupt motives hurt you?

_____

_____

Understand this: God doesn't need a motive to love you! He chooses to simply love you out of His great and incredible goodness! Do you love God this way, or do you have a motive attached to your love for Him? I bet if you were honest with yourself, you would even find that you have a motive for loving your husband or wife!

Luke 14:21 says, "*So the servant came back and reported these things to his master. Then in anger, the master of the house told his servant, 'Go out quickly into the streets and alleys of the city, and bring in here the poor, maimed, blind, and lame'*" (HCSB). Even if those first invited to the feast refuse, there will still be a feast; the Master will not go to all this preparation for nothing.

My friends, please realize that there are many who make excuses to God sitting next you in church every Sunday—there may be some sitting among us right now. They are in your family!

Are you ready to receive the invitation to come? Or will you make excuses? What about the type of people whom the Master sent His servant out to get? Will you make excuses, especially when you know what sort of people will be there? How powerful it is to realize that it will be redeemed sinners who are the maimed and the lame and blind.

Luke 14:22–24 ends this way:

> "*Master,*" the servant said, "*what you ordered has been done, and there's still room.*" Then the master told the servant, "*Go out into the highways and hedges and make [compel] them come in, so that my house may be filled. For I tell you, not one of those people who were invited will enjoy my banquet.*" (HCSB)

So why did Jesus say, "compel them to come in"? *Compel* means to convince. These wanderers and outcasts would need to be convinced that they were really welcome—just as we all needed to be. The devil tactfully uses the guilt of our sin to convince us that there is no way we can be redeemed—he compels us to accept that we are permanently lost. We must compel them yes—but let it be done in love, as Christ so compelled us.

We've talked about excuses, rationalization, and motives. Now it's time to examine our hearts right now to see how we have used these three methods to allow self to reign in our hearts. Stop making excuses to God: He has never made one excuse to you—our God only makes promises, and then He delivers on those promises.

Friends, it all starts to change when we stop making excuses to God. If you can do that, you will also stop making excuses to your spouse, your kids, your parents, your boss, and your friends. An excuse will never reveal Christ in your life.

Activities

1. Read Acts 5:1–11 and examine the story of Ananias and Sapphira.

Q: Can you identify what was in their hearts?

_____

_____

_____

_____

Q: What did you see in Ananias and Sapphira—excuses, reasons, motives?

_____

_____

_____

_____

2. Our heart is most often driven by selfish motives and desires.

Q: In what ways have you seen this evident in your own life?

_____

_____

_____

_____

_____

Q: Based on your usual pattern of decision-making, how is your heart different from theirs?

_____

_____

_____

_____

_____

_____

_____

_____

Chapter 8

The Good Fight

Too often in the last 20 years of my Christian walk, I have seen a lot of good men and good women just give up.

What I mean by this is that, at some point, something in the gospel became too offensive for them to tolerate. Christ's Holy statutes for how we should live were ultimately too strict, or worse, their love for something or someone in their lives was more important to them than God was. Because they could never surrender or put down what they loved most, their desire to be submitted and obedient to God's will was abandoned or was never really a priority to begin with. Their focus was off, and priorities were lost.

Oftentimes, when something slips away or is lost, we are too blind to see it. Maybe these people wanted the benefits of being known as a Christian, but their tree and their fruit never quite matched because Jesus was never their first love. While their mouths professed Christ, their hearts were actually far away from Him.

In addition, they put all their hope in what they did or what they gave away and foolishly thought that their empty works would be enough. The blindness that kept them from seeing what had been lost also kept them from knowing what real hope looks like, for men cannot produce real hope, only faith in Christ can. Without true faith in their hearts, they were unable to produce true works, so their counterfeit works became nothing more than false fruit tied to the Vine, only to be later pruned away by the Vine Dresser, who is God the Father. And a branch that has been cut from the vine soon dies, because apart from Christ, we can do nothing, not even live. (John 15:1–11)

Here's how we usually see this process happen:

- It began with a person lying to themselves. While trying to fool others, they only made fools of themselves. Their hope was in their works, as if to earn God's approval, but works without faith are always dead and empty (James 2:17–18).
- They made only temporary investments, not eternal ones.
- They denied the truth because it wasn't popular or convenient.
- They simply gave up or gave in; it doesn't matter which, because both have the same terrible end result—separation from God.

Do any of these bullet points describe what your heart looks like?

The Bible has much to say about "loving the world" or anything of it more than God. In James 4:4, the half brother of Jesus, calls us adulterous people and warns us that *"friendship with the world is enmity with God."* (In the Greek, *enmity* is a hostility, a reason for opposition, even hatred.)

Furthermore, the Apostle John tells us, *"If anyone loves the world, the love of the Father is not in him"* (1 John 2:15–17). It is impossible for the Christian to love both God and the world. A heart that is divided is a heart soon defeated.

And in Romans 1:25, the Apostle Paul tells us that God's wrath will be poured out on those who *"exchanged the truth about God for a lie and worshipped and served the creature rather than the Creator who is blessed forever! Amen."* (Read Romans 1:18–32.) Unfortunately for us, it doesn't take too much to make this horrible exchange in our hearts. When the human heart is consumed with self, the exchange is almost automatic. It simply comes down to choosing whom we are going to serve. And our entire human history provides for us irrefutable evidence that we are really good at being loyal to self and terrible at being loyal to God.

Q: Write a list of your priorities: Is God at the top of the list where He always should be?

_____

_____

Q: Are you willing to love Christ enough to put Him first in your life? Y/N _____

Q: How often do you quit something when it starts to get difficult or requires more of you than you initially expected?

_____

_____

Coincidently, over the years I have tried to talk to people who usually have this one stumbling block in common—they get hung up on what they don't know about God. This then becomes an excuse to lean on their own understanding (the exact opposite of what God commands in Proverbs 3:5–6); this tendency opens the door wide to accept doubt and fear from the enemy and the "life advice" of nonbelieving friends or relatives. Soon the world becomes their new gospel.

They blame God for what they don't know, and when God's Word conflicts with their lifestyle choices, they refuse to accept what has been revealed. This type of reasoning is self-contradictory, because first they get mad for what they don't know, and then when truth is revealed to them, they get mad all the more at what they then **do** know!

To me this sounds like madness! "God, you haven't told me what I want to know," which then leads to, "God, I don't agree with what your Word says on this topic." This is going to sound harsh, but this is not just madness but also a form of self-imposed ignorance and laziness. All of this is completely rooted in the person's selfish desire to have everything in the world agree with their terms or be aligned with their point of view.

I can confidently call this approach ignorance because everything we need to know to live a godly life has already been revealed to us _"through the knowledge of him who called us to his own glory and excellence_ (2 Peter 1:3). Some people simply refuse to accept or acknowledge God's Word and believe that's enough to make it false. They are ignorant. I also call this laziness because if a person doesn't take time to know God and study His Word, then these things will certainly remain unknown to them!

Why should this type of person invest their time to search out the truth, when they already believe they know the truth? Pride breeds laziness. But even if they did know, by itself just knowing is not enough. God requires us to not merely listen to the Word, and so deceive ourselves, but to do what it says (James 1:22).

And know that the knowledge of God comes with a price—the highest level of accountability (to whom much is given, much is required), as Jesus Himself says in Luke 12:48. This is yet another reason people sometimes avoid or deny the truth: They know they will be held accountable to the truth.

Thus, as believers, we must accept that God has made it clear that He has chosen not to reveal some things to us; this is something we must learn to welcome through our faith unconditionally. I can tell you that for me, this is just fine, and it is not in any way a game-changer for my faith; rather, it has strengthened my faith because I can fully trust that He knows everything.

Consider what Ecclesiastes 11:5 says, *"As you do not know the path of the wind, or how the body is formed in a mother's womb, so you cannot understand the work of God, the Maker of all things"* (NIV). Also, in Isaiah 55:8–9 God states: *"For my thoughts are not your thoughts, neither are your ways my ways, declares the LORD. For as the heavens are higher than the earth, so are my ways higher than your ways and my thoughts than your thoughts."*

Q: Has this truth ever been a problem for you?

_____

_____

As you contemplate this question, remember that we are in no position to ever question God or demand anything from Him. Another verse you can read to support this is Deuteronomy 29:29; somehow in my selfish and stubborn heart, God has brought me great peace through this.

Pursuing the Fight

Ultimately, we must confront the arduous task of fighting for the truth, and it most certainly is a fight, because the entire world stands vehemently against it. In order to fight the good fight, we must throw some blows:

> *Therefore I do not run like someone running aimlessly; I do not fight like a boxer beating the air. No, I strike a blow to my body and make it my slave so that after I have preached to others, I myself will not be disqualified for the prize.*
>
> —1 Cor. 9:26–27 NIV

My friends, the good fight begins with you and within you. The only way we can effectively live for Christ is to put self to death:

> *I have been crucified with Christ. It is no longer I who live, but Christ who lives in me. And the life I now live in the flesh I live by faith in the Son of God, who loved me and gave Himself for me.*
>
> —Gal. 2:20

Has your old nature been crucified with Christ, or are you still struggling like the lost people I have been describing above? We can easily live this life like a bystander, watching everything go on and pass us by, or we can take a stand for God and stand for holiness and righteousness—we can be His Holy warriors.

The bystander is a person who is present at something but does not take part in it. Now I don't see how true Christians can be bystanders; it just doesn't match who God says we are in Him. God did not make us to be "bleacher creatures." We all know what a warrior is—a brave and experienced soldier! And the warrior fights hard for his/her king.

Q: Are you a Christian bystander, or are you a Christian warrior?

_____

_____

There is both a purpose and a discipline that drives the Christian warrior forward, and God has promised His presence, His power, and His peace to be with us every step of the way.

62

Q: Do you believe that God's presence, power, and peace are with you? Y/N _____

I will tell you something I learned a long time ago: Whatever is worthwhile or valuable is never easy and is often very expensive. And when I want a good example to remind me, I immediately think of the cross. Here are a few important points we must never lose focus or desire for:

- Remember that this is a good and necessary fight: Paul tells us in 1 Timothy 6:12 that we are to *"fight the good fight for the true faith"* and *"hold tightly to the eternal life to which God has called you, which you have declared so well before many witnesses"* (NLT).
- Endeavor to persevere no matter what: *"Not that I have already obtained all this, or have already arrived at my goal, but I press on to take hold of that which Christ Jesus took hold of me"* (Philippians 3:12 NIV).
- Stay in the fight: Jude 1:3 says that the writer *"felt compelled to write and urge you to contend [fight]for the faith that was once and for all entrusted to God's holy people"* (NIV).

Q: Is Christ worth fighting for to you? Y/N _____

Q: Can you agree this is a good fight? Y/N _____

Q: Can you trust God enough to endure to the end? Y/N _____

Q: Do you realize what great reward is waiting for those who stay in the fight? Y/N _____

Let me remind you that Christ fought for us! He was willing to do whatever it took to reconcile His favorite creation to His Father. Now that sin and death have been defeated, He's asking you and me to fight for righteousness. This is the only good fight left for mankind—fighting for land, power, riches, authority, majority, or even principle no longer matters! Only the good fight of faith matters.

Dear friends, I'm writing this because I pray that you won't give up. I want you to find yourself rejoicing when life gets too hard. And when you find the gospel offensive, challenging, and difficult, remember that the work of the cross isn't asking for change: It demands change; that's why it offends. Remember that all God allows you to go through, wonder about, or struggle in is ultimately for your own good (James 1:2–4).

Finally, let your mind and your spirit be at peace with what the Apostle John writes in 1 John 5:13: *"I write these things to you who believe in the name of the Son of God that you may know that you have eternal life"* (NIV). We can actually know that we know—do you believe this?

The hope that we have now and for eternity in Christ cannot be taken from us, but you have to fight for it. You have to fight daily to avoid sin, go to war against our own bodies, and battle the temptations from the enemy. Now, I ask you to pray for those who appear to have given up. Be a faithful and loving witness to them. Be as supportive and forgiving to others as God has been to you. Remember the price of the cross, which bought our freedom, was paid in the blood of God's only Son; that's how much He loves us! Always fight as hard as you can for that.

This life is both a foot race and a spiritual fistfight, and if you want to finish well, you must be courageous enough and tough enough to run well to the end.

Chapter 9

The Man of Sorrows

He was despised and rejected by men, a man of sorrows and pain and acquainted with grief. And like One from whom men hide their faces He was despised, and we did not appreciate His worth or esteem Him.

—Isa. 53:3 AMP

In this lesson, we will look briefly at a couple of important segments from what Bible scholars refer to as, "The Passion of Christ." What we want to examine in particular is what Jesus experienced in the Garden of Gethsemane and then what happened on the cross while the two thieves were crucified on each side of Him.

In between these two major events, we will also examine the miracle of Lazarus being raised from the dead and the great impact I believe that had on Jesus's humanity. During these events, we can clearly see how deeply saddened Jesus was as He drew closer and closer to His destiny—the cross. We can especially see this emotion during His time of intense prayer in the Garden of Gethsemane. It was there that He agonized and wept, even sweat great drops of blood from the intense stress of what was to come. Yet He unconditionally committed Himself to do the Father's will by accepting the cup of suffering that would bring His death.

He was oppressed and He was afflicted.

—Isa. 53:7a AMP

God has given us the suffering of the Messiah in sobering detail in Isaiah chapter 53. If Isaiah's words in this chapter don't move you and stir your heart, I'm not sure what else would ever be able to. The detailed words describing the great suffering of the Messiah in Isaiah 53 were prophetic words spoken almost 700 years before they would be fulfilled. God's plan to redeem man had been laid out long before anyone ever knew there needed to be a plan for redemption. But God's plan to redeem mankind, the only creature in all of His creation to which He imparted His nature, was first and foremost a plan to glorify Himself. We must be sure to not forget that, since we so often have a tendency to read the Bible and think it's all about us. Nevertheless, God's goodness always overflows into everything contained in His amazing plans, and this is why we can say that anything He does for His glory is always for our greater good.

And even though I can say that I somewhat understand this, it still doesn't make the Passion story any easier to digest. The more I grow in love for our Savior the more His suffering for my sake hurts me and bothers me. Yet at the same time, I also find myself growing more and more thankful as well.

I have had this one disturbing thought more often than I would like, but I know God is using it to help me understand a little better, the reality of what my sin did to the Savior. I believe it came from a prayer I prayed years ago, right after I got saved. I asked God to help me truly grieve my sin. I wanted to be sure to never minimize it and wanted to understand how bad it really was. I have learned to be careful what I ask for.

I picture Christ appearing right next to me, opening His robe and pointing to His wounds, and saying, "These ones are yours, my son." Just thinking about this brings tears to my eyes. As I write this, I am thanking God for that thought and the image that comes with it. I thank Him because it has helped me to stay focused, and I truly know that I never want to hurt Him like that ever again, even though I know I probably will.

Here's what happened as recorded in the 22nd chapter of Luke's Gospel: The agony in the garden:

> *And he came out and went, as was his custom, to the Mount of Olives, and the disciples followed him. And when he came to the place, he said to them, "Pray that you may not enter into temptation." And he withdrew from them about a stone's throw, and knelt down and prayed, saying, "Father, if you are willing, remove this cup from me. Nevertheless, not my will, but yours be done." And there appeared to him an angel from heaven, strengthening him. And being in agony, he prayed more earnestly; and his sweat became like great drops of blood falling down to the ground.*
>
> —Luke 22:39–44

There's no doubt that Jesus knew what was coming; He knew that in just a few short hours, He was about to bear the tremendous weight of judgment for the sin of the world. This burden was like no other—no man before Him nor after Him would ever come close to experiencing anything like this. And Jesus knew that it had to be Him, and that no one else but Him could meet the payment, which was required to satisfy the sin debt of mankind. But He willingly accepted all of this in silence, not once trying to deliver Himself from it.

> *Yet He did not open His mouth [to complain or defend Himself]; like a lamb that is led to the slaughter, and like a sheep that is silent before her shearers, He did not open His mouth.*
>
> —Isa. 53:7b AMP

To make matters worse, Jesus also knew that one of the twelve with whom He had lived and walked for the three plus years of His ministry was going to betray Him. Jesus even washed his betrayer's feet. Even though He knew this, I have to believe that it still brought sadness to His heart. It's not God's desire that anyone should perish, but as Jesus said, *"Many are called, but few are chosen"* (Matt. 22:14). Whether we realize it or not, we each have a role to play in this life, and God's will and His ways will always be what get fulfilled in the end.

Judas's story is a sad and tragic one—one that we need to learn from. How many people like Judas have decided they will only accept Jesus on their own terms, or they try to make Him into something He is not for their own gain? Sadly, too many already have, and human nature dictates that there will be many more. Whether they end up at the end of a rope like Judas or die empty some other way, they will be spiritually separated from Jesus forever, which is the worst ending there is.

Needing a solitary place to pray, Jesus entered the Garden of Gethsemane with the remaining eleven apostles, leaving eight at the entrance, while taking His three closest friends, Peter, James, and John, into the garden with Him. He needs them to just stay awake—to stay awake and pray. Instead, they fall asleep not once, but twice. During the three times that Jesus knelt down to pray, He was beginning to see what was coming. As He petitioned the Father, the reality of the cross was surely coming into view.

I believe His appeal to His friends to stay awake and pray is not a rebuke as it may have seemed due to the urgency of His words. No, instead His appeal comes to them as a brother, one who needs His closest friends to be there for Him in prayer. Oh, how many times already in my own life have I had this very same need! Jesus needed support, and He needed community because He knew that very soon He would be alone.

Sweating great drops of blood is a medical condition called hematidrosis. Jesus really did sweat great drops of blood. This was not a made-up condition or a play on words to add drama to the agony our Lord was experiencing in the garden. The cause of hematidrosis is described as follows: "extreme anguish and intense mental contemplation and physical strain, are its most frequent causes." The pressure from severe stress can cause small blood vessels or capillaries to burst and be expelled out through the pores with sweat.

How real and heavy was our sin debt? How real was the cross? How serious was Jesus about being obedient to God? So much so that it caused Him to sweat great drops of blood in anticipation of what He was about to endure.

Q: When was the last time you experienced extreme stress, and who did you turn to for help or relief?

_____

_____

_____

_____

_____

An angel appeared from heaven to strengthen him: Jesus's human nature was in agony. Many people had seen that His miracles were evidence of His divine nature. And it was not unusual for God to send an angel to divinely sustain Him. What a beautiful passage. God is just so good. The Father wasn't going to leave His Son without comfort during this time.

Q: As you read the details of these events, what comes to your mind? Does it bother you that Jesus went through all this? Explain.

_____

_____

_____

_____

_____

What happens after He was arrested is darker than the most horrible horror movie, yet even when we try to envision it, what He experienced was actually much worse. I have personally seen the horror of war and have asked myself for years since what is it that can draw a human being to that level of cruelty. But even after experiencing all that, I am convinced that the cross and the road that led our Savior there were still somehow mankind's darkest hour ever.

The reality is that Jesus cried out terribly in agony from the fury of God's wrath as it was being poured out on His sinless body. His was the absolute extreme of human suffering, beyond what any mere man could bear. And it was carried out through the most brutal form of organized torture and execution ever known to mankind. Take notice of the language used to describe our Lord's suffering:

But he was **pierced** because of our rebellion,
crushed because of our iniquities;
punishment for our peace was on him,
and we are healed by his wounds.

We all went astray like sheep;
we all have turned to our own way;
and the LORD has punished him
for the iniquity of us all.

—Isa. 53:5–6 CSB; emphasis added

I'm certain that the ripping and tearing of His flesh as He was being brutally beaten goes beyond the description of human words. But the sheer weight and intense pain of the sin of the world must have been so much worse. Once again, He accepted it willingly, and it was all endured for the glory of God and our benefit. It was because He was perfect that He had to be the sacrifice, a lamb without spot or blemish, meant beforehand to pour out His perfect blood for the sins of all men as the holiest of all offerings.

Q: No matter how we approach the cross, the fact that Jesus accepted it all willingly has to blow our minds. Why do you think He did this?

_____

_____

_____

We should be careful not to overlook the fact that the "Passion of Christ" was also a tremendous display of the supreme and sovereign power of the Living God. Think about this for a moment: Satan felt that if he could kill Jesus, he would also be killing any chance of man being redeemed. And certainly, Satan hates God and, whatever God creates, Satan tries to poison, pervert, or destroy. But the truth is God played Satan for a fool all the way to the cross! God even used Satan as a tool, and gave him a starring role in it all, to help bring forth His righteous plans. Do you still have any doubts about who is really in control of all things?

This is the ultimate evidence that God's ways are always high and above ours, and yes, Satan's too. I love what Jesus says in John 10 to affirm this power:

> *This is why the Father loves me, because I lay down my life so that I may take it up again. No one takes it from me, but I lay it down on my own. I have the right to lay it down, and I have the right to take it up again. I have received this command from my Father.*
>
> —John 10:17–18 CSB

Because of this, no true believer should ever lose sight of or become complacent about the cross. We must realize the importance of the cross every day we live. It is at the cross where eternal life begins, and death forever ends. It is at the cross where good conquers evil, and love destroys hate. And what happened at the cross cannot be undone—evil hasn't been merely pushed aside, as if waiting for a chance to return one day. No, the permanence of the cross canceled death and put evil forever on the run. It is at the cross where the sovereign power of God was put on display for all to see, forever separating us from sin and death.

Here's where we break things down and look at some important specifics of what Jesus accomplished on the cross.

Jesus Is Our Perfect High Priest

Jesus is not only the perfect example of obedience; He is our perfect High Priest. Jesus was a Perfect Priest, and most obedient servant:

> *In the days of his flesh, Jesus offered up prayers and supplications, with loud cries and tears, to him who was able to save him from death, and he was heard because of his reverence. Although he was a son, he learned obedience through what he suffered. And being made perfect, he became the source of eternal salvation to all who obey him, being designated by God a high priest after the order of Melchizedek.*
>
> —Heb. 5:7–10 (emphasis added)

Pastor John MacArthur tells us more about the significance of the cross:

> The cross was a masterpiece of wisdom. God solved the problem which no human or angelic mind could have solved. What He did was also consistent with His holiness, for God showed on the cross His hatred for sin. It was consistent with His power, being the greatest display of power ever manifested. Christ endured for a few hours what will take an eternity for unrepentant sinners to endure. It was consistent with His love, in that He loved the world so much that He gave His only Son for its redemption. Finally, what He did was consistent with His grace, because Christ's sacrifice was substitutionary. The work of salvation was totally consistent with God's nature. It was entirely fitting for Him to have done what He did.[1]

Jesus was fully God and fully man. Jesus wasn't born with original sin and therefore had no sin nature: "*Therefore just as through one man [Adam] sin entered into the world, and death through sin, and so death spread to all men, because all sinned*" (Rom. 5:12 NASB 1995). This means that sin enters the family descendants through the father. Jesus had a human mother (though none of Mary's impurities or imperfections could be passed to Jesus because it is a medical fact that a child makes its own blood when in the mother's womb). Yet "He received His divine nature through God the Holy Spirit. Jesus is both God and man, was sinless, had no original sin, and was both fully God and fully man."

The first Adam brought sin and death; Jesus is the Last Adam, and from His cleansing blood flows eternal life. "*So it is written, The first man Adam became a living being; the last Adam became a life-giving spirit*" (1 Cor. 15:45 CSB).

Jesus Completely Understands Our Sin

Although Jesus completely understands our sin, He does not like it at all when we experience the results of it. Let's set the scene with the death and resurrection of Lazarus. In John 11 we find one of the most incredible and revealing miracles that Jesus performed. But even in His foreknowledge of what was going to happen, Jesus was still affected by the death of His dear friend.

John 11:33–36 tells us that "When Jesus saw her [Mary] weeping, and the Jews who had come with her also weeping, he was deeply moved in his Spirit and greatly troubled. And he said, 'Where have you laid him?' They said to him, 'Lord, come and see.' Jesus wept. So the Jews said, 'See how he loved him!'"

I believe this was the "tipping point" in Jesus's humanity: Imagine all the suffering and death He had seen during His earthly ministry. He had seen it all: poor and oppressed people, some suffering sickness and incurable disease, brutality and death. All were under tyrannical rule, while their own leaders were sellouts to the Romans, just so they could have a comfortable seat in their nation's captivity. Meanwhile, the common people were suffering in every way possible.

Lazarus was a man whom Jesus loved. In my opinion what happened to Lazarus could have been the last measure of the suffering from sin that Jesus was going to tolerate.

Notice that John describes Jesus as **"deeply troubled."** Here's where an understanding of the language can help us see that Jesus's feelings went beyond being deeply moved with sympathy. In Greek, "deeply moved" suggests anger or emotional indignation, meaning that Jesus was extremely upset with what sin had done to the human condition. The game changer was that He knew He was the only one who could do something about it. After Jesus raises Lazarus from the dead, He is laser focused on His mission to get to the cross. And He knew it was the cross that would end the reign of sin over the eternity of men.

As believers we can clearly see the compassion and understanding that Jesus has for our suffering, and we can and should take great comfort in this. God does not overlook our pain, He does not ignore our suffering, nor does He turn His back on our trials—He is always there because He always cares.

> *You have taken account of my wandering; Put my tears in Your bottle. Are they not recorded in Your book?*
> —Ps. 56:8 NASB 1995

Did you know that God has taken account of all our weariness and wandering and has also recorded all the times we have experienced pain, hurt, and suffering? He has even saved every tear that has flowed from our eyes because even our tears and what they represent matter to Him.

Q: Can you now see a little of what Jesus was feeling in His heart when He arrived at Lazarus's tomb? Y/N _____

Q: Do you believe that your pain, suffering, and trials matter to Jesus? Y/N _____

As stated above, the death and resurrection of Lazarus marked a change in Jesus's ministry. Interestingly enough, the result of this miracle was the chief priests' plot to kill Jesus and Lazarus, and the Bible tells us that Jesus *"no longer walked openly among the Jews"* (John 11:54). He began to teach the disciples differently, too—everything was now cross-centered. He would return to Jerusalem for the last time and finish what He had been born to do.

Brief notes on the scourging and crucifixion:

- Crucifixion is the most painful death ever invented my man; this is where we get the term *excruciating*.
- Jesus was most likely crucified naked.
- Within a few minutes of being placed on the cross, Jesus's shoulders were dislocated. Minutes later, His elbows and wrists became dislocated.
- All of this was due to the position and posture His body was forced into. He had to push down on the nails in His feet to raise His body in order to exhale (breathe out air from his lungs).
- Each strike of the whip carried the weight of the sin of the world with it.

Jesus and the Thieves on the Cross

This has always been one of the most incredible events for me in the entire Bible. So often I have felt just like these men, lost and broken by my own sinful choices, and knowing for certain that I deserved death. But what this story confirmed for me is that the heart that finds Jesus receives grace and mercy instead. Even when I was at my absolute worst, He stretched out His nail-pierced Hand, and said, "It's OK; come here, my son."

Let's look at what happened on that great and terrible day:

> *Two others—criminals—were also led away to be executed with him. When they arrived at the place called The Skull, they crucified him there, along with the criminals, one on the*

right and one on the left. Then Jesus said, "Father, forgive them, because they do not know what they are doing." And they divided his clothes and cast lots. The people stood watching, and even the leaders were scoffing: "He saved others; let him save himself if this is God's Messiah, the Chosen One!" The soldiers also mocked him. They came offering him sour wine and said, "If you are the king of the Jews, save yourself!"

An inscription was above him: THIS IS THE KING OF THE JEWS.

Then one of the criminals hanging there began to yell insults at him: "Aren't you the Messiah? Save yourself and us!"

But the other answered, rebuking him: "Don't you even fear God, since you are undergoing the same punishment? We are punished justly, because we're getting back what we deserve for the things we did, but this man has done nothing wrong." Then he said, "Jesus, remember me when you come into your kingdom." And he said to him, "Truly I tell you, today you will be with me in paradise."

—Luke 23:32–43 CSB

Jesus Always Stayed on Mission

Jesus stayed on mission until His work was completely finished. Even in the midst of tremendous pain and suffering, He remained coherent enough to ask God to forgive His murderers and to grant mercy and forgiveness to the thief who was hanging on the cross beside Him. He was still doing the work of the advocate even while He was on the cross.

Let me say that again: There was no limit to His goodness, even while He was dying on the cross! And it was at the cross where God through the death of His Only Son was making the biggest statement ever to mankind: Because of Jesus, all who believe in Him will receive mercy (be relieved from the punishment we deserve). Because of Jesus, all who believe in Him will receive grace (the unearned, undeserved favor of God). Because of Jesus, all who believe in Him will receive eternal life. What the repentant thief on the cross just realized was that death wasn't the end for him—for the first time because of Jesus, this man was about to really start living. As he hung dying on a cross, he had the beautiful realization that his past no longer mattered and because of Jesus, his fear gave way to a peace beyond comprehension.

Take a look at the diagram below: Read the description of each man and examine their physical and spiritual condition.

- **Man on the right:** Tired of sin and living in fear.

- **Jesus:** Chose to bear the sin of the world to conquer death and fear.

- **Man on the left:** Tired from sin and living in fear.

- Broken heart filled with *sorrow and repentance.*

- Broken heart filled with the sin of the world and the ability to remove it.

- Broken hearted filled with *pain and bitterness.*

- Feeling the weight of his sin being *lifted* off him.

- Feeling the weight of the sin of the world *being laid on* him.

- Feeling the weight of his sin crushing him.

- Glad the struggle with the flesh is almost over.

- Glad the victory over sin and death is near.

- Terrified that he is about to die and can do nothing about it.

- Is embracing the coming of God's forgiveness and being in paradise.

- Is embracing being reunited with the Father.

- Is surrounded and overcome by the fear of death and the unknown.

Q: I'm sure it's obvious as to who's who here based on Luke 23:32–43. What stands out to you the most about each of them?

_____

_____

_____

_____

_____

_____

_____

Q: Now, which one of these two criminals are you?

_____

_____

_____

_____

_____

_____

_____

Chapter 10

Individual Spiritual Assessment

Note: The material in this lesson was adapted from *Ten Questions to Diagnose Your Spiritual Health* by Donald S. Whitney.[1]

Today, we will examine the health of our spiritual life. When was the last time you did an honest "individual spiritual assessment"? Do you regularly give yourself a tune-up? I believe that self-assessments are not only beneficial but necessary from time to time, in order to assure that we stay as spiritually healthy as possible.

It is no secret that when the spirit gets sick, the rest of us eventually will, too. An unhealthy spirit can sooner or later manifest in us through an emotional or physical state of unwellness, and it can even affect our mental health.

Your spirit is the only part of you that has been designed to live eternally. But when we are physically born, we possess a dead spirit in us, since we are all born with the curse of original sin. The Bible confirms this in Romans 5:12: *"Therefore, just as sin entered the world through one man, and death through sin, in this way death spread to all people, because all sinned"* (NIV).

This also means that with our spirit in this dead state, its eternal destination is in fact separated from God, and therefore condemned. Since we are born with a dead spirit that is essentially being carried around inside a dying body, I think it is safe to say that we are technically "zombies." I don't know about you, but this doesn't sound good to me—I don't want to be a zombie; I don't want to be condemned, and I certainly do not want to be separated from the Living God.

So how can we overcome this? Is it even possible? Yes! The Bible says we must be "born again" (read John 3:3–21). The term *born again* means, "born from above," and it speaks in reference to rebirth through salvation: This means that the only way our spirit can ever live again is to be "born again" through trusting Jesus Christ as Lord and Savior. We need a change of heart—a literal spiritual transformation, and the condition we are born in is not one that is at peace with God, once again, because of sin. Therefore, new birth, or being born again, is an act of God, whereby eternal life is imparted to the person who believes. How beautiful is that?! Being born again has many complex parts, but God has made it simple to understand. And being born again means everything, because it costs everything.

The Bible tells us, *"But God shows his love for us in that while we were still sinners, Christ died for us"* (Rom. 5:8). This means that the sin debt we owed God, which we were unable to pay, has been paid in blood through the life of His Only Son, Jesus Christ, given for us on the cross.

Being "born again" means we become children of God through placing our trust in the name of Jesus Christ. It also means that we have our sins forgiven and now have a relationship with God. Understand that at one time, you and I were enemies of God, but being born again makes us His friends.

Being born again is the most important thing that can ever happen to you.

I took some time to go over that again because I want you to see how important it is that we stay spiritually healthy. After we are born again, we become new creatures. That means that old habits, unhealthy ways, and dangerous living become a part of our past—that is now our old nature, if you will. It's just not who we are anymore. In saving us, God has given us a new heart with new desires. I love how the Apostle Paul describes it here in these two passages:

> *Therefore, if anyone is in Christ, he is a new creation; the old has passed away, and see, the new has come!*
> —2 Cor. 5:17 CSB

79

I have been crucified with Christ, and I no longer live, but Christ lives in me. The life I now live in the body, I live by faith in the Son of God, who loved me and gave Himself for me.

—Gal. 2:20 NIV

So, I see an individual spiritual assessment as important and required maintenance to the most important part of who we are. If we fall spiritually ill, not only can it be harmful to ourselves, but it can also be harmful to others. In another chapter, I talked about how God has given each one of us a "sphere of influence." We have influence in the people groups that we are members of, and if we bring an unhealthy spirit into these groups, we not only damage our witness for Christ, but potentially even push others away from Him, too.

Our longing for God can be described as an intense hunger or a thirst that grows as we pursue knowing Him, but it can also wane when we allow our hearts to be drawn toward other pursuits and pleasures. In his book, *Ten Questions to Diagnose Your Spiritual Health*, Donald S. Whitney described the longing for God as thirst of a particular type of soul, through the description of three kinds of spiritual thirst.[2] This really inspired me to dig deeper into what I felt needed to be examined in my own heart. Inspired by Whitney, I began to map out an abbreviated assessment that could be completed in a relatively short time, so it could be used right away in counseling. I would like to note that I was the first to use this assessment and, from the assessment along with Whitney's book, I learned an awful lot about myself and what I needed to work on. To my surprise, I found that my soul had actually gone through all three phases included here at different times in my life, so I believe that I was able to describe them—because at some point I had lived them. I thank Mr. Whitney for showing me the way. My prayer for you is that this will be another tool to help you grow spiritually stronger and healthier in your relationship with our King. Let's get started.

Q: Do you have a hunger or thirst for God? Explain.

_____

_____

_____

_____

_____

_____

_____

_____

_____

_____

_____

_____

_____

Taste and see that the LORD is good. How happy is the person who takes refuge in Him!

—Ps. 34:8 CSB

As a deer pants for flowing streams, so pants my soul for you, O God.

—Ps. 42:1

Which one of the following describes your need for God?

a. The drought of a barren soul: This type describes a person who constantly feels like their inner man is trapped in a desert. The lack of desire to know God has unknowingly dried up every single well within. In desperation, they find themselves in pursuit of anything that will moisten the deep, dry void inside. They remain consumed by an endless search for satisfaction and fulfillment through the temporary distractions and pleasures of the world. Exhausted and unsatisfied, they find no lasting peace and contentment in them, and as a result, their soul ends up feeling like dry, cracked earth. They just seem to have a constant thirst for all the wrong things.

b. The frustration of a contaminated soul: This type of person is one who has tasted the goodness of the Living God but has spent more time drinking from the "well of the world." He or she is now saturated with a feeling of spiritual unwellness, because the things of the world and the things of God just don't mix. This contaminated state then produces a sense of frustration, because they know God is so close but somehow just can't reach Him. Yet even in the midst of this reality, they continue to try to drink from both wells.

c. The peace of a satisfied soul: This type of person continues to hunger and thirst for God because he or she has found complete satisfaction in Him as their only life-giving source. Their spirit has been enlightened and illuminated in the goodness of His perfect nourishment. The world has no hold on this soul because knowing Christ well spiritually can completely satisfy any appetite. This believer understands that no person, possession, or experience will ever be able to produce the spiritual completeness that is found only in Him.

Q: Describe the "state of your thirst" that is in your heart right now. Give as much detail as you can.

_____

_____

_____

_____

_____

Q: Is your life increasingly structured and driven by God's Holy Word?[3] Y/N _____

> *For the word of God is living and effective and sharper than any double-edged sword, penetrating as far as the separation of soul and spirit, joints and marrow. It is able to judge the thoughts and intentions of the heart.*
> —Heb. 4:12 CSB

By now, I'm sure you have deduced that the three definitions described above represent three different types of souls. The first one is someone who doesn't care to know God, the second is someone who wants to try to have both the world and God, and finally the last one is someone who wants God and nothing else.

Believe it or not, all three of these soul types require some manner of commitment. Obviously only one of them is ideal, so let's examine how we can get there together.

Many professed Christians today have little to no relationship with God through His Holy Word. They may carry a Bible with them to church, but they cannot tell you much about it because they do not take time to study it. The most people do today is spend a few minutes reading a short daily devotional and then immediately go and live the rest of the day however they choose.

A daily relationship with God's Word, when pursued with a sincere heart, is life-changing. And a strong relationship can only come through discipline and devotion. Many Christians claim that they never hear from God, but many of these same folks are not reading their Bibles—that is why they do not hear from God. Remember that a person who can be content with only a few routine interactions with God's Word may be in danger of something far worse than just spiritual decline.

Q: Do you regularly seek to be in God's presence? Y/N _____

Q: Describe what being in God's presence means to you.

_____

_____

_____

_____

_____

_____

Q: Are you at all sensitive to His presence?[4] Y/N or I don't know _____

Therefore, brothers, since we have confidence to enter the holy places by the blood of Jesus, by the new and living way that He opened for us through the curtain, that is, through His flesh, and since we have a great priest over the house of God, let us draw near with a true heart in full assurance of faith, with our hearts sprinkled clean from an evil conscience and our bodies washed with pure water.

—Heb. 10:19–22

The LORD appeared to him from far away. I have loved you with an everlasting love; therefore I have continued my faithfulness to you.

—Jer. 31:3

Jesus promised us in Matthew 28:20 that He would be with us always. But do we deliberately seek to be in the presence of God? Do we truly want to be with Him always? Many of us live as if He is far away; we ignore Him when times are good in our lives and usually only cry out to Him when we find ourselves in some sort of crisis. It is important that we understand that if we have an insensitivity to the presence of God, it usually means we are more tuned in to something else. Remember that something or someone almost always has our attention—but are we focusing on the right one?

In 1 Samuel 16:13–16 (CSB), we see two distinct movements of the Spirit of God: one when He left King Saul and the other when He entered David.

So Samuel took the horn of oil and anointed him in the presence of his brothers, and the Spirit of the LORD came powerfully on David from that day forward. Then Samuel set out and went to Ramah. Now the Spirit of the LORD had left Saul, and an evil spirit sent from the Lord began to torment him, so Saul's servants said to him, "You see that an evil spirit from God is tormenting you. Let our lord command your servants here in your presence to look for someone who knows how to play the lyre. Whenever the evil spirit from God comes on you, that person can play the lyre, and you will feel better."

What stands out to me here in this passage with regards to King Saul is that he seems more concerned with the spirit that is now tormenting him than with the One that had left him. When the Spirit of the Lord left Saul, he lost his covering. That means that now it's open season on Saul's soul, and all it took was for God to leave Saul for the enemy to jump in there and begin to torment him. And what is Saul's plan to deal with this? *"Go get me someone to come and play some soothing music for me."* If you ask me, that wasn't the decision that was going to change anything.

I believe that God allowed this to happen because Saul had disqualified himself as king through his disobedience. But the crazy thing to me is that Saul doesn't seem to be aware of what all has happened. In a previous chapter, I mentioned that evil and sin can be very effective distractions to the Christian, and I think our spiritual sensitivity is one of the areas where we get hit the most. In the final analysis, we human beings are pretty much the same. As Solomon said over and over in the book of Ecclesiastes, "There's nothing new under the sun." What I am saying is that we fall into sin and distraction just as fast (if not faster because of technology) as our OT brothers and sisters did.

But here's where we have the advantage: We have a different relationship with God than the OT saints did! Now He dwells in us. Are we completely missing out on this? I'm not saying we are able to "keep tabs" on God or always know where He is, but I am saying that when we truly know Him, we will often recognize when He is near. And remember, He promised to never leave us or forsake us (Deut. 31:6).

But when we allow ourselves to become insensitive to His presence, that can cause us to be less concerned with restraining sin in our lives. Was Saul so self-consumed that he totally missed the absence of the Holy Spirit after He left him? We can easily become just as self-consumed—at least I know I can. I can testify that God has used other people and certain situations in my life to remind me of or alert me to His presence. My friend, I am thoroughly convinced that God wants us to be aware of His presence because it is a key component of our relationship with Him. Allow me to share one more personal nugget with you—I call it a nugget because what God did was pure gold. I had experienced some very traumatic events while serving in the military. Most of the worst ones happened to me before I had given my life to Christ. Almost immediately after I was saved, God brought those events to my memory and through His Spirit showed me how He had preserved and protected me through them all! As I was experiencing this recall, His Spirit poured over me, and I had never felt that safe, that loved, or that valuable in my entire life.

His presence is real because He is real. I would stake my life on that fact.

Dig deep in your heart and examine yourself: Is where you are right now a place that is putting distance between you and God? Be honest and answer this question and then be determined to not forget God or ignore the peace of His presence anymore.

Now that we understand where the problem might be, we need to do something about it. So, how do we do this?

Start by Talking to Him through Prayer

Quiet time with God in prayer is as essential to the health of our faith just as breathing is to our bodies.

- Learn to say thank you: Too many Christians live more with an expectation from God than they do with a spirit of thanksgiving to God. We have so much to be thankful for and if we are honest, we will admit that we regularly take most of it for granted.
- Seek Him where He is always found: Go often to the place where God has revealed Himself the most—you will always find Him in the Bible. God's Word can also help guide your prayers. I have learned a lot about prayer from the psalms.
- Seek the right environment for prayer: Some people have a prayer closet, or prayer room, but I have always felt closer to God outside for some reason. Early on in my faith, I would venture outdoors, often at night, and search for God, and when I saw the stars, for some reason, He felt closer to me. The same thing has happened to me in the woods. I believe He has just allowed me to connect with Him more through His creation in nature.

Look for Him in Congregational Worship

Wherever His Word is faithfully preached and worship to Him is genuine, He will be there. Church attendance and participation must be a priority for you (Hebrews 10:25).

Continue to affirm within yourself that He is always with you, especially when you don't "feel" that He is near. Learn to trust your faith more than your feelings and believe what scripture confirms about our omnipresent God.

Find Him through Loving and Serving Others

Q: Do you have a growing concern for the needs of others?[5] Y/N _____

> *My brothers and sisters, if any among you strays from the truth, and someone turns him back, let that person know that whoever turns a sinner from the error of his way will save his soul from death and cover a multitude of sins.*
> —James 5:19–20

Scripture clearly teaches that we are to have love and concern for others and their needs. A selfless heart is some of the best evidence of a sanctified soul. At no other time are we more like Jesus than when we selflessly love and serve others and genuinely put their needs above ours.

There must be nothing in it for you: This manner of service must have no concern for personal gain or recognition. It is service that must be approached with the sole desire to serve God first as we go about caring for others.

Our Lord came to the earth with the sole purpose of glorifying God through the redemption of mankind. While Jesus's primary mission was to meet our eternal need, He most certainly did not ignore our temporary needs.

True service to others will often require us to move outside of our comfort zone: There will be times when God asks us to make not only a spiritual investment in others but a physical and emotional one as well. Galatians 6:10 commands: *"Therefore, as we have opportunity, let us work for the good of all, especially for those who belong to the household of faith"* (CSB). As ambassadors for Christ, we have been given a very unique opportunity to show the love of Christ through service to others: We have a responsibility in a sense to do exactly what Jesus did—care for others fully and completely. *"Carry one another's burdens; in this way you will fulfill the law of Christ"* (Gal. 6:2 CSB).

So, what does this look like? Through the declaration of our testimony (not just by our words, but also by how we live), we lay out the road map to salvation, and we are a witness, an assistant, or a guide to a person in their discovery of God. Always be confident that God has already prepared for us the opportunity to love and serve others. We have this promise from scripture: *"For we are his workmanship, created in Christ Jesus for good works, which God prepared ahead of time for us to do"* (Eph. 2:10 CSB).

Finally, having a genuine growing concern for the needs of others also comes with a promise: *"And the King will answer them, 'Truly I tell you, whatever you did for one of the least of these brothers and sisters of mine, you did for me'"* (Matt. 25:40 CSB).

Hate Our Own Sin More Than We Hate the Sin of Others

Let me illustrate what I mean by this statement. I certainly hate what Adolf Hitler did to the Jews during WWII; it was worse than atrocious, and I haven't met anyone who would disagree with me about this yet. But because I am not accountable for any of it, I have no right to place it above my own sin. God will certainly judge Hitler for all he did, and God will hold me accountable for my sin as well. For this reason, I must hate all sin, but especially my own. Remember, your sin is what messes with your sanctification, not anyone else's. We must be careful to not let anyone else's sin cause us to judge others more severely than ourselves.

Q: Do you still grieve over sin?[6] Y/N _____

> For godly grief produces a repentance that leads to salvation without regret, but worldly grief produces death.
>
> —2 Cor. 7:10 CSB

It is a fact that the closer you get to Jesus, the more you will grow in hatred for sin. And the more you hate sin, the more genuinely will you grieve when you commit sin. Here's where we can easily fall into a trap: When we continuously bring to mind past sin and continue to grieve it, this is very dangerous and can become sinful, because this activity stands in direct conflict with the promises of God in scripture: *"If we confess our sins, He is faithful and righteous to forgive us our sins and to cleanse us from all unrighteousness"* (1 John 1:9 CSB).

Not only that but allowing ourselves to continuously grieve over past sin robs us of our God-given joy today. Once we sincerely confess sin and turn away from that sin pattern, it is gone. God has promised that.

True and sincere confession, marked by true repentance of the heart, is never heartless nor mechanical. We must completely understand that every sin we commit is committed against God first, and so our immediate desire must be to make peace with God right away. We should hurt for a time every time we hurt God! It should be our very grief over sin that compels us to repentance.

Finally, a heart that truly loves God will hate the things He hates and will hurt every time God is offended by sin. And a person that truly loves Him will also never allow themselves to forget the eternal death sentence from which God has delivered them.

We Must Always Be Quick to Forgive Others.

Q: Are you quick to forgive others?[7] Y/N _____

> *And be kind and compassionate to one another, forgiving one another, just as God also forgave you in Christ.*
> —Eph. 4:32 CSB

It is sad to say that for many professed Christians forgiveness of others is often not an option. Forgiveness is a chief attribute in the heart of the sanctified person, and truly a mark of a changed life in Christ. When we refuse to forgive quickly, that is sin; and when we hold back forgiveness, we then quickly become bitter, and that too is sin.

Imagine where you and I would be right now if God chose to be slow or absent with His forgiveness. We would be in some serious trouble and would be faced with a debt that we have no way to pay.

Be sure to understand this: When you have been wronged by someone, the issue of forgiveness is between you and God **before** it is with the one who has hurt or offended you. Why? Because forgiveness is a holy command given to us by God and when we refuse to obey it, we place ourselves in disobedience to God.

God wants your heart to respond to the issue of forgiveness in obedience, so that you may then faithfully go and implement the act of forgiveness with your neighbor.

Q: Do you have a deep desire for heaven and to be with Jesus one day?[8] Explain.

_____

_____

_____

_____

_____

_____

_____

My soul thirsts for God, for the Living God; When shall I come and appear before God?

—Ps. 42:2

Surely goodness and mercy shall follow me all the days of my life, and I shall dwell in the house of the LORD forever.

—Ps. 23:6

The heart of every truly saved Christian desires one main thing: to be in the presence of God—to see His face and to be with Him forever. Too many Christians, though, are more concerned with the things of this world. They have more interest in their money or their stuff, or they have invested all of themselves into a job, a relationship, their kids, or even worse the temporary pleasures of a temporary world.

Ask yourself these questions:

- When it comes to my death, am I only concerned about not going to hell, or do I actually long to be in the perfect presence of the Living God?
- Is salvation all I want from God? If that is the case, then you may not really have it.
- Will the only place we find your name be on a rock in the dirt or will your name be found in the Lamb's Book of Life also?

Jesus died not only to save you but to have a loving relationship with you. Our love for God must grow past the benefits of the cross and must become a love that simply exists because of who He is—not just for what He has done.

Take time to reflect on your answers and be prepared to develop a plan to change and improve the areas where you find yourself lacking.

And don't worry, you won't have to do this by yourself!

PART 2

Being a Christian offers me the blessed opportunity to serve the LORD. We are to submit to each other as unto the LORD. Submitting means that I want what the Lord wants for me, more than what I want for myself. With this mindset, I want to walk with Christ and carry out what He has for me.

—Pastor Ron Smith, BT Church

Chapter 11

The Power and Authority of Christ

Today, we will look in detail at two examples of the power and authority of Jesus Christ.

Each believer should have working knowledge of Christ's authority so they can confidently navigate the challenges of this world. When we are absolutely sure of who Christ is and the power and authority He controls, we are less likely to be overwhelmed or fooled by the lies of the world or be discouraged by man's unrighteous use of the authority given to him.

I'm also sharing this with you because we all struggle to some degree with our submission to God's authority. We all test the boundaries of His grace in ways that we most certainly should not. It is important that we examine every area of our heart that would try to challenge the authority of Christ, because left unchecked, we might challenge Him to death.

Finally, we must have the right view of Christ, and that view should be one where we find ourselves on our knees expressing great reverence to Him as the Sovereign God, while at the same time being fully aware that we are not. Let's start with a few questions:

Q: What do the words *power* and *authority* mean to you?

_____

_____

_____

_____

_____

Q: What comes to mind when you think of power and authority? For instance, you might think of privilege, control, or responsibility.

_____

_____

_____

_____

_____

The Bible makes it clear that God is absolutely sovereign over all things, but interestingly enough, it was just that exact same authority that Jesus set aside in order to enter into this world in the form of a flesh and blood man. His plan, from the beginning, was to redeem mankind through offering Himself as a perfect, sinless sacrifice. He didn't have a problem with humbling Himself to death, in order to do it. Let's look at this beautiful piece of scripture:

> *Adopt the same attitude as that of Christ Jesus, who, existing in the form of God, did not consider equality with God as something to be exploited. Instead he emptied himself by assuming the form of a servant, taking on the likeness of humanity. And when he had come as a man, he humbled himself by becoming obedient to the point of death—even to death on a cross. For this reason God highly exalted him and gave him the name that is above every name, so that at the name of Jesus every knee will bow—in heaven and on earth*

and under the earth—and every tongue will confess that Jesus Christ is Lord, to the glory of God the Father.

—Phil. 2:5–11 CSB

What Christ expressed through emptying Himself to assume the form of the servant is nothing less than an incredible expression of power. Think about this for a moment: Our God who is perfect in every way imaginable, made Himself **less,** so He could save us—now, that is power.

He was able to conquer death because of who He is as the Apostle Paul so beautifully explained to the Colossian church:

> *He is the image of the invisible God, the firstborn over all creation. For everything was created by him, in heaven and on earth, the visible and the invisible, whether thrones or dominions or rulers or authorities—all things have been created through him and for him. He is before all things, and by him all things hold together. He is also the head of the body, the church; he is the beginning, the firstborn from the dead, so that he might come to have first place in everything. For God was pleased to have all his fullness dwell in him, and through him to reconcile everything to himself, whether things on earth or things in heaven.*
>
> —Col. 1:15–20 CSB

It was through the absolute power and authority of Christ that everything was reconciled to Himself.

Q: God chose to redeem us by sentencing His Only Son to die on the cross as payment for our sins. Can you say that you understand why Jesus had to be our sacrifice? What does it mean to you?

_____

_____

_____

_____

_____

The Power of Christ

On that day, when evening had come, he told them, "Let's cross over to the other side of the sea." So they left the crowd and took him along since he was in the boat. And other boats were with him. A great windstorm arose, and the waves were breaking over the boat, so that the boat was already being swamped. He was in the stern, sleeping on the cushion. So they woke him up and said to him, "Teacher! Don't you care that we're going to die?" He got up, rebuked the wind, and said to the sea, "Silence! Be still!" The wind ceased, and there was a great calm. Then he said to them, "Why are you afraid? Do you still have no faith?" And they were terrified [filled with awe] and asked one another, "Who then is this? Even the wind and the sea obey him!"

—Mark 4:35–41 CSB

Setting the scene:

- Jesus and His disciples were on the western shore where all the larger cities were, and they wanted to cross over to the eastern shore where there were smaller towns and fewer people.
- Jesus needed a break from continuous preaching, teaching, and healing; simply put, He was tired.
- The Sea of Galilee is more like a large lake, and it sits about 700 feet below sea level and is surrounded by hills, which allow the wind to get trapped over the low-lying water so windstorms like this one were not uncommon.
- And this storm, which apparently whipped up very quickly, was obviously a bad one to so easily have frightened the disciples who were experienced fishermen.

Q: How many times have you allowed the storms of life to be greater than God?

Q: Can you say in your heart that you usually default to trusting in Him when hard times come?

I find what the disciples said in verse 38 to be very interesting: *"He was in the stern, sleeping on the cushion. So they woke Him up and said to Him, 'Teacher! Don't You care that we're going to die?'"* This is a perfect example of how quickly we forget about the complete authority of Jesus over all things. In fact, just a short time before this happened, the disciples had witnessed Jesus performing countless miracles, signs, and wonders! Look at what is recorded only one chapter earlier in Mark's Gospel:

> *Then he told his disciples to have a small boat ready for him, so that the crowd wouldn't crush him. Since he had healed many, all who had diseases were pressing toward him to touch him. Whenever the unclean spirits saw him, they fell down before him and cried out, "You are the Son of God!" And he would strongly warn them not to make him known.*
>
> —Mark 3:9–12 CSB

After being witness to all of this, they are still ready to resign themselves to death! "The storm is just too big! Master, how can You just lie there and sleep when we are about to die?"

> *See now that I, even I, am he, and there is no god beside me; I kill and I make alive; I wound and I heal; and there is none who can deliver out of my hand.*
>
> —Deut. 32:39

I can just picture Jesus, the Creator of everything He's encountering at that moment—the howling wind, the raging seas, and the whining disciples—Jesus even created the tree from which the cross came from! I can just picture Him, getting up slowly but deliberately, walking out to the main deck of their tiny boat that's probably almost half underwater, and He calmly says, "Peace. Be still." And everything stops.

Now, that is power. That is authority.

And then He has to ask that question: "Do you still have no faith?" How about you, friend? Where's your faith when the world is crashing down all around you and your life is being flipped upside down? After all that Jesus has made known to you about Himself—after all He has done for you and what you have seen Him do for others—after all He endured for you on that horrible cross—do you still have no faith?

Activity

Describe briefly in your own words a life event that really shook you up; I'm not asking you to relive it, just to briefly describe it, and how you reacted to it.

After you have written that down, stop and offer that event to Christ. Give Him authority over it, whether it has been resolved or not. If you didn't trust Him through it, repent for that. Ask God to give you peace in your heart over this matter. Finally, write a short prayer of thanksgiving to God for His goodness.

_____

_____

_____

_____

_____

_____

The Authority of Christ

Then they sailed to the region of the Gerasenes, which is opposite Galilee. When he got out on land, a demon-possessed man from the town met him. For a long time he had worn no clothes and did not stay in a house but in the tombs. When he saw Jesus, he cried out, fell down before him, and said in a loud voice, "What do you have to do with me, Jesus, Son of the Most High God? I beg you, don't torment me!" For he had commanded the unclean spirit to come out of the man. Many times it had seized him, and though he was guarded, bound by chains and shackles, he would snap the restraints and be driven by the demon into deserted places. "What is your name?" Jesus asked him. "Legion," he said, because many demons had entered him. And they begged Him not to banish them to the abyss.

A large herd of pigs was there, feeding on the hillside. The demons begged him to permit them to enter the pigs, and he gave them permission. The demons came out of the man and entered the pigs, and the herd rushed down the steep bank into the lake and drowned.

When the men who tended them saw what had happened, they ran off and reported it in the town and in the countryside. Then people went out to see what had happened. They came to Jesus and found the man the demons had departed from, sitting at Jesus's feet, dressed and in his right mind. And they were afraid. Meanwhile, the eyewitnesses reported to them how the demon-possessed man was delivered. Then all the people of the Gerasene region asked him to leave them, because they were gripped by great fear. So getting into the boat, he returned. The man from whom the demons had departed begged him earnestly to be with him. But he sent him away and said, "Go back to your home, and tell all that God has done for you." And off he went, proclaiming throughout the town how much Jesus had done for him.

—Luke 8:26–39 CSB

Setting the scene: Nowhere else in scripture do we receive such a detailed description of a demon. Here we find the classic profile of demonic possession. It would appear that this man has been demon possessed for a very long time. The effect of his possession had caused the man to live like a sub-human, wild animal:

- He didn't wear clothes; in fact, he tore them off.
- He lived in a cemetery, bound in shackles and chains. He was so strong that he broke the chains and everything else the townspeople tried to tie him up with!

- When a demonic spirit takes up residence in a human body, at times it will exhibit its own personality through the person of the host body.

Whether we want to believe it or not, this is how the devil can torment a human being. Today, we are seeing a cultural phenomenon that is growing, and in many places, it is seen as a normal expression—of what I have no idea. The phenomenon is self-mutilation. It includes people hanging themselves up using meat hooks in their flesh and finding pleasure in that—that is not what God intended, and I don't think anyone who is in a healthy state of mind does this. This is one of the ways that the enemy works in us—overwhelming the operations of one's body and causing a person to do strange and grotesque things.

People often ask me, "Can a Christian be possessed?" My answer is this: I believe no, a truly saved person cannot be possessed. For a true Christian to be possessed by the devil, the devil or demon would have to be able to remove the presence of the Holy Spirit from that person, and I don't believe that can happen. No matter what form he takes or how many he brings with him, the enemy cannot overwhelm the Spirit of the Living God! Remember, greater is He who is in you than he that is in the world!

But a saved Christian can be **oppressed** by an evil spirit—that is, they can be "strongly influenced."

> *When he saw Jesus, he cried out, fell down before Him, and said in a loud voice, "What do You have to do with me, Jesus, Son of the Most High God? I beg You, don't torment me!" For He had commanded the unclean spirit to come out of the man.*
> —Luke 8:28 CSB

- Notice that the very first thing the demons did was acknowledge the authority of Christ! *"I beg You, don't torment me!"*
- Satan, his demons, and all the enemies of God are fully aware of the power and authority of Jesus Christ!
- They know that they have no power or authority over the Living God.

Q: Sadly, we often overlook or even forget this. Are you prone to allow the enemy to deceive you in this? If yes, why?

_____

_____

_____

"Many times it had seized him," and though he was guarded and bound by chains and shackles, he would snap the restraints and be driven by the demon into deserted places.

> "What is your name?" Jesus asked him. "Legion," he said, because many demons had entered him. And they begged him not to banish them to the abyss.
>
> —Luke 8:30–31

- The demon known as "Legion" begged Jesus not to banish them to the abyss.
- It is important for us to realize that the demons are fully aware of the coming judgment; they know they will eventually end up in the abyss!
- Proverbs 16:4 says, "The Lord has made everything for its purpose, even the wicked for the day of trouble."

Areas of Personal Authority

As we contemplate this short study on the power and authority of Jesus Christ, we must come to grips and accept ownership and responsibility for the things over which we have authority in this life. And according to scripture, there are only three things you and I actually own and have authority over: our thoughts, our words, and our actions.

Our Thoughts

> You have heard that it was said to our ancestors, Do not murder, and whoever murders will be subject to judgment. But I tell you, everyone who is angry with his brother or sister will be subject to judgment. . . . You have heard that it was said,

Do not commit adultery. But I tell you, everyone who looks at a woman lustfully has already committed adultery with her in his heart.

—Matt. 5:21–22a, 27–28

In case there was any doubt, pretty much every sin is born on the battlefield of the mind. But oftentimes, our thoughts remain just thoughts (they never "graduate" to words or actions), but all those unholy or impure thoughts are still sin, and we will be held accountable for them one day. We truly are what we think.

Q: Have you noticed a pattern of bad thoughts in your thought life? Y/N _____

We all have bad thoughts, but we do not deal with them as we should.

Q: Have you repented to God for your bad thoughts and struggled to renew your mind as often as needed in obedience to the commands of scripture (e.g., Romans 12:2, 2 Corinthians 10:3–5)? Y/N _____

Our Words

Brood of vipers! How can you speak good things when you are evil? For the mouth speaks from the overflow of the heart. A good person produces good things from his storeroom of good, and an evil person produces evil things from his storeroom of evil. I tell you that on the day of judgment people will have to account for every careless word they speak. For by your words you will be acquitted, and by your words you will be condemned.

—Matt. 12:34–37 CSB

Whoever insults his brother or sister, will be subject to the court. Whoever says, "You fool!" will be subject to hellfire [literally the fire of hell].

—Matt. 5:22b CSB

104

Words can and do cut deep, and when they are not edifying words or words "that give grace to all who hear," then they are dangerous and hurtful words. As the Bible says, what comes out of our mouths is truly a direct reflection of what is in our hearts.

Q: Do you use bad language or speak in ways that do not bless the ears of others? Y/N _____

Q: How would you generally describe the content of your speech—wholesome or unwholesome? Building up or tearing down? Hurtful and condemning, or blessing and encouraging? (Circle the appropriate answers.)

Q: If this is something that you struggle with, have you sought out accountability through a close friend or someone you can trust to hold you accountable? Y/N _____

If no, why not?

_____

_____

_____

Our Actions

> *I also saw the dead, the great and the small, standing before the throne, and books were opened. Another book was opened, which is the book of life, and the dead were judged according to their works by what was written in the books.*
> —Rev. 20:12 CSB

Isn't it interesting that what we own starts out as a thought, progresses to words, and often ends up as actions? And just like our words, our actions become evidence of the condition of our heart. It is sad that many a good Christian witness has been torn down through sinful words and actions.

How can the world see us as different if these three areas of our lives are not brought into submission to the power and authority of Jesus Christ?

Q: How well are you managing your own thoughts, words, and actions?

_____

_____

_____

Q: As a believer, would you say that are you still "playing" with sin? Y/N _____

Q: Are you right now prepared to give account to the Living God for the quality and character of your thoughts, words, and actions? Y/N _____

In Matthew chapter 28 Jesus says that He has been given authority over everything in heaven and on earth. As supreme ruler over the universe, God has the right to do whatever He wants, and He has complete control over everything that happens.

In direct contrast to this, our authority in this life is tiny, yet still capable of destroying us. When we truly believe and understand that Jesus is sovereign over all, then we can relax and not worry about trying to control everything, and that frees us so we can live in this truth and be a light to a lost world that is constantly crying out for true order.

Let us strive to live every day in the reality that Jesus is in fact sovereign over all.

> _As you do not know the path of the wind, or how the body is formed in the mother's womb, so you cannot understand the work of God, the Maker of all things._
>
> —Eccles. 11:5 NIV

Chapter 12

Standing at the Crossroads, Part 1

For most people, the quest for peace and happiness in this life ends up becoming a long series of heartaches, disappointments, struggles, and exhaustion. What we end up with versus what we think we are entitled to are never the same. We seem to be really good at dreaming bigger than the limits of our temporary reality!

At some point, most people have looked at their lives and their goals and pursued them through the eyes of the world; as a result, they have obtained only what they saw in their own half-blind perceptions. If we are honest with ourselves, we are still way out of focus. Even if the plans we drew up in our heads were somewhat noble and may have even been inundated with miles of good intentions, we continuously fell short.

Be honest. How often have we caught ourselves saying, "One more year . . . just one more try; I know I can make it." "Once I get that promotion, or that pay raise . . . then I will be there." Or maybe you are there and are saying, "I don't get it . . . I have the car, the house, the job, the money, the spouse . . . everything I thought would make me happy . . . but why does my life feel so empty?" Worse yet, how about when those "well-laid plans" go wrong and not only hurt you but also your family? We need to reevaluate our priorities.

He who loves money never has enough; whoever loves wealth is never satisfied with his income; this too is meaningless.
                                                    —Eccles. 5:10 NIV

Many are the plans in a person's heart, but it is the Lord's purpose that prevails.
                                                    —Prov. 19:21 NIV

Q: What is your "formula" for making decisions? Describe what is involved in this process.

_____

_____

_____

Q: How often do you seek outside assistance or counsel when having to make big or complicated choices? If you are one who does not seek counsel, why not?

_____

_____

_____

If you have had most of your plans backfire in your face, you are certainly not alone. With our misaligned priorities, we will seek futile and essentially meaningless dreams and goals that will either amount to nothing and pass away during our lifetime or never be as fulfilling as we originally hoped. The truth is, what we seek in the here and now is only temporary, and our earthly plans will have no value in heaven. We need to reevaluate our priorities.

Q: Please list your top five priorities here.

_____

_____

_____

_____

_____

Ask yourself how successful has your quest for peace been on your journey so far? What exactly is true peace—do you even know what it is?

In my own life these questions have burned inside me like an unquenchable fire. For the past several years, I have been on a journey, a quest if you will, a calling I received from the Lord. He called me into Christian ministry and after years of me telling the Lord God Almighty no time and time again, He bent the knee I refused to bend before Him. I must admit it was more than a bit painful.

> *Humble yourselves, therefore, under the mighty hand of God, so that he may exalt you at the proper time.*
> —1 Pet. 5:6 CSB

God offers us the opportunity to humble ourselves, to willfully submit to Him, and it even comes with a promise—God is the One who eventually (in His time) exalts you: He will lift you up and establish you. And if the Living God lifts you up, who will be able to tear you down?

Through this assurance, I finally began to see a small piece of what He has planned for me. Now I'm starting to see more, like why He made me and why He let me experience all that I have been through in my life—both the good and the bad.

Let me tell you that I have already carried a variety of crosses on my journey as a "learning disciple." I say "learning" because in my journey, I realize that I have been the one picking up all the wrong crosses!

I have come to realize that God is the One who chooses the crosses—not me. I like the comfortable ones that only look heavy or make me look like I'm a great guy. But I found out it can be like putting on razor blade–lined socks and underwear.

The things He has planned for me (and for you) are first and foremost totally for His glory, and we must be OK with that. He picks the crosses and if you carry them, they accomplish His plans, not yours. But what is so wonderful is that His great glory is full of nothing but the best for us in every way.

So, what is your calling? Have you made it your mission to seek out the unique way He designed for you to bring Him glory? Here's an example of the attitude we must have:

Not to us, O LORD, not to us, but to your name goes all the glory for your unfailing love and faithfulness.

—Ps.115:1

Q: Describe what you believe is your "calling" in life.

_____

_____

_____

Q: Have you picked up the cross in that calling yet? If yes, how do you know?

_____

_____

_____

Q: Explain your understanding of making temporary investments versus eternal investments.

_____

_____

_____

Q: What investments have you made in both these areas?

_____

_____

_____

As I sit here writing this, I am a fifty-something-year-old guy who is a truly blessed and grateful husband of the most amazing woman I know, and the father of two of the most incredible children (now adults), and grandfather to the most precious granddaughter a man could ever possibly ask for.

I'm going to share with you what I have learned through my short, complicated existence, and a lot of you are going to be able to draw comparisons and relate to the parallels of a regular guy's life on this earth—be it ever so brief.

If you are older, you can say, "Yeah, I've been there," and you may find yourself surprised that you have made it through so far. If you are younger, please take heed and try to use this short read as an opportunity to take an honest look at yourself and where you are in relation to God right now.

Oftentimes, this life can be so painful, yet our gracious God who made us has us right where we are for a reason, even if we have taken more than one wrong turn.

No matter what age you are when you read this, stop for a moment and pull down the walls you have built up around yourself and lay aside your huge pride; let the gentle presence of the wonderful Comforter, the Holy Spirit, show you what you need to see now. If you are at a crossroads in your life, whether it is the first time or the hundredth time, if you will let Him be God, He surely won't disappoint you. I guarantee that if you seek Him with your whole heart, you will find the peace of God, *"which surpasses all understanding, [which] will guard your hearts and your minds in Christ Jesus"* (Phil. 4:7).

Preparing for War

> *Rejoice, O young man, in thy youth; and let thy heart cheer thee in the days of thy youth, and walk in the ways of thine heart, and in the sight of thine eyes; but know thou, that for all these things God will bring thee into judgment.*
>
> —Eccles. 12:9 KJV

Life is a strange gift; for us to put so much energy into living while working against time and a body that gradually declines and will ultimately fail us, can certainly be an enigma. It would seem that an existence such as ours would be a pure waste if we were merely created just to exist.

Yet, a lot of us live as if the only reason we are alive is to do just that—exist. But human beings seem to be driven by extremes. For many, just living isn't enough. Since the beginning of time, countless people have ascribed to the concept of the "get it now, no matter what the cost" mentality: This manner of thinking can be very dangerous and has even been responsible for starting wars. Few today actually seek to live for the purpose for which they were created; in fact, many don't even believe they were created on purpose, let alone for a purpose! Unfortunately, the sad truth is, most would much rather prefer to live for their own purpose instead. God has warned us from the beginning of time about the deadly attraction to "loving our own life" more than anything else. Choosing to live only for self will result in permanent separation from God.

That's why God had to send His Son to save us from ourselves—to save us from the consequences of our selfish choices—to save us from eternal death. How many times did you gamble with your life, just for the thrill of it? As a history buff, I have read numerous books on the Founding Fathers and often reflected on a simple pearl of wisdom from Ben Franklin, who said, "Work as if you were to live a hundred years, Pray as if you were to die tomorrow."[1] This was a profound nugget of wisdom that meant nothing to me until I woke up one day and realized I had only been paying attention to the first part.

Looking back, what stood out is the selfish, self-destructive string of years that I wasted trying to fill up the God-shaped hole inside of me. Without a relationship of submission and service to the Lord Jesus, time does not heal all wounds, and the scars on your heart are continuously painful and bloody. Life at that point is literally exhausting, and you begin to tell yourself that there is no such thing as true meaning and purpose.

Q: What is your definition and understanding of death?

_____

_____

_____

Q: What do Psalm 139:16 and Hebrews 9:27 mean to you?

_____

_____

_____

Q: Does death frighten you? Why or why not?

_____

_____

_____

_____

*Many are the plans in the mind of man, but it is the purpose of
the* Lord *that will stand.*
—Prov. 19:21

As a combat veteran I thought I knew the meaning of "preparing for
war." I thought that if I worked and studied hard enough, I could defeat
anyone or any situation. I also thought that after having experienced a taste
of war that nothing in my life would ever come close to being so horrible or
so difficult. Well, as usual, I was wrong.

There were several things in my life I was not prepared for. I was not
prepared to be a father, and I was already on my way to being a lousy
husband. I had no idea how to make the transition from being a soldier to
being a civilian, especially since I had spent the majority of my adult life up
to that point as a soldier; it was all I knew how to do. Worse yet, I carried
some real hard parts of war inside, and for years that has robbed me of a lot
of sleep and sometimes my sanity.

As I struggled to provide for my family and find my place in the
"civilian world," I collapsed under the pressure and fell back into drinking
to try to cope. It seemed I had already lost the fight before it even began.
The dark place I crawled into was built by all the hurts, losses, and failures
I had experienced in my life, and it was poisoning my heart. I was stubborn
and arrogant on the outside, while beaten down, exhausted, frightened, and
alone on the inside.

My refusal to accept God's sovereignty over my life blinded me and even
fueled my selfishness and anger all the more—I kept telling myself that I
needed to fix this, but the more I tried, the worse it became. Yet every day I
expected the judgment of my righteous God to be thrust down upon me for
my many sins, which I knew deep inside I deserved. I was a tormented man.

Q: Can you describe one example in your life where you thought you could "fix" all the problems that were surrounding you?

_____

_____

_____

What I thought was settled in my life was unraveling fast; the plain fact that everything was completely out of control was totally beyond my comprehension. I didn't know how to live a life totally submitted and obedient to God, and I wasn't prepared for the fight that came against me. Without knowing it, I had abandoned God and the faith in my Savior that had once comforted me, and I replaced it with old guilt and new regrets.

> _There is a way that seems right to a man, but its end is the way of death._
>
> —Prov. 14:12 KJV

How tragically sad it is when we fatally take the wrong stand, for the wrong things, at the wrong time—over and over again. As we repeat this process, a piece of us slowly dies inside each time. Could it be that's what it felt like for Adam and Eve immediately after the Fall—to be suddenly overcome by the painful sting of mortality? Life hurts, and it can really beat you up sometimes. And oftentimes, as in my case, I was the one constantly punching me in the face.

We could probably get points for our pathetic consistency, but they would be worth nothing. If only we could wake up from the delusional state of mind we are in and just simply point our compasses toward the "true north" in life—Jesus. Instead, we choose to suffer and arrange our lives just as if we had planned to carry water in a bucket full of holes.

Q: What have your life experiences taught you so far?

_____

_____

_____

Q: Which decision in your life has backfired on you the most? What did it cause you to change?

_____

_____

_____

_____

My story is just a brief summary of some of what took place over a 20-year period of my life. Many of you can most likely relate to at least half of the emotions and situations I described. We all have a past and a story, with the future chapters yet to be written by a gracious and forgiving God. Let's move forward together and remove the chains we have been wearing like slaves for so long. We must learn to submit so we can fulfill our mission to serve; as I have said, we must reevaluate our priorities.

> *Think of all the hostility he endured from sinful people; then you won't become weary and give up. After all, you have not yet given your lives in the struggle against sin.*
> —Heb. 12:3 NLT

In some manuscripts Hebrews 12:3 reads, *"Think of how people hurt themselves by opposing Him."* Notice the slight contrast between these two versions, yet God offers us a lesson of hope through them both. It is almost impossible for us to comprehend the extreme physical punishment Jesus suffered on the cross. But what is truly beyond our understanding is this: the sheer weight of unseen spiritual suffering caused by the debt of human sin. He paid it all. We now draw hope that we can endure, knowing it would certainly be worse on every level, to oppose Him, or to try to live and then die without Him.

When you come to Spiritual Crossroads in your life, choices have to be made: "Which way do I go?" To go either left or right at these crossroads will lead us deeper into self or into the world. To turn around and go south will just return us to the broken man who has already hit every hole in the road thus far. To not move at all will not be safe, either. Complacency will also kill you: Leaving the good undone is sin.

Please understand that choosing not to move is choosing to deny living the life for which God has created you.

We must go north! In order to do so, we must reevaluate our priorities.

The crossroads are where we can decide to leave all the garbage behind. Pointed north our eyes will be made clear, our bodies will be strengthened, our will becomes more determined, and our hearts will be full of good, godly courage. And the peace we long for will be ever on the horizon before us. This is the peace that Jesus has promised, but He demands all of you and me. We must be all His, holding nothing back for self, leaving nothing attached to this world.

Jesus says, "*Whoever is not with me is against me, and whoever does not gather with me scatters*" (Matt. 12:30 NIV). The crossroads are a place of choices:

We must **choose** to move forward in our faith.
We must **choose** to grow in our trust for God.
We must **desire** a deeper relationship with Him.
We must **submit** our whole life to His perfect authority.
We must **honor** His sovereignty through our continued obedience.
We must **choose** to ignore the distractions of the world.
We must **hate our sin more** than we do the sins of others.

The love of Christ must abound in our hearts and overflow into all we say, think, and do. We must be His example in the way we care for and serve others. We must strive to be holy as He is holy!

Q: A Spiritual Crossroads is one of the most important places you will ever find yourself. Do you realize this? Does it matter? Why or why not?

_____

_____

_____

_____

_____

Q: What is your decision(s) going to be?

_____

_____

_____

_____

_____

Q: Do you realize that you must choose a direction of travel? Y/N _____

_____

_____

_____

_____

Chapter 13

Standing at the Crossroads, Part 2

It's surprising how unprepared we are when it comes to the most important things in life. Oh, we usually prepare adequately for the big meeting with the new client or the job interview, and we will definitely prepare well in advance for such events as the Super Bowl or even a simple weekend BBQ—but for the things that have eternal value, very little to no concern is given until we get really hurt, really sick, or find ourselves attending someone's funeral.

When it comes to things in life to which we assign value or things that present an opportunity for personal gain, we definitely make sure we are prepared. You may be asking right now, "Am I selfish?" The answer is a definitive yes; but guess what, we all are. It is in our fallen nature to be this way, but we do not have to remain this way.

We foolishly think we have a system, or a formula, as to how things are supposed to work in life. But in our selfish minds, the geometry of this ridiculous formula is shaped like a simple circle: 360 degrees that start with me and end with me.

Christian men and women are literally shocked when things in their life don't go as they planned or even as they prayed. Notice here the word *planned* is purposely placed before the word *prayed*. In the minds of most people (even Christians), that is the natural order of things. These same folks freak out, as if to assume that being a Christian means everything falls into line with their plans no matter what, and that this sinful world, the enemy, or our bad choices should not or could not have anything to do with the outcome!

They say, "OK, I will plan this out, and since it seems logical to me, and what I want or need isn't going to hurt anyone, it should work out; and if I hit a snag, that's when I need to pray. I'm a good guy or a good gal; it's only fair and right that I get what I expect." Sounds more like a demand than a hopeful expectation.

Please do not miss the point here; we fail simply because we do not submit—or we are just submitting to all the wrong things. Many of us are quick to submit to the desires of our hearts but when it comes to submitting to the commandments and statutes of the Living God, that is where we say [in our self-righteousness], "I need to pray about this"; or "I'm not sure I'm ready," or "I'm not good enough for God, so I can't." We are all excellent liars, especially to ourselves.

Q: Can you right now admit this? Y/N _____

Q: Who do you find yourself lying to the most? Why?

_____

_____

_____

_____

Q: We are all professional rationalizers. Do you see how you use rationalization in your life?

_____

_____

_____

_____

Q: And we are all quick to move toward compromise. How and in what areas of your life have you compromised your relationship with God for something personal?

_____

_____

_____

_____

The sad reality is that many people we know will choose to live their lives their way and then die having never experienced what God had intended for them. The prophet Isaiah was delivering a dire warning when he instructed the people in Isaiah 55:6 to _"seek the LORD while he may be found; call upon him while he is near"_ (NIV). It is fair to deduce that what Isaiah was saying here was the Lord will not always be near—and there will come a day when He cannot be found!

Your continued relationship with sin that you secretly feed and protect may one day make Him unreachable—your prayers will either drift off quietly into emptiness, or they may not even reach beyond the roof of your house. Your refusal to forsake sin and submit to Christ will one day force you outside a locked door, and no matter how fervently you knock on it or no matter how hard you pound on it, that door may never be opened or answered. Sin may one day separate you permanently from the perfect goodness of the Living God.

The truth is we all have a calling and a mission in our lives to be fulfilled. And God has made us part of a beautiful, glorious plan, which is designed for us to live a life that gives Him glory and that will always be for our greatest good!

Paul confirms this for us in Ephesians 2:10: _"For we are God's handiwork, created in Christ Jesus to do good works, which God prepared in advance for us to do"_ (NIV).

Q: Do you have trouble believing that you have a calling and a purpose? Y/N _____

As much as we may want to deny it, we cannot escape accountability to our calling, and if you are determined to ignore His call on your life, you will most certainly be accountable to Him one day, face-to-face. A life lived without Christ results in one thing—eternal death. Now that that's been said, let's examine Romans 8:28, which plainly tells us, *"And we know that for those who love God all things work together for good, for those who are called according to his purpose."*

What God sees as good for us is the ultimate good, and it goes far beyond what we can understand as to what "good" or "right for us" really is.

His goodness is perfect and just and when He lays it on our lives, it is called a blessing. This is a lot different than buying a good car, landing a good job, or even finding a good husband or wife—He knows our real needs and how to meet them. We understand that we must be called to "His purpose" in order to receive Him—that means putting aside our agendas and canceling our plans in exchange for His perfect one. And because He is sovereign, everything that happens to us (good or bad) is for a wonderful purpose. Remember, it's about God's glory first, not ours.

Since we serve a sovereign God, giving up control to Him when we never really had it in the first place is still a very hard concept for most people to grasp. As we look at learning to submit, it might be good for us if we pause for a moment and reflect on what we need to surrender in our lives. Here's a short list of some of the hard ones:

You are not in control of the following:

- Your marriage
- Your finances
- Your health
- Your children
- Your spouse
- Your job
- Your life

Q: The seven aspects of our lives listed above are some of the most important priorities for us. How many of these have you turned over fully to God?

James tells us, "*Whatever is good and perfect comes down to us from God our Father, who created all the lights in the heavens. He never changes or casts a shifting shadow*" (James 1:17 NLT). All the areas listed above are blessings from God in our lives. No person is ever guaranteed any one of them, let alone all of them in life. Please understand that while you may have some influence over these areas, you are not and never will be, in full control of them.

Yet God graciously blesses whom He chooses, promising to never leave us or forsake us if we will trust Him. And He does not leave us ill prepared for the challenges that come with being a father, mother, husband, wife, provider, or even the steward of our bodies; He has left us His instruction manual—the Holy Bible.

I've had to learn to trust God on a deeper level in my life recently, during times when He was my only hope. I had to stop and submit to Him as my first and best option, and not use Him like a last resort or a "911 service" as I did in the past. It's amazing how your faith can grow when you not only submit, but actually believe He is in control. And as Jesus Himself told us, "*Anything is possible if a person believes*" (Mark 9:23 NLT).

Sin and self, a couple of our greatest obstacles, both stand directly opposed to our ability and desire to trust God. Faith is the key, and yet even the ability to believe is a gift from Him! Hebrews 11:6 says this: "*Now without faith it is impossible to please God, since the one who draws near to him must believe that he exists and that he rewards those who seek him*" (CSB).

In order to trust God, we are going to have to confront our sin and be determined through faith, to be ready for all-out war against sin and self!

> *Therefore do not let sin reign in your mortal body, so that you obey its desires. And do not offer any parts of it to sin as weapons for unrighteousness. But as those who are alive from the dead, offer yourselves to God, and all the parts of yourselves to God as weapons for righteousness. For sin will not rule over you, because you are not under the law but under grace.*
>
> —Rom. 6:12–14

It is important for us to remember that it is our own flesh that lures us into sin (James 1:13–15): The enemy can only tempt us; we are the ones who make the final choice to embrace sin or to walk away. Let's break down the types of sin and examine them a little closer and see how they can affect our ability to trust God. Without trust in God and submission to Him, we will be stuck at these crossroads.

Definition of Willful Sin

Since all sin is an "act of our will" and a transgression of the law. Let's break down what it means to sin willfully:

a. (To) Sin: The present tense means that sin is being practiced.

b. Willfully: Something done with presence of mind and a desire to do so and then carried out without restraint. The good conscience is directly overridden. Willful sin can also be identified with not acting at all when we know we should. This is called "leaving the good undone." James 4:17 says, *"So whoever knows the right thing to do and fails to do it, for him it is sin."*

c. The Bible calls willful sin "transgression."

d. Definition of *iniquity*: Sin that is or has been preplanned.

Q: Do you realize that transgression and iniquity don't have to exist in our lives? Y/N _____

These two types of sin are CHOSEN by us—we need to remember this.

Pride—the Enabler of All Sin

One of the main characteristics of pride is a sense of self-entitlement. Self-entitlement is an attitude that says, "I deserve this," and therefore enables us to adopt a mentality that is totally self-serving. For both men and women, this takes selfishness to a whole new level, allowing us to rationalize into existence just about anything we want to do—because "we deserve it." Remember, we are constantly at war with our flesh, and your mind will figure out a way to get your body whatever it wants if you submit to the desire to do so.

Q: How has pride affected your life? Do you see yourself as a prideful person? Why? Why not?

a. Rationalization—the great compromise. This can be a conscious or unconscious defense mechanism in which perceived controversial behaviors or feelings are logically justified and explained in a rational or "logical" manner in order to avoid any confrontation with the truth.

b. By allowing ourselves to make bad decisions consciously tolerable or even admirable and superior, we then lose focus on reality and work to implement our choices by any conceivable means.

c. Rationalization encourages irrational or unacceptable behavior, motives, or feelings that create false fantasy scenarios in our minds—basically, how we want the situation to be played out. This process ranges from fully conscious (e.g., to present a defense against ridicule from others or to fulfill lust, desire, or greed) to subconscious (e.g., to create a block against internal feelings of guilt).

"Who, by their unrighteousness suppress the truth" (Rom. 1:18).

d. People rationalize for various reasons. Rationalization may be used to differentiate the original deterministic explanation of the behavior or feeling in question. It is also an informal fallacy of reasoning.

e. Sometimes, rationalization occurs when we think we know ourselves better than we actually do, but most often it occurs when we think more of ourselves then we should (pride, self-righteousness).

For by the grace given to me I say to everyone among you not to think of himself more highly than he ought to think, but to think with sober judgment, each according to the measure of faith that God has assigned.

—Rom. 12:3

What Is Trust?

Trust is the trait of believing in the honesty and reliability of others. Real trust exhibits the following:

a. Acceptance of suffering (John 16:33).
b. Acceptance of the inevitability of death.
c. The ability to have an eternal view and a desire to make eternal investments now.

d. Having daily appointments with God and trusting that He is and will be our source of provision in all things. This is focused prayer throughout the day, not just quiet time.

e. During prayer, practice listening more and talking less, and trust that God will somehow answer your prayers. This will require great discipline and faith to wait to hear God.

f. Trust allows your discernment to be checked by an elder brother in the faith. It requires submission and willingness to be vulnerable in relationships.

g. Daily offering your complete and unhesitating obedience to Jesus.

Memorize this acronym for trust:

Totally
Relying
Upon the
Savior's
Timing

The essential elements of trust are:

a. Faith – Hebrews 11:1
b. Humility – 1 Peter 5:6
c. Repentance – 1 John 1:9
d. Submission – James 4:7
e. Obedience – John 14:15

Q: Which of the five essential elements of trust are lacking in your life right now?

_____

Q: What do you suppose is keeping you from fully trusting God?

_____

_____

Finally, understand that once you find yourself standing at the crossroads of life (and sooner or later, we all will), you cannot go back. If you were to turn around and go straight back, you would be returning to the sinful patterns and disobedient ways that brought you to the crossroads in the first place.

That would be returning to sin, and the Bible says if we do that, we will be worse than we were before (Matt. 12:43–45).

Setting our hearts on the course of "true north" (Jesus) and committing ourselves to trust God no matter what is our best option for both now and for our future.

> *Enter by the narrow gate. For the gate is wide and the way is easy*
> *that leads to destruction, and those who enter it are many. For*
> *the gate is narrow that leads to life, and those who find it are few.*
> —Matt. 7:13–14

Notice that Jesus speaks of broad and narrow gates—these are what lie at the entrance of the broad and narrow roads that we choose to walk in life. The left or the right lead to a broad, smooth, and easy road—this is the way of the world, and it promises everything to you that this life says you need to have.

All that it offers is temporary—fame, promises of wealth and comfort—and it also says there is no accountability as to how you choose to live your life. This path is already filled with many, many travelers, and they will be constantly calling you to join them. Yes the smooth road is beautiful but also full of distractions: Once we step onto that road, it can be very hard to step off. And you will not be able to get off by yourself. You will need divine assistance.

Q: Will you accept divine assistance? Y/N _____

But if you choose to continue straight, you will encounter a rough, narrow, and rugged path, which will be difficult to negotiate, and it will challenge you in everything and every way possible. It will be a hard journey, with many uphill battles as well as valleys marked with low, dark days. But it will also be here in the midst of trials where perfect peace can be found: The journey offers strength for the body, clarity in your mind, and a sure confidence in your steps.

And most importantly, please understand this: You will not be making any part of this journey alone. The Holy Spirit will be with you to teach you, guide you, and protect you. Finally, at the end of the rough, narrow, and rugged path you find the outstretched, nail pierced hands of the One who loves you more than could ever be measured. And He will welcome you, safely home, blessing you with His sweet words of approval: *"His master replied, 'Well done, good and faithful servant! You have been faithful with a few things; I will put you in charge of many things. Come and share your master's happiness!'"* (Matt. 25:23 NIV).

Q: Which path are you on right now—the narrow road or the broad, smooth road?

_____

_____

Q: Are you willing to submit fully to God and trust in Him in every aspect of your life? Explain.

_____

_____

_____

_____

_____

_____

_____

_____

_____

_____

_____

_____

Chapter 14

The Need for Trust in Discipleship

Trust is one of the most important elements in any relationship. In our relationship with God, it is paramount that we continuously strive to fully trust Him at all times. I have identified five elements that make up trust, and I believe if we lack in any one of these elements, we will have a difficult time trusting God.

> Proverbs 3:5–6
> Luke 9:23–24
> Isaiah 55:7

Five Obstacles to Trusting God:

1. Identity crisis
2. Fear (1 John 4:18)
3. Pain and suffering (John 16:33)
4. Believing the lies of the enemy (Job 19:25)
5. Living a life of defiance

If you call yourself a Christian, then being a disciple is not optional!

Five Elements of Trust

Faith

It all starts with faith. Hebrews 11:6 says, *"And without faith it is impossible to please him, for whoever would draw near to God must believe that he exists and that he rewards those who seek him."*

Faith is so much more than "positive thinking"; positive thinking cannot produce faith. In fact, Romans 12:3 tells us that God has given each of us a "measure of faith." Is your faith struggling right now? Stop resisting His gifts and believe. Jesus has already done all the work for us. Acknowledge God now by believing and living out your faith.

Q: Who is your faith really rooted in?

_____

Q: Can you say that your faith is strong enough to trust God no matter what happens in your life? Y/N _____

Humility

We cannot place our trust in God until humility is expressed in our hearts and our lives. The Apostle Peter tells us the first step is to *"humble yourselves under God's mighty hand, that he may lift you up in due time"* (1 Pet. 5:6 NIV).

God is offering you an opportunity to humble yourself. Believe me, He has no problem humbling you Himself if you will not accept His gracious gift and learn to do it yourself. Jesus expressed the perfect example of humility when He chose to step down from His place in heaven and put aside His godly authority to save us (Phil. 2:6–8).

Q: Do you struggle with being humble? If so, how?

_____

_____

_____

_____

Q: What steps must you take to help put your pride in check? How do you need God to help you in this?

_____

_____

Repentance

If we are to draw near to God, we must turn from our sin. Any sin we hold on to proves that we trust ourselves for satisfaction more than we trust God and also proves that we love our sin more than our Savior.

This should not be so, especially since we are assured that if we would confess and repent, *"He is faithful and just to forgive us our sins and cleanse us from all unrighteousness"* (1 John 1:9). He is "just" because God Himself defines and embodies perfect justice and has released us from the sentence of eternal death through payment of the best He had—His precious Son. Always strive to be quick to repent because He is so willing and swift to forgive when you do.

Q: Do you know the difference between godly sorrow and worldly sorrow? (See 2 Corinthians 7:9–11.)

_____

_____

_____

Q: When you sin, are there any delays in your repentance? If yes, why?

_____

_____

_____

Submission

Submission means to surrender (James 4:7). You will never fully trust someone to whom you do not submit in some manner. Husbands and wives learn to submit to one another in love through the trust that is formed by God through the marriage covenant. We submit daily to the rules, regulations, and laws of society and if we do not, we are punished.

Why should we then submit to self before we submit to God? Will He not righteously chasten (discipline) us? Why not *"taste and see that the LORD is good; blessed is the one who takes refuge [trusts] in him"* (Psalm 34:8)? Christian, your trust in God will fail unless you fully submit to His perfect authority.

Q: Submission is especially hard when we are used to getting our way: Is this true of you? If yes, explain.

_____

_____

_____

_____

Q: Jesus requires full submission (Matt. 12:30). Are you ready to finally and fully submit to Him? Y/N _____

Obedience

Jesus plainly says, *"If you love me, you will keep my commandments"* (John 14:15). Do we love our precious Savior enough to simply obey Him? It was His perfect example of obedience that has stayed the death angel.

By obeying His Father, Jesus paid with His life to buy our freedom from the penalty of eternal death: *"Not my will, but yours be done"* (Luke 22:42).

Q: Our lack of obedience to God can be indicative of our lack of love for Him. Is this true of you? Y/N _____

Q: What is hindering or stopping you from striving for full obedience to God?

_____

_____

_____

_____

Q: Jesus proved at the cross that He was "all in" for you. Are you "all in" for Him? Explain.

_____

_____

_____

_____

_____

_____

Conclusion

If we lack in any one of these five elements, we will not be able to fully trust God.

Trusting God the way Christ did means knowing without a doubt that God loves you, and that He is perfectly good whether or not He intervenes in the midst of your problem, your pain, or your suffering. Trusting God also means that you will put God first in all things. Christ must be your first line of defense, your lawyer and advocate, and your most secure confidante. That means He's plan "A," my friend, not B or C, or whatever letter gets your leftovers.

Activity

Take a piece of paper and trace an outline of your hand: On each finger, write one of the elements of trust. As you do the work to examine what areas of trust you struggle in, imagine that the area(s) where you lack trust would actually cost you a finger!

This is a worthwhile activity because your hand would become less useful each time you lost a finger. If you do the activity and end up with an incomplete hand, imagine having an incomplete heart, because that is what a lack of trust in God will produce in you. You may lose your peace, you may lose your joy, or something else just as valuable to both you and your faith.

Trusting God fully and completely must be a priority for all of us.

Chapter 15

Basic Indicators of Pride

Today, we will examine ourselves for the sin of pride. It is a fact that we all struggle with pride in one form or another. Even if you only recognize and agree with one or two of these points please know that that is enough to do you great harm spiritually. It is important that we do business with this issue, or it will eventually end up doing business with us.

In his book, *The Hazards of Being a Man*, Jeffrey E. Miller outlines twelve potentially harmful hazards, which if not managed, can set a man on course for spiritual disaster. I must say that this book inspired me greatly. As a pastor and counselor, I wanted to isolate the sin of pride in particular and also approach it as a non-gender-specific sin, since pride is not just a male problem—it is a human one. Therefore, I chose seven of Miller's twelve hazards that I believe are most directly rooted in pride and defined and applied them as reflected in my counseling experience.[1] As I stated above, any one of these if left unchecked will bring great harm into a person's life.

Activity
Take a moment to read the definitions and questions carefully. Allow the Holy Spirit to help you honestly answer these questions and then pray for a plan to manage them in your life.

After you have answered the questions, sit down with someone you trust who knows you and isn't afraid to tell you the truth. Together, develop a plan to combat the areas in which you struggle and allow this person to hold you accountable to your plan.

Deflecting Responsibility for Our Thoughts, Words, and Actions

Pride tells us that others are usually to blame for everything we do because we are too good or simply not capable of making mistakes. If we do acknowledge the sin of pride, it is only because we had a reason or excuse for the sin to have occurred; it's just never fully our fault. Deflecting responsibility is one of the ways we enable ourselves to hold on to sin, whether they are secret sins, or otherwise. This is also one of the first acts of deception that we accept in ourselves when we embrace pride.

Q: Has this bad habit been a part of your life? Do you find it hard to accept the blame for your own thoughts, words, and actions? If so, how and what has it done to your relationships with God and others?

_____

_____

_____

_____

Manipulation of Others

By this we mean that we use others and manipulate them to fulfill our own desires or perceived needs. We can even manipulate others through their own guilt and mistakes. It is a completely self-centered pride trait that is very damaging to all involved once the truth has been uncovered. No one likes to be used.

Q: How have you used others for your own benefit? What has it cost you to do so?

_____

_____

Misplaced Priorities

Since we are so selfish and driven to satisfy our own needs and desires, we often lose track of what is important and forget that everything must be done in a proper order. Simply put, we have our priorities in the wrong perspective.

Q: Has your selfishness and pride caused you to put your desires before your responsibilities to God, your family, or your job? What has it cost you? Explain.

_____

_____

_____

_____

_____

Lust

Submitting to the desires of the flesh can lead to addictions to sex, pornography, adultery, fornication, self-gratification, homosexuality, substance abuse, and even self-mutilation. All of these are the lowest points of human degradation. For most, lust is a means of escape from deep hurts in order to avoid having to deal with a painful past or a severely messed up present. What this path does ensure, though, is a hopeless future.

What you may see as a simple harmless pleasure of gawking at girls from a distance, casually looking at porn on the internet, or polluting your body with drugs and alcohol is actually the process of poisoning your heart, soul, and mind.

Q: Have you given in to lust in your life? How do sexual sins and other sins against the body affect your relationship with God and others? What has it cost you?

_____

_____

_____

The Sin of Partial Obedience

When we refuse to honor God with our complete obedience, we are saying that His ways are not sufficient to completely direct our lives. Our pride is so deceptive that we tell ourselves that partial obedience is enough. Acceptance of this lie in our hearts lays down the foundation for self-righteousness. We cannot pick and choose which of God's laws we will obey and which ones will be governed by self. Choosing to acknowledge only parts of the truth means to accept the lie, and God will not allow this rebellion to go on in our lives without consequences.

Q: Examine your heart to see whether you have compromised your relationship with God by choosing to govern yourself. Are you willing to be obedient to the death for God as Jesus was for you? How has partial obedience hurt you? What has it cost you?

_____

_____

_____

_____

_____

Unresolved/Unrighteous Anger

Unrighteous anger is a broad gateway to pattern sin. This type of anger causes tremendous damage to self and others through expressions of physical and verbal abuse; it is the "Velcro" for other sins (such as rape) to run along with. For example, a man may have an argument with his wife and through his anger may rationalize that it is his "right" to look at porn. Unrighteous anger never walks alone; it is one of the main links to the primary ingredients of pride, which is self-entitlement.

Anger fuels the "I deserve this or that" mentality and pushes us emotionally toward the need to justify our thoughts, words, or deeds as well as the desire to carry out our own brand of justice. Finally, anger is often overlooked and even accepted as "part of us" because it is an emotion, so we rarely ever honestly address it.

Q: Anger can be an issue for everyone; take a moment to reflect on the damage that has been done by your words and your actions. What has it cost you?

_____

_____

_____

_____

Unteachability

Would people who know you say that you are unteachable? Are you often seen as the "know-it-all"?

If you allow it, your pride will convince you that you know enough or at least you have all you need to run your life. As we fall deeper into arrogance and confusion, our pride feeds us, our hearts become unmoved to truth and the true wisdom of God, and His Holy Word no longer penetrates and convicts us. Established patterns of sin and denial become the broken plains and shaky ground on which the fallen man struggles to exist. In fact, the simple but life-changing message of the gospel of the cross no longer has any impact or relevance.

Q: Do you think you know it all or at least enough that you no longer need the wisdom of God's instruction? Has your heart become so hard that you are no longer moved by the beautiful expressions of God's love for you, which are so purposefully laid out in His Holy Scriptures? Are you missing the supernatural God as He moves in and around your little natural world? What has this hardness of heart cost you?

_____

_____

_____

_____

_____

_____

Chapter 16

Fruit of the Spirit: Patience and Kindness

But the fruit of the Spirit [the result of His presence within us] is love [unselfish concern for others], joy, [inner] peace, patience [not the ability to wait, but how we act while waiting], kindness, goodness, faithfulness, gentleness, self-control. Against such things there is no law.

—Gal. 5:22–23 AMP

Today, we will examine the spiritual fruit of patience and kindness.

Q: What does patience mean to you?

_____

_____

_____

_____

_____

The Fruit of Patience

Patience is biblically defined as a quality or virtue that is represented as either forbearance or endurance. It is a quality of self-restraint or of not giving way to anger, even in the face of provocation; it exists in perfection in God and in more selfish and much lesser degree in man. Godly patience is closely related to mercy and compassion.

Godly patience is not merely the ability to wait, but it is defined by how we act while we are waiting.

> *Therefore, every one of you who judges is without excuse. For when you judge another, you condemn yourself, since you, the judge, do the same things. We know that God's judgment on those who do such things is based on the truth. Do you really think—anyone of you who judges those who do such things yet do the same—that you will escape God's judgment? Or do you despise the riches of his kindness, restraint, and patience, not recognizing that God's kindness is intended to lead you to repentance?*
>
> —Rom. 2:1–4

We often see the word *longsuffering* in the Bible as a representation of patience. But what exactly is longsuffering, according to the scripture? The word *longsuffering* in the Bible is made up of two Greek words meaning "long" and "temper"; literally, "long-tempered."

So, to be longsuffering is to possess self-restraint when you are tempted to express anger. A longsuffering person does not immediately retaliate or punish; instead, he or she has a "long fuse" and patiently forbears. Godly longsuffering does not surrender to circumstances or succumb to trial. Longsuffering is also associated with mercy and hope.

- **Mercy:** Colossians 3:12–13 says, "*Therefore, as the elect of God, holy and beloved, put on tender mercies, kindness, humility, meekness, longsuffering; bearing with one another, and forgiving one another, if anyone has a complaint against another; even as Christ forgave you, so you also must do*" (NKJV).

139

- **Hope:** Matthew 24:10–13 says, *"And then many will be offended, will betray one another, and will hate one another. Then many false prophets will rise up and deceive many. And because lawlessness will abound, the love of many will grow cold. But he who endures to the end shall be saved"* (NKJV).

Real hope can only exist in the heart of the Christian through the God-given ability to be longsuffering—waiting simply for the sake of waiting is both ridiculous and useless. But patiently waiting, and practicing self-restraint, all because of the anticipation and the hope for something greater than the situation and greater than ourselves—even greater than anything we can understand or comprehend—now that is worth it.

The Bible makes it clear that God is the source of longsuffering because it is part of God's character. Scripture confirms He is patient with sinners: *"The Lord does not delay His promise, as some understand delay, but is patient with you, not wanting any to perish but all to come to repentance"* (2 Pet. 3:9 CSB). However, God's longsuffering can come to an end, as seen in the destruction of Sodom and Gomorrah and the need to repeatedly send Israel into captivity.

> *Don't be deceived: God is not mocked. For whatever a person sows he will also reap because the one who sows to his flesh will reap destruction from the flesh, but the one who sows to the Spirit will reap eternal life from the Spirit.*
> —Gal. 6:7–8 CSB

The Bible also tells us that the process of learning godly patience is one with a purpose—patience is not something we do simply because God wants us to be opposite of who we are right now. His plan is to make us more like His Son. God's desire that we possess all the fruit of the Spirit is most certainly for a purpose:

> *Dear friends, don't be surprised when the fiery ordeal comes among you to test you as if something unusual were happening to you. Instead, rejoice as you share in the sufferings of Christ, so that you may also rejoice with great joy when His glory is*

revealed. If you are ridiculed for the name of Christ, you are blessed, because the Spirit of glory and of God rests on you. Let none of you suffer as a murderer, a thief, an evildoer, or any sort of criminal [in response to persecution], or as a troublesome meddler interfering in the affairs of others.

But if anyone suffers as a Christian, let him not be ashamed but let him glorify God in having that name. For the time has come for judgment to begin with God's household, and if it begins with us, what will the outcome be for those who disobey the gospel of God? And if a righteous person is saved with difficulty, what will become of the ungodly and the sinner? So then, let those who suffer according to God's will entrust themselves to a faithful Creator while doing what is good.

—1 Pet. 4:12–19 CSB

All Christian suffering is definitely for a good purpose, but sadly most Christians do their best to avoid suffering at all any way they can. Because of the cross, we now have access to something greater, which is yet another perfect gift from God that fills in the gaping holes of our flawed humanity when it comes to our ability to be longsuffering.

It's called grace. It is only through the gift of God's perfect grace (i.e., His unearned favor), which has been poured out upon us, that we are able to be in each other's presence right now. We are living examples of those who have received and experienced the longsuffering, perfect patience of God:

His divine power has given us everything required for life and godliness through the knowledge of him who called us by his own glory and goodness. By these he has given us very great and precious promises, so that through them you may share in the divine nature, escaping the corruption that is in the world because of evil desire.

—2 Pet. 1:3–4 CSB

Right here, the Apostle Peter, through divine instruction from the Holy Spirit, tells us that God has given the believer everything that is needed to live a life of godliness. And because the believer in Jesus Christ has been

141

given and received the very life of God in us (the Holy Spirit), we have access to His divine nature. That life in us produces certain characteristics (fruit) that must be displayed in the believer as we obey the Holy Spirit who lives within us. The expressions of this fruit serve not only to glorify God but also to confirm our genuine rebirth in Him.

Our Bible simply calls this trait "patience," but we know it is much more than that. Longsuffering is to be expressed and must be put on display as part of our new godly character in all believers.

Q: What does your ability to be patient look like?

_____

_____

Q: Are you seeking to be longsuffering because you have been called to, for your own personal gain, or for the glory of the Living God?

_____

_____

Q: Have you ever taken the grace of God for granted? Y/N _____. If yes, how did that affect you?

_____

_____

_____

_____

The Fruit of Kindness

True kindness is Holy Spirit–produced. It is a supernaturally generous orientation and expression of our hearts toward other people, even when they don't deserve it or respond with kindness in return.

In fact, godly kindness does not seek anything in return. But the truth is, only God Himself is truly kind in this way. The main purpose of His kindness is to lead people to repentance, which implies they haven't yet turned to Him and are separated by sin or are still His enemies.

Kindness is an attribute of God and a quality that is certainly most desirable but unfortunately not consistently found in humans. Godly kindness is a supernatural quality, and once we examine its attributes, we will easily be able to differentiate between His divine kindness and our self-serving human kindness, which always seems to fall short.

Human Kindness

Human kindness is very one-dimensional. It is most often expressed by us once we have made an assessment of the situation and decided it to be a low enough risk for us to take. We either express kindness to get it over with or do it for some form of reward (like making ourselves feel good just by doing it).

Human kindness is rarely given without expecting something in return. Human kindness often seeks a platform and loves to get noticed, recognized, or applauded. Let's be honest, most of the time, when we seek to step out and express kindness through service or sacrifice, we are often doing it for one of the reasons I have already identified. Sometimes, we want to check off the box and appease our conscience (and be able to say, "I was kind to him/her today") and guess what—for most of us and for most of the time, that is enough.

Now, you may be saying, "Wow, Pastor Mike. You are certainly slamming humanity and its ability to be kind." OK, yes, I am. But I am only telling you like it is from my own heart and from what I have experienced in my life as a man who has more often been looking to receive kindness rather than having the desire to unconditionally give it away. Scripture proves my words to be true:

For people will be lovers of self, lovers of money, proud, arrogant, abusive, disobedient to their parents, ungrateful, unholy, heartless, unappeasable, slanderous, without self-control, brutal, not loving good, treacherous, reckless, swollen with conceit, lovers of pleasure rather than lovers of God.
—2 Tim. 3:2–4

For they all seek their own interests, not those of Jesus Christ.
—Phil. 2:21

For where jealousy and selfish ambition exist, there will be disorder and every vile practice.

—James 3:16

Whoever closes his ear to the cry of the poor will himself call out and not be answered.

—Prov. 21:13

Do you not know that if you present yourselves to anyone as obedient slaves, you are slaves of the one whom you obey, either of sin, which leads to death, or of obedience, which leads to righteousness?

—Rom. 6:16

Q: What does the kindness that you give away look like? Is it self-seeking in some way? Is it a conditional gift, meaning you expect something in return? Explain.

_____

_____

_____

_____

_____

_____

_____

My friend, if we seek to only express human kindness, then we will become slaves to its selfish limitations. But if we seek to express godly kindness, then we can experience the transforming process of His love through the full expression of His power—not ours.

Godly Kindness

In contrast, godly kindness is multidimensional. One facet of Divine kindness is expressed through what is called "common grace." God is generously kind to all He has made, even when His creation rejects Him or acts ungrateful and wicked. But His kindness is intended to lead people to repentance, not to the rejection of Him.

Luke 6:35 instructs us this way: *"But love your enemies, do what is good, and lend, expecting nothing in return. Then your reward will be great, and you will be children of the Most High. For He is [kind] and gracious to the ungrateful and evil"* (CSB).

Does that sound like anything you or I would be able to do on our own, without expecting some sort of reward or benefit in it for ourselves?

I would say no, we would not.

God's kindness completely transcends every part of our simple understanding; His kindness has the ability to completely change hearts. This is because God's love, which is the source from which His kindness flows, is unconditional and does not keep score of our wrongs. And even though sin has clouded our understanding in regard to this, that did not stop God from moving on our behalf.

> *For while we were still helpless, at the right time, Christ died for the ungodly. For rarely will someone die for a just person—though for a good person perhaps someone might even dare to die. But God proves his own love for us in that while we were still sinners, Christ died for us. How much more then, since we have now been declared righteous by his blood, will we be saved through him from wrath. For if, while we were enemies, we were reconciled to God through the death of his Son, then how much more, having been reconciled, will we be saved by his life. And not only that, but we also rejoice in God through our Lord Jesus Christ, through whom we have now received this reconciliation.*
>
> —Rom. 5:6–11 CSB

This is without a doubt the best and most incredible evidence of the kindness God has for us! The fact is we were born into sin and tainted by all of its poisons and imperfections. This was same curse that completely separated us from God. When it came time for God to collect debts, we had nothing to offer Him. And there isn't anything in our humanity that would draw Him to us.

What is so amazing is that God did not save us because He felt sorry for us—He saved us because He loves us! And because of His great love, God's kindness is expressed in ways not only related to salvation from the guilt and punishment of sin. His kindness is seen in His deliverance of the believer from affliction, fear, addictions, and all manner of trouble. The gift of His perfect peace comes to us through His kindness because He truly wants our hearts to be at peace no matter what.

He even gives us kindness (once again through the gift of grace) when we don't recognize or acknowledge His intercession on our behalf. God's kindness is also expressed in the fact that He always provides a way back to Himself, no matter what has been done against Him.

> *Seek the Lord while he may be found; call to him while he is near. Let the wicked one abandon his way and the sinful one his thoughts; let him return to the LORD, so he may have compassion on him, and to our God, for he will freely forgive.*
>
> —Isa. 55:6–7 CSB

Once again, God is providing us that same way back—and for the Christian person, the sanctified heart must constantly be seeking the face of God. It is through the Holy Spirit that we can obtain the possession and expression of the Holy fruit of His most excellent character. Let the words of David in Psalm 119:36 be your constant prayer to our incredibly kind and patient, loving Father: *"Incline my heart to your testimonies [O Lord], and not to selfish gain!"*

Activity

Write a prayer to God in your own words and ask Him to give you a portion of His patience and His kindness. Then ask Him to teach you how to give it away freely to others.

_____

_____

_____

_____

_____

_____

_____

_____

_____

_____

_____

_____

_____

_____

_____

Chapter 17

The Fruit of Self-Control

Today, we are going to examine in detail a very critical element of our Christian walk called the fruit of self-control.

What we first need to realize is that in and of ourselves, we do not possess any true form of self-control. In fact, true self-control is a fruitful work of the Holy Spirit in us and is something that goes way beyond mere behavior modification. Let's look at what scripture has to say, and then we can move forward together in allowing the Holy Spirit to build in us the fruit of self-control.

> *But I say, walk habitually in the [Holy] Spirit [seek Him and be responsive to His guidance], and then you will certainly not carry out the desire of the sinful nature [which responds impulsively without regard for God and His precepts]. For the sinful nature has its desire which is opposed to the Spirit, and the [desire of the] Spirit opposes the sinful nature; for these [two, the sinful nature and the Spirit] are in direct opposition to each other [continually in conflict], so that you [as believers] do not [always] do whatever [good things] you want to do.*
>
> *But if you are guided and led by the Spirit, you are not subject to the Law. Now the practices of the sinful nature are*

clearly evident: they are sexual immorality, impurity, sensuality (total irresponsibility, lack of self-control), idolatry, sorcery, hostility, strife, jealousy, fits of anger, disputes, dissensions, factions [that promote heresies], envy, drunkenness, riotous behavior, and other things like these. I warn you beforehand, just as I did previously, that those who practice such things will not inherit the kingdom of God.

But the fruit of the Spirit [the result of His presence within us] is love [unselfish concern for others], joy, [inner] peace, patience [not the ability to wait, but how we act while waiting], kindness, goodness, faithfulness, gentleness, self-control. Against such things there is no law. And those who belong to Christ Jesus have crucified the sinful nature together with its passions and appetites.

—Gal. 5:16–24 AMP

The Bible defines *self-control* as physical and emotional self-mastery, particularly in situations of intense provocation or temptation.

Christ—Our Perfect Example

Early in the Gospel of Matthew, two very important events occur.

Chapter 3 concludes with Jesus being baptized by John the Baptist in the Jordan River, signaling the beginning of His earthly ministry. Maybe like me you have wondered why Jesus didn't baptize John instead—after all, He is the Master, right? But Jesus has always been our example for all things, and His baptism was a necessary part of the righteousness He secured for sinners.

During that amazing moment, the Holy Spirit descends and rests on Jesus in the form of a dove, while God the Father proclaims, *"This is my beloved Son, with whom I am well-pleased."* Christ connects with us through this beautiful act of obedience and in it, we are given the privilege of witnessing the miraculous presence of the Holy Trinity in affirmation of Jesus and His ministry! And right after His baptism, Matthew 4 opens with the Holy Spirit leading our Lord out into the desert for 40 days, where He is to be tempted.

It is there that Jesus encounters the devil face-to-face. Of course, Satan's goal is to disqualify Jesus as the perfect sacrifice by tempting His humanity to sin against God.

As Christians we must remember that tests, temptations, and trials are allowed by God as opportunities for us to glorify Him through our reliance on His Holy power in us to resist, endure, and overcome them.

Jesus willingly faced temptation first and foremost for us, and the Bible tells us that through the power of the Holy Spirit, "He chose **not** to sin." He resisted every single temptation, so that He could prove to us that through God, it can be done:

> *Then Jesus was led by the Holy Spirit into the wilderness to be tempted by the devil. After He had gone without food for forty days and forty nights, He became hungry. And the tempter came and said to Him, "If You are the Son of God, command that these stones become bread." But Jesus replied, "It is written and forever remains written, 'MAN SHALL NOT LIVE BY BREAD ALONE, BUT BY EVERY WORD THAT COMES OUT OF THE MOUTH OF GOD.'"*
>
> *Then the devil took Him into the holy city [Jerusalem] and placed Him on the pinnacle [highest point] of the temple. And he said [mockingly] to Him, "If You are the Son of God, throw Yourself down; for it is written,*
>
> *'HE WILL COMMAND HIS ANGELS CONCERNING YOU [to serve, care for, protect and watch over You]';*
>
> *and*
>
> *'THEY WILL LIFT YOU UP ON THEIR HANDS,*
>
> *SO THAT YOU WILL NOT STRIKE YOUR FOOT AGAINST A STONE.'"*
>
> *Jesus said to him, "On the other hand, it is written and forever remains written, 'YOU SHALL NOT TEST THE LORD your GOD.'"*
>
> *Again, the devil took Him up on a very high mountain and showed Him all the kingdoms of the world and the glory [splendor, magnificence, and excellence] of them; and he said to Him, "All these things I will give You, if You fall down and worship me." Then Jesus said to him, "Go away, Satan! For it is written and forever remains written, 'YOU SHALL WORSHIP*

THE LORD YOUR GOD, AND SERVE HIM ONLY.'" Then the devil left Him; and angels came and ministered to Him [bringing Him food and serving Him].

—Matt. 4:1–9 AMP

Notice that the description of this most critical event begins by telling us that *"Jesus was led by the [Holy] Spirit into the wilderness to be tempted by the devil."* This time in the wilderness had to be experienced, for both Jesus and for us. God shapes and sharpens us through trials, and Jesus proved to us that through God's power, temptation can be overcome.

Do you find it interesting that the devil tries to tempt Jesus with everything that He [Jesus] Himself had created!

Sin the Corruptor—Satan the Destroyer

Here are some important facts for us to remember:

- The devil is not a creator—he cannot make anything except a mess, let alone anything new.
- But he is, however, the corruptor and the destroyer.
- He poisons and perverts everything good, perfect, and pure.
- Remember that all the enemy can ever offer you is a sick, distorted, unhealthy, and unholy version of something God has made.
- There isn't meant to be any lasting peace or good permanence in anything he has to offer. Satan's goal through the temptation of the flesh is to entice you and distract you long enough so that you will choose to betray and insult the Living God and the Spirit of Grace by choosing sin.
- Satan takes God's perfect gift of sex, meant only to be expressed and shared in the union of marriage, and turns it into every manner of degradation, perversion, adultery, fornication, and pornography.
- Through the perversion of the gift of sex, child abuse, rape, sexual self-mutilation, and sadomasochism have become some of the most destructive mental and physical addictions that exist in society.
- Satan takes the gift of food, herbs, and medicine, which God intended for us to use for health and healing, and turns them into addictions.

- Drug addiction and alcoholism, food addictions, and numerous other forms of chemical addictions and abuses (household cleaners, compressed air dusters, inhaling paint, drinking antifreeze) are killing people by the hundreds of thousands worldwide.
- We have become so corrupted by the pleasures of intoxication that people will stick just about anything into their body to get high.
- Satan even easily manipulates our God-given emotions and tempts us to express all forms of unrighteous anger and commit countless variations of senseless violence and destruction.

Self-Control Affects the Whole Person
Physical Self-Control

The flesh does not rule over you, but in fact you rule over it. God expects us to go to war against the flesh if need be in order for us to bring it under control. If you are like me, it's an ongoing battle!

> *So I do not run like one who runs aimlessly or box like one beating the air. Instead, I discipline my body and bring it under strict control, so that after preaching to others, I myself will not be disqualified.*
> —1 Cor. 9:26–27 CSB

Using lust as the example, it's not the first look but the second look that determines the willingness of the heart to pursue sin. Does the first look hurt our sanctification? I don't know, but I know the second one sure does.

> *For this is God's will, your sanctification: that you keep away from sexual immorality, that each of you knows how to control his own body in holiness and honor, not with lustful passions, like the Gentiles, who don't know God. This means one must not transgress against and take advantage of a brother or sister in this manner, because the Lord is an avenger of all these offenses, as we also previously told and warned you. For God has not called us to impurity but to live in holiness.*
> —1 Thess. 4:3–7 CSB

Mental Discipline

Often, before we commit sin, we have already mentally given ourselves the "OK" to do it—please understand that the very thought of acceptance of sin is itself the first sin act!

Having an attitude of indifference toward sin is also dangerous: If you do not see sin as something deadly, then you really must stop and reevaluate how you see things. Just because something isn't a temptation to you right now does not mean it's harmless or that it won't be a struggle for you in the future.

> So prepare your minds for action, be completely sober [in spirit—steadfast, self-disciplined, spiritually and morally alert], fix your hope completely on the grace [of God] that is coming to you when Jesus Christ is revealed.
>
> —1 Pet. 1:13 AMP

> The end and culmination of all things is near. Therefore, be sound-minded and self-controlled for the purpose of prayer [staying balanced and focused on the things of God so that your communication will be clear, reasonable, specific and pleasing to Him].
>
> —1 Pet. 4:7 AMP

> Be sober [well balanced and self-disciplined], be alert and cautious at all times. That enemy of yours, the devil, prowls around like a roaring lion [fiercely hungry], seeking someone to devour.
>
> —1 Pet. 5:8 AMP

Controlled Speech

Your mouth will always reveal a lot about who you are and what you truly believe because it is the voice box of your heart. A corrupt heart will eventually produce a diseased tongue and sick lips. Evil spreads from within outward. Don't be the one who glorifies the devil with foul and unholy talk.

> Set a guard, O LORD, over my mouth; Keep watch over the door of my lips [to keep me from speaking thoughtlessly].
>
> —Ps. 141:3 AMP

Understand this, my beloved brothers and sisters. Let everyone be quick to hear [be a careful, thoughtful listener], slow to speak [a speaker of carefully chosen words and], slow to anger [patient, reflective, forgiving].

—James 1:19 AMP

He who guards his mouth and his tongue, Guards himself from trouble.

—Prov. 21:23 AMP

Do not be hasty with your mouth [speaking careless words or vows] or impulsive in thought to bring up a matter before God. For God is in heaven and you are on earth; therefore let your words be few.

—Eccles. 5:2 AMP

Not many [of you] should become teachers [serving in an official teaching capacity], my brothers and sisters, for you know that we [who are teachers] will be judged by a higher standard [because we have assumed greater accountability and more condemnation if we teach incorrectly]. For we all stumble and sin in many ways. If anyone does not stumble in what he says [never saying the wrong thing], he is a perfect man [fully developed in character, without serious flaws], able to bridle his whole body and rein in his entire nature [taming his human faults and weaknesses]. Now if we put bits into the horses' mouths to make them obey us, we guide their whole body as well. And look at the ships. Even though they are so large and are driven by strong winds, they are still directed by a very small rudder wherever the impulse of the helmsman determines. In the same sense, the tongue is a small part of the body, and yet it boasts of great things.

See [by comparison] how great a forest is set on fire by a small spark! And the tongue is [in a sense] a fire, the very world of injustice and unrighteousness; the tongue is set among our members as that which contaminates the entire body, and sets on fire the course of our life [the cycle of man's existence], and is itself set on fire by hell (Gehenna). For every species of beasts and birds, of reptiles and sea creatures, is tamed and has been tamed by the human race. But no one can tame the human tongue; it is a restless evil [undisciplined, unstable], full of deadly poison. With it we bless our Lord and Father, and with it we curse men, who have been made in the likeness of God. Out of the same mouth come both blessing and cursing. These things, my brothers, should not be this way [for we have a moral obligation to speak in a manner that reflects our fear of God and profound respect for His precepts]. Does a spring send out from the same opening both fresh and bitter water? Can a fig tree, my brothers, produce olives, or a grapevine produce figs? Nor can salt water produce fresh.

—James 3:1–12 AMP

We All Have Sin Triggers

Sin triggers are internal or external factors that can stimulate a sin response in a person. It is important to understand that all sin triggers are given permission beforehand [by you] to exist in you; nothing can trigger you that you don't either want or allow.

Q: Have you ignored certain sin practices in order to protect your sin triggers?

Believe it or not, many people find pleasure in sin triggers. It can be like hiding a pornographic picture in your phone and sneaking away every once in a while to look at it. There is pleasure in the anticipation (that's the sin trigger) of actually looking at the photo, and then a temporary satisfaction when it is actually done (that's the sin act). Both the trigger and the act are poisonous and deadly to us.

Consider these facts about sin triggers:

- Sin triggers are easily tripped if we are habitual excuse-makers.

Q: Is this you? Are you constantly making excuses for unholy behavior?

- Rationalization can also be a sin trigger; when we constantly look for excuses to exercise bad behavior, it isn't too long before it develops into pattern behavior.

Q: Do you find yourself frequently rationalizing your responses to difficult, uncomfortable, or stressful situations, so as to excuse your bad behavior?

_____

_____

- God has given every believer the power to overcome their sin triggers. When we deny His power, we are denying Him and His ability to give us true victory over sin.

Q: Have you willfully denied the power of the Living God and in so doing denied Him and all that was purchased at the cross for you?

_____

_____

Self-Control Is the Mark of a Wise Person

The Bible says there are only two types of people in this world: those who are wise and those who are fools.

How sad to be proved the fool without even realizing that we have deceived ourselves into thinking that we can control any form of sinful behavior. But the truth is, we all have done this in one form or another.

In contrast to this, a wise person is honest with themselves and aware of their weaknesses and is willing to take any steps necessary to correct or eliminate potentially deadly behavior. A wise man or woman even seeks out accountability for these weaknesses in order to help prevent a personal disaster.

We have to see sin for the deadly beast it is and be aware of how it not only affects our personal behavior but also our relationship with God. Do we want to live in a way that disgraces the cross of Christ? Are we going to allow ourselves to be OK with thoughts, words, and actions that attempt to rip open fresh wounds on the body of Christ?

Q: Do you see yourself as a foolish person or a wise one? If you have trouble deciding, simply recall your most recent thoughts or actions to help you.

_____

_____

A [shortsighted] fool always loses his temper and displays his anger, But a wise man [uses self-control and] holds it back.

—Prov. 29:11 AMP

The proverbs (truths obscurely expressed, maxims) of Solomon son of David, king of Israel:

To know [skillful and godly] wisdom and instruction; To discern and comprehend the words of understanding and insight, To receive instruction in wise behavior and the discipline of wise thoughtfulness, Righteousness, justice, and integrity; That prudence (good judgment, astute common sense) may be given to the naive or inexperienced [who are easily misled], And knowledge and discretion (intelligent discernment) to the youth, The wise will hear and increase their learning, And the person of understanding will acquire wise counsel and the skill [to steer his course wisely and lead others to the truth].

—Prov. 1:1–5 AMP

Self-Control Is a Critical Aspect of Christian Character

I like to regularly challenge people with these three questions because I believe the correct response will ensure a desire for Christian character:

1. Is what I am thinking or about to say or do going to glorify God?
2. Does what I am thinking, doing, or saying set me apart from the rest of the world?
3. Is what I am thinking, doing, or saying increasing my sanctification?

For the [remarkable, undeserved] grace of God that brings salvation has appeared to all men. It teaches us to reject ungodliness and worldly (immoral) desires, and to live sensible, upright, and godly lives [lives with a purpose that reflect spiritual maturity] in this present age.

—Titus 2:11–12 AMP

For this very reason, applying your diligence [to the divine promises, make every effort] in [exercising] your faith to, develop moral excellence, and in moral excellence, knowledge (insight, understanding), and in your knowledge, self-control, and in your self-control, steadfastness, and in your steadfastness, godliness, and in your godliness, brotherly affection, and in your brotherly affection, [develop Christian] love [that is, learn to unselfishly seek the best for others and to do things for their benefit]. For as these qualities are yours and are increasing [in you as you grow toward spiritual maturity], they will keep you from being useless and unproductive in regard to the true knowledge and greater understanding of our Lord Jesus Christ. For whoever lacks these qualities is blind— shortsighted [closing his spiritual eyes to the truth], having become oblivious to the fact that he was cleansed from his old sins.

—2 Pet. 1:5–9 AMP

Therefore, believers, be all the more diligent to make certain about His calling and choosing you [be sure that your behavior reflects and confirms your relationship with God]; for by doing these things [actively developing these virtues], you will never stumble [in your spiritual growth and will live a life that leads others away from sin]; ¹¹for in this way entry into the eternal kingdom of our Lord and Savior Jesus Christ will be abundantly provided to you.

—2 Pet. 1:10–11 AMP

Q: Who is in control of your heart? Is it you or God? Maybe you let Him have control sometimes—what's the story here?

_____

_____

_____

_____

_____

_____

If Christ is indeed Lord and Master of your heart, then His Holy Spirit will be the source and power of self-control in you.

If you are constantly at war against God's Spirit in you or somehow seem to be in a constant state of "negotiations" for rule over your heart, you will struggle severely with self-control, and it will eventually have a huge impact on the quality and genuineness of your witness for Christ.

Q: Have you sought out an accountability partner to help you grow in self-control? Y/N _____

Q: What steps have you taken to recognize your sin triggers, and what steps have you taken to help keep them in check?

_____

_____

_____

_____

Q: The way back to God always starts with repentance, and He will turn no broken heart away. Have you made peace with God through repentance? Y/N _____

If no, why not? What are you waiting for?

_____

_____

_____

_____

Finally, submission means to surrender. God requires full submission of your heart. But let me also remind you that whenever God asks you to give something up for Him, He always gives you something back—even greater.

Q: Have you surrendered everything to Jesus yet? Y/N _____

Q: If no, why not?

_____

_____

_____

_____

_____

_____

_____

_____

_____

_____

Remember that God loves you so much and will never, ever abandon you, so don't abandon Him. Allow Him to give you the fruit of self-control.

Chapter 18

Discipleship Disciplines

Today, we will review some basic ideas that you can add to your daily routine in order to ensure that your Christian walk stays on track.

I call these principles "discipleship disciplines" because each one will require some level of discipline on your part in order to make them a reality in your life. Several years ago, I had the opportunity to do a group study. It was discipleship-focused, and we worked together through Greg Ogden's magnificent book, *Discipleship Essentials*. It helped me to outline for myself a workable routine that grew into my own daily devotion. Since then, I have built a template around some of these basics because they are just that good and important.[1] But the sad fact is, very few Christians possess the discipline required to keep these basic principles with Christ healthy.

I believe that these simple tasks and daily life adjustments are some of the most important things that you and I will ever do in our personal lives. Our dedication to God requires a steady commitment to the understanding that in order to have a relationship with Jesus, we must make regular investments in that relationship.

Please also understand that the disciplined life of the believer serves as some of the greatest evidence of one's calling and salvation. It is a fact that how you live your life will most likely have a bigger impact on those around you who don't know Jesus than any of your words will. I have broken these disciplines down into two categories: inward parts and outward parts.

Discipline in Our Inward Parts

Quiet Time, Bible Study, and Prayer

These are three of the most important disciplines in our relationship with the Living God and ones that every believer must make daily investments in so that this relationship can remain healthy and fruitful and be able to mature.

Jesus is our great example. Mark 1:35 tells us that *"Very early in the morning, while it was still dark, He got up, went out, and made His way to a deserted place; and there He was praying"* (CSB). Notice that Jesus had priorities, and I believe His biggest was His alone time with the Father.

To me this is the most important aspect of this discipline because this is where it all must start: making alone time for the Father and me. Please notice that I did not say "taking" alone time: In my mind, making time means that I am in control of my time, and this also means that I must choose to be alone with God. Remember, God doesn't need to discipline Himself to spend time with us; no one had to coax Christ to the cross. We are the ones who need discipline in this area.

My dear friend, **make** time; don't try to take time.

To me, "taking time" means that I have to go and get some time from somewhere else, and when I tried to do that, God always got cheated because I would never take time consistently. There was always something in life that would eventually take the time back from me (and God). When I allow my devotion to God to get tangled up with all my other responsibilities, God isn't always a priority. But when I **made** time for God, that was our time, and I was able to keep everything else out of the way. I realized that if I could make time for my second greatest priority, my wife, I could surely make time for God, whom I always claim is my number one everything.

If this sounds a bit strange or abstract to you, stop and ask yourself these two questions: Do I really want to spend time with God, and what am I willing to do to make it happen on a regular basis? Get it in your mind right now that making time for you and God to be alone can be done. As our perfect example, this is exactly what Jesus did. I recommend that you start by setting aside 30 minutes per day of uninterrupted time alone with God.

Here's a simple break down of what your time with God should consist of.

Quiet Time and Prayer

The material in this section is adapted from "If Quiet Time Is New to You."[2] A daily quiet time with the Lord is a critical factor in the growth and development of our faith. By now, you can tell that this is deliberate time made to be consistent daily.

Quiet time is when we offer the Lord praise and honor as we delight ourselves in the reality of His presence: Here we can spend time giving thanks as we contemplate His many blessings. Here we can freely offer up our deepest heartfelt confessions of our failings as well as humbly submit our requests and our needs. This is the place where the believer can find perfect peace and serenity in the quietness of His presence.

Our alone time with God is also the place where we hear from God Himself, as He speaks to and teaches our spirit, through the absolute perfection of His Holy Word. Coming to know God through personal experience in His Word will develop a deep hunger in you for more of Him, and it is in our quiet time that we see firsthand the love that God has for us as we come to experience it in His own words.

The Bible is meant to be both studied and read, but it doesn't end there—God wants us to meditate on His Holy Word as well. His Word, which contains the knowledge and understanding of the ages reveals to us everything we need to know about our past, present, and future. In Joshua 1:8, God commands that we *"Keep this Book of the Law always on your lips; meditate on it day and night, so that you may be careful to do everything written in it "* (NIV).

Benefits of Time Alone with God[3]

- We gain knowledge and important information during our time alone with God. The Bible is rich in teaching, wisdom, life lessons, and true account stories, which can help us understand and navigate through each one of life's challenges. If you are constantly looking for a nonfiction book that has romance, murder, intrigue, nasty bad guys, incredible acts of bravery, and amazing miracles, the Bible is the book you are looking for—it contains all these types of information and more! In fact, the more you read it, the more you will find that you have a lot in common with the men and women of the Bible!

The Bible also reveals the character and nature of God and shows us that His great plan to redeem mankind was carefully crafted before and throughout the ages.

- We gain healing, strength, and encouragement. God's Word is the source of all strength, truth, and real and complete freedom. Through His Holy Spirit, God inspires and empowers us as we grow in strength and knowledge of Him. Our personal prayer time with God allows us to be vulnerable and open to the guidance and correction of the Holy Spirit, which enables us to receive God's comfort and peace.

- We experience God's power. "Christ is the ultimate source and power and meeting with Him is essential to our receiving it."[4] It is through God's power that we learn how to live a life that glorifies Him, and that is always for our greater good. I have no doubt that each believer at some point in their lives will experience a personal touch of the Holy Spirit of God. In my own life I am grateful to attest that His touch has come in times when I needed it the most, and it has been powerful indeed.

- We experience pleasure. "Being alone with the person we love is enjoyable, and as we spend time with Christ we experience a joy that is unattainable anywhere else."[5] The pleasure that exists in a genuine relationship with Jesus is real, and I'm certain that He wants us all to be able to experience it.

Dedication to a daily quiet time, Bible study, and prayer will change and refine everything about you. God not only works on us, but in your quiet time, God will develop in you a growing concern for the spiritual and temporal needs of others. He teaches us to value the importance of quick repentance and forgiveness, and in time, He will enable us to see and love others the way that He does.

The Relationship between Repentance and Personal Sanctification

Consistent quiet time can help us understand the importance of quick and regular repentance and its relationship to our personal sanctification.

Repentance is a call to a personal, absolute, and ultimate unconditional surrender to God and His sovereignty. Though it includes sorrow and regret, it is more than that. In repentance, a person also makes a complete change of direction in thought, word, and action—all in obedience toward God.

Repentance is not only critical to the well-being of our spiritual health, but also to the growth in our personal relationship with the Father. When we repent, we are restored to a right relationship with God, which allows our sanctification to continue. First John 1:9 promises that *"If we confess our sins, he is faithful and just to forgive us our sins and cleanse us from all unrighteousness"* (CSB).

Sanctification means to be "made holy, free from sin, and purified." It is a progressive work of God, which is a lifelong process and one that God uses to make us more and more free from sin and more like Christ in our daily lives.

It is important to remember that sanctification is an internal process, which is continuous. We must cooperate with God in this process and continue to strive for obedience; this is why personal repentance is so important.

Sanctification does not mean that we will be perfect in this life, and sanctification can be greater in some people than it is in others. It all depends on how much we allow sin to overpower us. The Christian must rely on God's power to defeat sin daily. Remember the promise in 1 John 4:4: *"You are from God, little children, and you have conquered them, because the One who is in you is greater than the one who is in the world."*

Sanctification has three stages:

1. It begins at regeneration when we are saved. (1 Corinthians 6:11)
2. It continues throughout our lives. (1 Peter 1:15)
3. It is completed at death for our souls and then for our bodies when the Lord returns.

Q: Have you established for yourself a daily quiet time routine where you can get alone and study God's Word and pray?

_____

_____

_____

Q: If yes, describe what it consists of. If no, why not?

_____

_____

Q: If yes, what have you experienced in God so far?

_____

_____

Q: Do you daily strive to live a holy and set apart life before God?

_____

_____

Q: Are you quick to repent to God for your sin because you realize your role in your own sanctification?

_____

_____

Discipline in Our Outward Parts

This is where we take what we have learned in our faith and put it into action. While the five areas discussed in this section are very important, they certainly do not constitute all the outward disciplines that are required for a healthy Christian life. I chose these five because I feel that they are effective ways to build and refine our discipline in the outward parts, and they are effective ways to respond to the call of The Great Commission.

The Great Commission is the calling that God has put on every single believer, which Jesus proclaimed:

> _Jesus came near and said to them, "All authority has been given to me in heaven and on earth. Go, therefore, and make disciples of all nations, baptizing them in the name of the Father and of the Son and of the Holy Spirit, teaching them to observe everything I have commanded you. And remember, I am with you always, to the end of the age."_
>
> —Matt. 28:18–20 CSB

I love that this call also comes with a promise: *"And remember, I am with you always, to the end of the age."*

This is huge because what Jesus is telling us is that in the midst of this tremendous responsibility, we will find Christ right there in the thick of it all working with us. Our outward disciplines essentially reflect either the depth of our faith or the shallowness of it; this is why Jesus placed so much emphasis on a tree and its fruit. He said, *"Either make the tree good and its fruit will be good, or make the tree bad and its fruit will be bad; for a tree is known by its fruit"* (Matt. 12:33 CSB).

Let's now examine the five outward disciplines: worship, personal endurance and sacrifice, being in community with others, service to others, and forgiveness of others.

Worship

This material was inspired by *The Key to Authentic Worship of the Living God.*[6] Worship is one of the greatest privileges we have as human beings. Whether we do it alone, in a small group, or in a corporate gathering, God highly delights in the praise of His people. When we worship God, we please Him, and in turn, He shares His goodness and Holiness with us. All good things we were created for are amplified in us as we praise Him. Because God is so worthy, man can never praise Him enough. Holiness is the very nature of God—something only He possesses—and that sets Him apart from everything that was created. As we commune with Him in worship, He renews and refines our spirit, drawing us closer and closer to His perfect presence.

Authentic worship of the Living God serves not only as the righteous praise He so rightly deserves but it is also an affirmation of our understanding of who He is and that His presence is with us.

> *Sing to God! Sing praises to his Name. Exalt him who rides on the clouds—his Name is the LORD—and celebrate before him.*
>
> —Ps. 68:4 CSB

Personal Endurance and Sacrifice

Since the beginning, Christians have been called to endure in the faith in regard to the hardship or difficulties that we encounter in this life. All throughout scripture, God encourages, places emphasis on, even commands that believers endeavor to persevere:

> *Therefore, since we are surrounded by so great a cloud of witnesses, let us also lay aside every weight, and sin which clings so closely, and let us run with endurance the race that is set before us, looking to Jesus, the founder and perfecter of our faith, who for the joy that was set before him endured the cross, despising the shame, and is seated at the right hand of the throne of God.*
>
> —Heb. 12:1–2

The writer of Hebrews is referring to the beautiful examples we find in what is called "The Hall of Heroes" as recorded in Hebrews chapter 11. The suffering of these men and women is given so that we will be encouraged and strengthened by their examples to persevere and endure. In addition to this great encouragement, God has even set aside a special reward for those who endure unto the end:

> *Don't be afraid of what you are about to suffer. Look, the devil is about to throw some of you into prison to test you, and you will experience affliction for ten days. Be faithful to the point of death, and I will give you the crown of life.*
>
> —Rev. 2:10 CSB

The hope that we carry in us, which is written with a promise in our hearts by the Holy Spirit, is a guaranteed hope and one that no amount of hardship or suffering can erase. This hope must be a visible component of our outward discipline as believers.

Christ is the ultimate example of what full and perfect sacrifice looks like, and scripture has recorded this in detail for us in both His life and death. He expects us as believers to be ready and willing to sacrifice for the needs of others. Real personal sacrifice can only come from a heart that has been renewed by God, and this is one of the most powerful ways that we can show a lost world what the love of Jesus looks like.

We must be ready and willing to make sacrifices in this life for the betterment of others who are less fortunate than ourselves. By honoring

God in faithfully using our time, talents, and treasures for the benefit of others and the furtherance of His kingdom, we are giving God great glory.

Being in Community with Others

Hebrews 10:25 give strong direction about *"not neglecting to gather together, as some are in the habit of doing, but encouraging each other, and all the more as you see the day approaching"* (CSB). God expects us to be both connected and involved with a community of like-minded believers. Being in community assures us that we will have access to help, encouragement, and accountability. Community means gathering together for corporate worship, small group meetings, and even one-on-one fellowship and discipleship.

Service to Others

In James 1:26–27 (CSB), the half brother of Jesus writes this:

> *If anyone thinks he is religious without controlling his tongue, his religion is useless and he deceives himself. Pure and unde-filed religion before God the Father is this: to look after orphans and widows in their distress and to keep oneself unstained from the world.*

I believe that what the Holy Spirit is saying through James is that our personal conduct in respect to how we show our love for God is not expressed in merely hearing God's Word, but also by obeying it. James uses the example here of bridling or controlling the tongue as a marker of evidence of our obedience.

But that's not all he has to say: Evidence of our faith can also be seen in how we love and serve others. He is saying that our walk with God is useless if it does not affect and change the way we live and treat others. A powerful example of this can be expressed simply by helping the needy and keeping oneself unstained by the world's corruption.

Forgiveness of Others

Ephesians 4:32 commands this: *"Be kind to one another, tenderhearted, forgiving one another just as God in Christ forgave you."*

Forgiveness of others is one of the most important and powerful attributes of a truly changed heart. God expects us to give away love, kindness, and forgiveness to others in the same way He gives those things to us—freely and generously, without any strings attached. Since forgiveness is our way back to God, it only makes sense that it would be just as important in our human relationships. Take a moment to think about all that God has released you from—all your sin through the beautiful and incredible act of forgiveness. This exercise will help you realize how important it is that we strive to practice forgiveness just as God does.

- Do you worship God outside of church? If no, why not?
- Do you find it hard to endure the hardships and trials of this life?
- Have you taken your issues to God and allowed Him to help you endure?
- Have you gone out of your way to make sacrifices for those who are less fortunate than you?
- Are you part of a community of believers outside of church? If no, why not?
- Have you shared your faith through the service of others? If no, why not?
- Do you realize that forgiveness is a command, not an option for us?
- Do you find it difficult to forgive others? If yes, why?
- Do you realize how much God has already forgiven you? Explain.
- What type of fruit would you say that your tree produces most often?

Chapter 19

Spiritual Quicksand

One of my greatest fears related to my walk of faith is falling into a state of spiritual complacency. I've had my days when spiritually I felt like I was walking with cement blocks on my legs, and I did not like it one bit. So, what is complacency?

Complacency, as defined by our friend Webster means "a feeling of quiet pleasure or security, often while unaware of some potential danger, defect, or the like." Imagine finding yourself in a spiritual version of something like this—as I said above, to me this is truly scary. The sad thing is, we slip into complacency more often than we even realize.

Because complacency takes us to a place of "quiet pleasure and security," it is easy to see how complacency can also create a false sense of security for us. Here's an important question we need to address before we go further:

Q: Have you ever noticed that your relationship with God grew as a result of your need to draw nearer to Him during a severe trial, loss, struggle, or crisis? Y/N _____

If your answer to this question is similar to mine, we can agree that difficult times in our lives are often God's ways of getting our attention and are meant to help us snap out of the dangerous, complacent places we carelessly sink into. Complacency can be likened to quicksand: very rarely does one know they are stuck in it in advance.

Spiritual complacency is silent and sneaky, and I like to say it comes upon us kind of like the flu. And like the flu, we never see the virus or bacteria coming, and we only realize it when our bodily defenses have been compromised and we start to experience the nasty symptoms of the sickness.

Likewise, we cannot pinpoint or recall exactly how we became spiritually sick or why it even happened in the first place—but more times than not, complacency happens because at some point, we separated ourselves from our regular devotion to God. And to make matters worse, complacency can be kept alive through distractions, addictions, or other forms of willful sin. If left in place long enough, these distractions can cloud and distort the promptings and urgings of the Holy Spirit.

We will find ourselves stuck in spiritual quicksand fairly quickly if we allow ourselves to engage in the following:

- Lose interest or perspective on what God has called us to.
- Allow things in life to override our commitment to the discipline required to walk effectively as a true Christ follower.

Spiritual quicksand will also hinder your ability to see everyday things as they really are because there is no clear, confident place to step in quicksand—every move in any direction becomes suspect, and every single thought is bombarded by speculation.

And just as bad, many times we make the struggle worse through excuses such as, "There are too many things that I have to do right now," or "I am a single parent—I don't have time to have quiet time; I'm good," or "I can address this/that later."

Even worse, because of spiritual quicksand's ability to make everything a burden, if we do give God some of our time, we often choose to give God the last moments of our day when we are tired and worn out.

Q: Is it fair to God if the only time we give Him is when we are exhausted, and that's when we try to pray and study His precious Word? Y/N _____

Remember that spiritual quicksand works on us gradually. When we compromise on our discipline or forsake regular devotion and communion with God because we think that in the moment we are content, that's when we quietly slip away from our relationship in Him.

Because of this, the enemy doesn't need to cause a huge distraction or weave some elaborate temptation to draw you—he just needs to capitalize on the selfishness of your temporary contentment. What is truly sad is that most Christians slip in their walk with Christ and even neglect it when everything is going the way they want. Unfortunately, this is why so many "believers" only have a "911 relationship" with the Savior.

When we feel like we are stuck or not moving spiritually yet we allow ourselves to believe it is because of something else and not our own neglect, we have become truly complacent. I have been in that state of spiritual complacency, and it is no place I ever want to be in again.

You can turn off the TV, you can shut off the computer or iPad, you can put down the video game, you can put down your phone; your life does not have to be dictated by your job.

Understand that you yourself are enough of a distraction to allow complacency to exist in your life.

Q: Have you noticed complacency in your spiritual life? Y/N _____

Q: Just because your relationships or your finances are "healthy" right now doesn't mean your walk with Christ is. Have you placed as much effort in your spiritual life and walk with Christ as you have with everything and everyone else?

_____

_____

If you truly love God, you can and you will discipline yourself to set aside time in your day to strive to know your Creator. Consider what Proverbs 4:23–27 has to say:

> *Keep (protect, preserve) your heart with all vigilance, for from it flow the springs of life.*

Friends, the evidence of who your heart is truly faithful to will always be revealed by every word that comes out of your mouth and how you live daily before others. It's called fruit— it's either healthy or rotten.

Put away from you crooked speech, and put devious talk far from you (compare verses 23 and 24 to Matt. 12:33–37). *Let your eyes look directly forward, and your gaze be straight before you.*

—Prov. 4:25

Friends, keep your eyes focused on Jesus, not on the world and its desires that are already passing away.

Ponder the path of your feet; then all your ways will be sure.

—Prov. 4:26

Strive to seek God's counsel every day, watch where you step in life, and continuously offer your praise and prayers to Him throughout your day. Seek accountability through community; seek out one-on-one discipleship with someone who is more spiritually mature than you. (An easy, simple verse to memorize for building a good daily pattern is Romans 12:12.)

Proverbs 4:27: *"Do not swerve to the right or to the left; turn your foot away from evil."* God's path is straight; stay focused. Flee from (run away from, avoid at all costs) evil.

Psalm 34:4 says, *"I sought the LORD, and He answered me and rescued me from all my fears"* (NASB).

When the trials of life come, we must find ourselves already firmly rooted in a relationship with Christ: If we are, we will not allow ourselves to slip into or get stuck in spiritual quicksand. A sold-out heart for Christ must abide in us, and our heart must be overflowing with a love that exists more for who He is, rather than what He has done for us; this is a critical element of a Christ-centered relationship.

Spiritual maturity is marked by loving Jesus for who He is, not just for the gift of salvation. We are less likely to stumble into spiritual quicksand if we are constantly finding ourselves amazed by the person of Jesus. There is no temporary pleasure that can do this. If you somehow cannot find yourself in love with the person of Jesus, you may need to seriously evaluate your relationship with Him.

A constant pursuit of Jesus will keep you well away from the random and erratic trails that meander off into spiritual quicksand.

Please remember that we have not been given a passive faith; we were purposely created to live a life that glorifies God first, and the way we do this is to seek to truly know Him as much as our human minds possibly can.

Finally, in Psalm 27:8 David writes, *"When You said 'Seek My face,' my heart said to You, 'Your face, O Lord I shall seek'"* (NASB 1995).

Q: Are you seeking to know Him with your whole heart today? Y/N _____

Don't fall into the quicksand because you were not paying attention to where you were walking, and do not allow your heart to drift away from Him because you got too comfortable or complacent in this life.

Take inventory of who you are spending time with and what you are investing in: Carefully examine what you count as valuable in this life.

Too often, we are prone to commit all our resources to temporary investments instead of eternal ones, because the human heart has a short attention span and a long list of wants, needs and desires.

> *Seek the LORD and his strength: seek his face continually.*
> —1 Chron. 16:11 KJV

I love the following promise from God found in Proverbs 8:17. Our God is a promise keeper who is faithful to every covenant He has made with mankind. If God said it, you can count on it.

> *I love those who love me; And those who diligently seek me will find me.*
> —Prov. 8:17 NASB

You may ask, "Why would we need to know that God is a promise keeper?" Believe it or not, I have actually been asked this question. My best answer has always been this: because what God says matters to Him, and He expects it to matter to us, because He fully intends to follow through. And He will keep you out of the spiritual quicksand if you can remain faithful in your intent to know Him.

Activity

Evaluate where you are standing right now, spiritually: Is God in focus and in sight as you continue to move toward Him, or are you stuck, distracted, or lost?

Only you will know.

And only He can change where you are standing.

Chapter 20

The "Our Father" Prayer

Here is a template for how we should pray as was given to us by our Lord Jesus Christ in Matthew 6:9–13 and Luke 11:1–13. I encourage you to commit to seek to know Him deeply through prayer daily and cling to what He taught us as we study the details of this beautiful "formula." Remember, prayer is both communication and communion with God.

1. **Our Father who is in heaven:** As you begin to pray, seek out, recognize, and worship the presence of God, know that through His amazing and perfect attributes, He is omniscient, omnipotent, and omnipresent. Thank Him for His never-ending presence and have peace in the fact that there are no private moments. (Ps. 139:1–16)

2. **Hallowed (Holy) be Your name:** Our God is holy and set apart and emanating a purity that cannot even be comprehended. How amazing is it that He wants to share His holiness with us. So, how should you respond to this? We respond through worship and obedience. During this part of your prayer time, thank Him for His holiness and the fact that all good, pure, and perfect things come from Him, especially His love. Read and meditate on the vision Isaiah had of the Lord in Isaiah 6:1–7.

3. **Your kingdom come:** Here we pray not only for God's coming kingdom, which is a real, literal place, but also for His spiritual kingdom, which rules over our hearts right now. As His bondservants, let us be thankful that we serve such a perfect, righteous King. (Ps.145:13)

4. **Your will be done, on earth as it is in heaven:** We must first desire to seek His will, and our prayers should be a combination of thanksgiving for His perfect will (since God's will always results in His glory revealed, and His glory revealed is always for our greater good) and striving to make our plans match His. (Matt. 6:33)

5. **Give us this day our daily bread:** We must believe that Jesus is the only One who can meet all our needs and also that He is more than willing to do so. An important part of this aspect of our prayer is asking for the wisdom and maturity to clearly see the difference between our needs and our wants. Seeking to be fully satisfied in Jesus must be the ultimate goal of our lives just as David so clearly expressed in Psalm 23.

6. **Forgive us our trespasses:** We need to be relieved of the guilt and the shame, and we need to be relieved of the punishment that unrepentant sin brings. Jesus knows this, and this is why He instructs us to pray this way. Know that any sin we commit is done first and foremost against God. As you pray and repent, meditate on Psalm 51:1–12 as you pour out your heart to our merciful God.

7. **As we forgive those who trespass against us:** Forgiving others is really more about you and God than you and the person(s) who offended you; know that your own forgiveness depends on how you forgive others. Holding on to pain and resentment will create bitterness in you, and that is sin, also. Pray to be like Jesus and be quick to forgive. (Matt. 11:25)

8. **Lead us not into temptation but deliver us from evil:** Jesus commands us to run to Him in desperation (believing that He will provide protection, endurance, or a way out) and an expectation (believing He will do all that He has promised us). That is why He instructs us to plead for help in trials and protection when evil comes against us. Friends, we are not designed to, or meant for, standing up to temptation and evil by ourselves. Pray for and dwell in the shelter of the Most High. (Ps. 91:1–12)

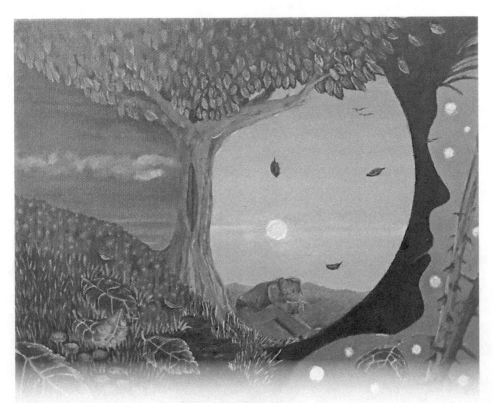

PART 3

Being a Christian is understanding that you have been given a gift that you don't deserve but get the amazing blessing of sharing.

—Pastor Isauro Medina, BT Church

Chapter 21

Giving God Our Obedience Instead of Our Works

Today, I would like to share with you from the book of Genesis 4:1–16, which is the story of Cain and Abel.

In the story of Cain and Abel, we get our first good look at pride, jealousy, and selfishness in the hearts of men, post-Fall. I will tell you that your heart, my heart, the heart of every living person is stained exactly the way that Cain's was so long ago. The human heart is one of the worst yet most protected parts of our human nature—the issue stems from the love of self, which is a flaw that we all nurture to some degree.

This is a story about motives.

When people choose sin, there is always a motive. Yes, I do believe people stumble into sin once in a while, but unfortunately, the majority of folks run to it, and we can even preplan it. This is not only true for nonbelievers but also includes Christians. I can honestly tell you that when I sin, it is usually something I allow or something I choose outright.

Thankfully, God doesn't leave us in our sin to rot—He prompts us to be restored to Him through repentance. James 4:17 is just one of many verses God has used in my life to wake me up; I find this passage to be a very sobering and convicting one, which thankfully prompts me to quick repentance. James 4:17 says, "*So whoever knows the right thing to do and fails to do it, for him it is sin.*"

What I have come to realize over the years is that if I can examine and adjust my motives ahead of time, maybe I can cut to the root of the problem and thereby fail God less. What I also need to realize beforehand is that I am going to have to deny self every time.

The "X factor" is going to lie in the things I don't want to give up. If we can be honest with ourselves for a moment, we all have secret sins and whether or not we want to admit it, we will often protect them. The interesting thing here is that there is usually a motive behind that.

So, what is the definition of motive? *Webster's* defines motive, as "a reason for doing something, especially one that is hidden or not obvious." As I said earlier, we all have motives. People rarely do something without some form of intent behind it.

Along with the fact that we sometimes don't have the right motives for what we do, some of us even have the wrong kind of motives for serving God. Many do it out of obligation, guilt, and compulsion or to receive something—I have even met people who serve the Living God out of some form of fear.

In total contrast to this, I have met a lot of Christians who truly find rest in their service to God and the difference maker is that these people are not chasing the gifts but instead are simply in love with the Giver, and a relationship with Him is all they want. Their motive is to just know Him!

I have found that typically Christians fit into one of three categories:

- The Fan: Loves the perks of calling themselves a Christian—they love the gifts. And like many Dallas Cowboys football fans, when their team starts losing, the jerseys come off!
- As soon as they are confronted by some challenging scripture, they are immediately offended. The minute suffering enters the picture, they tap out on God. Their faith was only ankle-deep at best.
- The Phony: They talk like a Christian, speaking perfect "Christianese," and they may even walk like one when being watched, but sooner or later, they return to their true self. These are the folks who use being a Christian for some form of gain.
- The Follower: These are the Luke 9:23 Christians—true followers no matter what.

Q: Which one of these are you?

_____

_____

Maybe you are asking, "You talked about people only being in love with the gifts—well, what GIFTS are you referring to, Pastor Mike?"

Many are in love with the gift of Salvation. You might say, "Well, what's so wrong with that? Salvation is a great thing, and who wants to go to hell?" I don't think anyone does, but for many Christians, salvation is all their faith is built upon. We have found in counseling that many, many people have walked the church aisle or said that special prayer simply out of guilt, condemnation, or fear of consequences—not because they wanted Jesus as King of their heart.

They did it because at that moment, their life was very hard, and they didn't want to suffer any more, or they didn't want to go to hell. I have to tell you these are not the right motives for coming to the cross. And if that is why you came to the cross, maybe you did not really find what you were looking for. Now, let's get into today's scripture and unpack this deeper with some more insight from God's Word.

So, this famous story starts out in a fairly normal manner. First, we have the birth of Cain, the older brother, followed by the birth of his younger sibling—a boy named Abel. From the way the story is written, we might assume that they were close in age; many Bible scholars have suggested that Cain and Abel were twins, since they appear to have been born so close together.

> _The man was intimate with his wife Eve, and she conceived and gave birth to Cain. She said, "I have had a male child with the LORD's help."_
>
> _She also gave birth to his brother Abel. Now Abel became a shepherd of flocks, but Cain worked the ground. In the course of time Cain presented some of the land's produce as an offering to the LORD. And Abel also presented an offering—some of the firstborn of his flock and their fat portions. The LORD had regard for Abel and his offering, but he did not have regard for Cain and his offering. Cain was furious, and he looked despondent._

Then the Lord said to Cain, "Why are you furious? And why do you look despondent? If you do what is right, won't you be accepted? But if you do not do what is right, sin is crouching at the door. Its desire is for you, but you must rule over it."

Cain said to his brother Abel, "Let's go out to the field." And while they were in the field, Cain attacked his brother Abel and killed him.

Then the Lord said to Cain, "Where is your brother Abel?"

"I don't know," he replied. "Am I my brother's guardian?"

Then he said, "What have you done? Your brother's blood cries out to me from the ground! So now you are cursed, alienated from the ground that opened its mouth to receive your brother's blood you have shed. If you work the ground, it will never again give you its yield. You will be a restless wanderer on the earth."

But Cain answered the LORD, *"My punishment is too great to bear! Since you are banishing me today from the face of the earth, and I must hide from your presence and become a restless wanderer on the earth, whoever finds me will kill me."*

Then the LORD *replied to him, "In that case, whoever kills Cain will suffer vengeance seven times over." And he placed a mark on Cain so that whoever found him would not kill him. Then Cain went out from the Lord's presence and lived in the land of Nod, east of Eden.*

—Gen. 4:1–16 CSB

Wow. If you are like me, you have either read or heard this story multiple times, but the content of it still grips me. We are then told about their occupations, both of which are respectable ones for the time. Verse 2 tells us that *"Abel became a shepherd of flocks, but Cain worked the ground."*

Notice how the younger brother is mentioned first: Why is that so? I believe that Abel is mentioned first because his occupation is representative of pastoral life. He is the shepherd, and this will become a very important occupation in the history of the people of Israel.

- Before David was king, he was a simple shepherd.
- Jesus is the King who became the Good Shepherd.

By contrast, Cain followed the occupation of agricultural life—he was a farmer. And given the way it is described here, we see a much different emphasis—possibly because this occupation follows the curse of God in Genesis 3:17.

But what happens next is huge. We find that both brothers are preparing to worship the Living God with an offering from their labors.

> In the course of time Cain presented some of the land's produce as an offering to the LORD. And Abel also presented an offering—some of the firstborn of his flock and their fat portions.
>
> —Gen.4:3 CSB

Now watch what happens here and keep your eyes open for motives.

> The Lord had regard for Abel and his offering, but he did not have regard for Cain and his offering. Cain was furious, and he looked despondent. Then the Lord said to Cain, "Why are you furious? And why do you look despondent? If you do what is right, won't you be accepted? But if you do not do what is right, sin is crouching at the door. Its desire is for you, but you must rule over it."
>
> —Gen. 4:4–7 CSB

God deserves your best, not your leftovers:

- We think we know what an acceptable sacrifice is. We think we know what God should expect and accept from us.
- Many Christians today are too content with offering some of what they have, instead of giving God the best of what they have. Remember, what God wants more than an offering is our obedience.
- There's a big difference between giving God the best of what you have and giving Him what you think should be acceptable.
- Here's another problem: Too often, we choose to worship God on our own terms, not His.

The Lord reaches out to Cain, seeing the condition of his heart:

> *If you do what is right, won't you be accepted? But if you do not do what is right, sin is crouching at the door. Its desire is for you, but you must rule over it.*
>
> —Gen. 4:7 CSB

- First, God gave this man a way out, by reminding him to *"do what is right."*
- Then came the warning: "Sin is crouching at the door. Its desire is for you." In other words, sin is like a hungry lion ready to pounce on Cain; it wanted him so bad.
- God was warning him that sin is waiting for him, and make no mistake, it wanted to master him, but it doesn't have to be that way.
- God saw the stubbornness and anger in Cain's heart and because of that, the Lord's instruction bounced right off Cain's hardened heart!

But sadly, that's all that Cain allowed himself to see—this is what he wanted. He was satisfied with an angry and bitter heart because he felt like he deserved to feel this way because God chose Abel's offering over his. Captured by his own anger, jealousy, and bitterness, Cain set out to get even with his brother for stealing God's favor from him! You see, Cain simply couldn't make sense of the situation:

- Abel gave God the best of what he had because his heart wanted to please God.
- In direct contrast, Cain gave God a random sampling of what he had and expected God to accept it.
- And not only just accept it—He expected God to find his offering to be superior to his brother's offering.

So, what happens next?

> *Cain said to his brother Abel, "Let's go out to the field." And while they were in the field, Cain attacked his brother Abel and killed him.*
>
> —Gen. 4:7 CSB

Q: Do you think Cain had a motive, or did he sin out of sheer impulse?

_____

You may think I just asked you an obvious question, but I need you to see that random sin acts rarely happen in our lives as Christians!

Q: Examine your heart for a moment and check and see what was truly behind your most recent sin. Was there a motive behind it, or did you simply give in and sin out of sheer impulse?

_____

_____

_____

Did Cain sin out of jealousy? Yes!

Did he sin out of envy? Yes!

Did he sin out of revenge? Yes!

It is so sad to see, but it's all there—the pride, the arrogance, the pain—all of this in Cain's heart. My friends, we do the same thing! And it doesn't have to come from any of the motives Cain had—we make our own motives so that what we do meets our own needs. We pick and choose our areas of obedience, and then we try to add to it or doctor it up through our works. We might say to ourselves: "Well, I know that I am a very good tither, and God knows I am a very good tither. So He should not have any problem with me looking at porn once in a while on my phone." Or someone might say, "I'm a good giver. . . . I am being obedient in that. God should be pleased with me."

Now Abel is dead.

The first field to ever become a crime scene now holds the evidence of the first murder in human history, and it's officially in the books. For the first time ever, human hands have shed human blood. And to make it worse, it was a brother who killed a brother on purpose. It wasn't a stranger, and it wasn't an accident.

In verses 9–10, _"The LORD said to Cain, 'Where is your brother Abel?'"_ The Lord came looking for His son, but He knew where he was, and Cain responds the same way we all still do today. He plays it off and responds as if God doesn't know what happened. *"'I don't know,' he replied. 'Am I my brother's guardian?' Then he said, 'What have you done? Your brother's blood cries out to me from the ground!'"*

There are several problems here. First of all, Cain does know where Abel is—he's the one who murdered him. Abel is lying dead somewhere out in a lush field, and his blood is crying out to God from the ground for justice. But here's one of the reasons God is asking: As the older brother, Cain is supposed to be his brother's keeper, and God is asking him, so Cain will realize that he has abandoned his responsibility as the older brother.

Culturally, the firstborn son has authority and responsibility for his younger siblings. And Cain has abandoned that responsibility in the worst way—allowing harm to come to the younger brother. Cain rejects the obligation to care for Abel and instead, he uses his authority as his protector to be the one who takes his life.

Cain, who once brought his sacrifice *"from the fruit of the ground"* and has shed his brother's blood on the soil, is now himself cursed *"from the ground."* No longer a farmer, Cain now becomes a wanderer, exiled from the fruitful soil and cursed to dwell in the Land of "wandering." He's lost everything—his family, his livelihood, and his home; he now dwells outside civilization as a hopeless drifter.

Here's another scary consequence of his actions: Where he wanders, there is no law or morality. So, he complains to God: *"Anyone who meets me may kill me"* (Gen. 4:14). This would be an apt punishment for a murderer. But God has compassion for Cain and gives him a mark so that no one will kill him. Cain will live on, but his existence is only a shadow of his former life.

We should all receive this story with a heart open to self-examination: There must exist in us a constant awareness of our motives, what they mean, and what they can potentially do to us and to our relationship with the Living God. What God wants from us is obedience, which He says is better than sacrifice. We have nothing He wants or needs, and there is nothing in us that would draw Him to us. Why?

God has already given His best to you!

- It's very different for us now—it's been different for every human being ever since the cross.

- There are no more temporary appeasements offered to God.
- The cross was the final, perfect effort, which set all who accept it free.
- That means we can no longer give God what we think He should accept.
- Church, do you realize that it was God who reached out to submit to our needs? Now, you may be saying, "Wait a minute, Pastor Mike, God doesn't submit to anyone!" Well, don't let the language here confuse you—He willfully offered the best He had for us.
- Jesus submitted to our need for a savior. Jesus said, *"No one takes it from me, but I lay it down on my own. I have the right to lay it down, and I have the right to take it up again. I have received this command from my Father"* (John 10:18). Just hearing these powerful words should reset your heart and all its current priorities.

> Just like Cain, it's easy to say it's all about me.
> Selfishness is probably our greatest character trait as humans.
> I see evidence of it every week in counseling: "Fix her, Pastor; she's the problem."
> "I'm a good person, I don't know why all of this is happening to me."
> "I don't deserve this—I deserve better."

My seminary education is primarily based in counseling. This is my 16th year counseling, and I've had the privilege of having my wife as my co-counselor for about the past 10 years. As you can probably imagine, we have seen a bit of everything in our time.

God sought Abel to provide justice, and God sought Cain to pronounce justice. It may be hard to see this with Cain, but it probably would have been better for him to die than to have lived with the curse his sin brought upon him.

I can confidently tell you that sin is and has always been the same with every person or couple we have counseled; the only difference is that it occurred in different places, on different dates, and with different faces. As scripture so accurately states, there is nothing new under the sun. When people choose sin, there is always a motive.

Take a few minutes to answer these questions:

Q: How have you responded to God's gift of His one and only Son?

_____

_____

Q: Have you received Him? Y/N _____

_____

Q: Have you flat-out rejected Him, or are you still saying, "No, not yet"? Sin has a huge debt, and God has tremendous wrath stored up for it.

_____

_____

We all must respond to the cross. A decision must be made. I urge you to respond to the giver today and take no concern for the gifts. If you have the giver, you have everything!

Activity

Our motives can set the course for sin, but God can still bring us back on track. Write down a brief example of a time when you acted with the wrong motives and then describe how God brought you back to Himself.

We all have these stories. When you are finished with your story, write a prayer of thanksgiving to God and thank Him for coming to find you as He did with both Cain and Abel.

_____

_____

_____

_____

_____

_____

Chapter 22

Lessons from the Conversion of the Apostle Paul

Today, we will take a close-up look at the conversion of Saul the Pharisee to Paul the Apostle of Jesus Christ (Acts 26:1–23).

Paul the Apostle was one of the greatest men who ever walked the face of the earth. Through his ministry, we can safely say that millions have heard the gospel he preached throughout the world. Paul was directed and inspired by the Holy Spirit to write 13 letters, or epistles, making him the largest contributor to the contents of the New Testament.

Through the book "The Acts of the Apostles" as written by Luke, we have an excellently detailed portion of Paul's life and ministry, which records how God used him to take the gospel to all men. God most certainly shocked the faithful when He said, *"This man is my chosen instrument to take my name to Gentiles, kings, and Israelites. I will show him how much he must suffer for my name"* (Acts 9:15–16 CSB).

What we will be looking at today is his conversion story as told by Paul himself to King Agrippa, while under arrest, as recorded in Acts chapter 26. Now, Paul's actual conversion took place back in Acts chapter 9, starting from verse 1, and I recommend that you go back and read the original event because it is quite an amazing piece of history in our faith.

What I like about the Acts 26 version is that it presents Paul himself talking about the kind of man he was before and after he had the amazing encounter with the Risen Savior on the road to Damascus that great and fateful day. Let's take a look together at Paul's defense as he tells his story to the Roman authorities:

Agrippa said to Paul, "You have permission to speak for yourself."

Then Paul stretched out his hand and began his defense: "I consider myself fortunate that it is before you, King Agrippa, I am to make my defense today against all the accusations of the Jews, especially since you are very knowledgeable about all the Jewish customs and controversies. Therefore I beg you to listen to me patiently.

"All the Jews know my way of life from my youth, which was spent from the beginning among my own people and in Jerusalem. They have known me for a long time, if they are willing to testify, that according to the strictest sect of our religion I lived as a Pharisee. And now I stand on trial because of the hope in what God promised to our ancestors, the promise our twelve tribes hope to reach as they earnestly serve him night and day. King Agrippa, I am being accused by the Jews because of this hope.

"Why do any of you consider it incredible that God raises the dead? In fact, I myself was convinced that it was necessary to do many things in opposition to the name of Jesus of Nazareth. I actually did this in Jerusalem, and I locked up many of the saints in prison, since I had received authority for that from the chief priests. When they were put to death, I was in agreement against them. In all the synagogues I often punished them and tried to make them blaspheme. Since I was terribly enraged at them, I pursued them even to foreign cities.

"I was traveling to Damascus under these circumstances with authority and a commission from the chief priests. King Agrippa, while on the road at midday, I saw a light from heaven brighter than the sun, shining around me and those traveling with me. We all fell to the ground, and I heard a voice speaking to me in Aramaic, 'Saul, Saul, why are you persecuting me? It is hard for you to kick against the goads.'

"I asked, 'Who are you, Lord?'

"And the Lord replied, 'I am Jesus, the one you are persecuting. But get up and stand on your feet. For I have appeared to you for this purpose, to appoint you as a servant and a witness of what you have seen and will see of me. I will rescue you from your people and from the Gentiles. I am sending you to them to open their eyes so that they may turn from darkness to light and from the power of Satan to God, that they may receive forgiveness of sins and a share among those who are sanctified by faith in me.'

"So then, King Agrippa, I was not disobedient to the heavenly vision. Instead, I preached to those in Damascus first, and to those in Jerusalem and in all the region of Judea, and to the Gentiles, that they should repent and turn to God, and do works worthy of repentance. For this reason the Jews seized me in the temple and were trying to kill me. To this very day, I have had help from God, and I stand and testify to both small and great, saying nothing other than what the prophets and Moses said would take place—that the Messiah would suffer, and that, as the first to rise from the dead, he would proclaim light to our people and to the Gentiles."

—Acts 26:1–23 CSB

Let's now look briefly at eight facts from the conversion of Paul:

1. Through the conversion of Paul, we see clearly the relentless pursuit by God of those whom He loves.

   Think about your own conversion story for a moment: I don't know too many souls who can say that it was they who ran to God to be saved—most if not all of us were running away from Him while we were chasing the desires of our own heart.

   Just why God seems to pursue some more intensely than others is a mystery. I don't know why He did not quit on me because I certainly gave Him every reason to. The truth is, God is the **initiator** of every spiritual pursuit and, therefore, He is the author of every spiritual relationship; Jesus confirms this through the parable of the lost sheep (Luke 15:3–10) and wants us to understand the goodness of God's heart and that He desires to know each one of us intimately.

Q: What stands out to you or what do you remember the most about God's pursuit of you?

_____

_____

_____

2. God will often take an enemy and convert him to an ally.

Saul was a murderous man who imprisoned and killed Christians, tore families apart, and ruined the lives of many believers. At that time, he was the greatest threat to the NT church, but God had other plans for him!

Q: Do you realize that at one time, you were God's enemy? Y/N _____

Q: What does it mean to you to now be called God's friend?

_____

_____

_____

3. God is able to cover anyone's sins.

God can save anyone! There is no one who can out-sin His grace; the blood of Christ is more than enough to not only cover but also wash away all of our sins! God made Saul into a new man. Second Corinthians 5:17 says, _"Therefore, if anyone is in Christ, he is a new creation. The old has passed away; behold, the new has come."_

Activity

Take a moment now and write down a name of a person who you think is unlikely to ever be saved (we all know at least one). Now commit yourself to pray for that person's salvation at least once a day going forward from this moment. We should never doubt that God can and will save even the most lost persons we know.

Write their name(s) here:

_____

_____

4. "It's difficult to kick against the goads [pricks]" (verse 14).

   This Greek proverb would be something familiar to the Jews and to anyone who worked in agriculture. An ox goad was a long stick with a pointed and sharpened metal tip on the end of it which would be used to "steer" the animal back to the right direction by pricking it with this instrument. A couple of pricks with this sharp instrument was usually all it took for the animal to correct its course.

   What Jesus was basically saying to Paul was that it is useless for him to rebel against Jesus—in fact, it was a losing battle. Yes, Paul had a sincere drive and passion against Christianity (he thought he was doing right), but he was not heading in the direction God wanted him to go. Jesus was telling him that it's difficult to continue in a direction that God does not want you to go, and that God will prick or goad you back into the right direction.

   This pricking or goading may be painful—usually, it has to be painful to get the animal (or us) to respond. But the pricks and goads that come from the Holy Spirit are administered in love and with our ultimate good in mind.

   Q: Has God had to prick or goad you into the right direction? Y/N _____

   Q: Can you recall a specific moment in your relationship with Christ when this happened? Explain.

   _____

   _____

   _____

5. God has a plan for us all in His will for the world.

   Just like Paul we have been saved from something and for something. God uses all whom He calls for His glory, which always results in our greater good. Remember that God makes plans, and we make choices. God's plans often include suffering: God is not cruel or someone who likes to watch His creation suffer, but He also knows that difficult times are what will draw the best out of us and enable us to grow and change. Paul would suffer more than any other ordinary man who would be called by God in the NT aside from Jesus, and it would all be for God's great glory. Remember God's own words regarding Paul as found in Acts 9:15–16 above.

Q: What has God called you to in this life?

_____

_____

_____

Q: Are you willing to accept all that His call may require of you? Y/N _____

6. Trusting in Christ also brings us into community with other believers.

Paul would not be left alone in the work his calling would require. God provided strong friendships with Luke, Barnabas, Silas, Timothy, and Mark throughout his ministry for support and encouragement—all through a genuine brotherhood that comes with our faith.

Q: How has God changed or enriched your life through relationships with other believers?

_____

_____

_____

Q: How are your Christian relationships different from other relationships in your life?

_____

_____

_____

7. Our salvation opens our eyes and shows us how lost we actually were before Christ.

   It is important that God show us what He has delivered us out of, and we must be fully aware of the transformation He is working in us.

   Q: Why is knowing this so important?

   _____

   _____

   _____

   Q: Have you stopped and taken inventory of who you were before Christ, and do you realize how much He has changed you? Y/N _____

   Look at Paul's description of himself in verses 9–12: *"In fact, I myself was convinced that it was necessary to do many things in opposition to the name of Jesus of Nazareth. I actually did this in Jerusalem, and I locked up many of the saints in prison, since I had received authority for that from the chief priests. When they were put to death, I was in agreement against them. In all the synagogues I often punished them and tried to make them blaspheme. Since I was terribly enraged at them, I pursued them even to foreign cities. "I was traveling to Damascus under these circumstances with authority and a commission from the chief priests"* (CSB).

8. God is always in complete control no matter how things may appear on the outside.

   In Acts 18 we find that Paul is having a rough time in Corinth, and he begins to fear for his life. What looked potentially bad to Paul on the outside wasn't how God saw it or how He wanted Paul to see it at all. The Lord spoke to Paul at night in a dream and not only encouraged Him but gave him instructions to keep on preaching: *"The Lord said to Paul in a night vision, 'Don't be afraid, but keep on speaking and don't be silent. For I am with you, and no one will lay a hand on you to hurt you, because I have many people in this city.' He stayed there a year and a half, teaching the word of God among them"* (Acts 18:9–11 CSB).

We can be confident that God is always in control and will not leave us nor forsake us. He will walk through even the darkest valleys and travel the most dangerous roads right beside us. His Word promises that His Holy Spirit will even give us the words we need to speak in our most difficult hour. Like Paul, we are called to take a stand for Jesus, and He does not want the proclamation of His Word to be characterized by either a spirit of fear or indecisiveness.

Q: Can you say that you trust God and that you fully believe that He is always in complete control, no matter what? Y/N _____

Q: What areas of your life are you having difficulty in giving God your complete trust?

_____

_____

_____

Chapter 23

Picking Up Your Cross Daily

If you find yourself experiencing the daily struggles, challenges, and trials of life, let me comfort you by reminding you that you are not alone.

Everyone in the human race is currently dealing with some type of crisis or problem right now across this big blue marble we call earth. It should bring us at least some relief to know this, and I hope it does for you. If you are a Christian, I have some additional news for you. For many of you this will merely be a reminder; but for some, it will be a tough pill to swallow until you can begin to fully submit to Christ and fully trust Him.

The news is this: In addition to everything else we must endure, we are going to suffer for what we believe. What?? Suffer? Yes. Before we get too worked up, let me take you to the Bible and expand on an often overlooked or misunderstood piece of scripture. My references will be from Luke 9:23 and 1 John 2:15–17.

First, in Luke 9:23, we read this: *"And he [Jesus] said to all, 'If anyone would come after Me, let him deny himself and take up his cross daily and follow Me.'"* In this extremely important verse, Jesus gives us the basic outline of what is required to become one of His disciples.

Death to Self Is Mandatory

In the first part, "let him deny himself," our Lord is stating that right away a major change must occur—we must change our minds about who is in charge of our life, and we must come to the conclusion that it can only be King Jesus.

"Denying self" requires a couple steps: First, this means you must remove yourself completely from the equation. This means it's not about you anymore, and your life is not just for you anymore. Second, Jesus must be placed in full and complete authority over every single area of your life. Simply stated, He is now King of your heart, and your life is now lived to honor and glorify Him first, not self. Now for most people if not all, this is no easy task, and it may even sound crazy or unnecessary. In fact, true self-denial remains one of the most difficult struggles Christians face today, but this is because too often self is never fully surrendered.

It seems that a lot of us live in a realm of constant negotiations with God. We say, "OK, God, you can have this part of my life, but not that part (let's clarify with some practical examples here): You can have my language and clean that up, but I want to maintain control over my eyes. I don't lust too much."

Or, we say, "You can have authority over my finances, but not my alcohol use." When all of self is not surrendered, when all of self is not regularly denied, and when Christ is not permanently allowed to reign on the throne of your heart, you will not be able to follow Him. I am not saying you and I must be perfect, because that is impossible. But when we willfully deny Christ access and control to any part of ourselves or think we can negotiate with His Lordship, we will not be able to be His disciple.

Q: As you read through this, is it all still about you? Y/N _____

Q: Right now, what areas of your life are you unwilling to give Him full authority over?

_____

_____

Jesus's words are very clear: *"he must deny [all of] himself."* My dear friends, please understand this: Jesus is either Lord of all in our lives, or not Lord at all.

Willfully Pick Up Your Cross? Yes.

The second part of denying yourself is often where some confusion comes in. During Luke's time, the statement Jesus makes next, *"Take up his cross and daily follow me,"* would definitely invoke a brutal, savage, and fearful image in the minds of those who heard it, since crucifixion was well-known and very feared.

In those days, if you saw a man carrying a cross, it basically meant "dead man walking," and you and everyone else who saw it knew that. That scene would tell you without words that a man was going to die arguably the worst death of all time, most likely for a very high crime.

But Jesus said this to mean something else. It meant that truly following Him would bring suffering. This type of suffering isn't limited to the kind of suffering common to everyone on earth as a result of the curse of sin. This would be a suffering for righteousness' sake: This means that abiding in Christ fully and completely puts you totally against the entire world and all that it can throw at you.

Because of the world's hatred for Christ, we will suffer, and Jesus is saying that choosing to follow Him means choosing to accept all the hurt that comes with it. In 1 John 2:15–17, the Apostle John clearly tells us the following:

> *Do not love the world or the things in the world. If anyone loves the world, the love of the Father is not in him. For all that is in the world—the desires of the flesh and the desires of the eyes and pride of life—is not from the Father but is from the world. And the world is passing away along with its desires, but whoever does the will of God abides forever.*

Q: Have you ever contemplated what it must have been like for Jesus to bear the physical, emotional, and spiritual burdens of the entire world on the cross? Y/N _____

Q: Have you ever stopped to consider just how much your sins contributed to that terrible burden? Y/N _____

Taking up our cross daily removes from us the love of a world that as John points out is already *"passing away."* You may ask, "So what is passing away?" I believe that what God is saying here is that anything apart from

Him will always be temporary. When you die, there will not be a trophy shelf for you to display all your worldly accomplishments. They just won't matter and will, like everything else temporary, pass away.

But once again accepting this task of "cross bearing" is not an easy one, and many Christians do their best to avoid it, either ignoring it through belief in fraudulent doctrine, through denial, lack of self-control, or just plain laziness.

Some Christians just say, "No, I refuse to accept suffering." When I hear this, I ask them to tell me what Paul meant in Galatians 2:20 (CSB), and then next comes silence.

> I have been crucified with Christ, and I no longer live, but Christ lives in me. The life I now live in the body, I live by faith in the Son of God, who loved me and gave himself for me.

My friends, that clunky, jagged, dirty, and heavy cross will give you new life, if you have the courage to pick it up. I also want you to take notice of the fact that Jesus said, *"Take up your cross,"* not "choose" which one you want to pick up! We cannot choose what cross we will carry in this life. However, there is no doubt that "our own unbelief and sin can become the master carpenters of our cross"[1] as Charles Spurgeon so adequately puts it.

This means that your sin can become the cross which will ultimately crush you—your own self-imposed cross will become the tool of your own self-destruction! In direct contrast to this are the crosses Christ intends for us to carry in this life, and they are God-designed and appointed for us in divine love. God requires that we accept them not only willingly but also with a cheerful heart.

Friends, we must make sure not to carry our crosses as an outward "badge of burden."[2] Your cross is not meant to become your own public pity party. Nor do we allow ourselves to carry them with an attitude that could lead us to a place where we end up blaming God or resenting Him. Simply put, God will not honor whining and complaining about the burdens He asks us to bear.

Notice that not once did Jesus ever complain about anything the Father asked Him to do: He never complained once even though His burdens were much greater than ours will ever be, and on a level we will certainly never be able to comprehend.

Every Christian must take up their crosses in this life—it is a gloriously mandatory and beautifully unavoidable duty. And, as Spurgeon reminds us, our crosses will never be made of feathers or covered with velvet, or in any manner be comfortable at all.[3] This is a true and sobering fact for us all. I believe I have spent enough time talking about the crosses we must bear in this life. But allow me to finish with three very important things:

First, remember that it is Christ who actually bears your burdens (crosses) and mine. He carries them with us and for us.

Second, enduring suffering actually makes you and me better—it is part of our sanctification.

Third, eternal blessings are promised to you and me for being obedient and having endured all through His great love!

I leave you now with some of my favorite scriptures below. The rest you can look up and read and study on your own. I suggest you commit as many as possible to memory, so they can be your strength and encouragement toward each step you take carrying your divinely appointed burdens:

Blessed [happy, spiritually prosperous, favored by God] is the man who is steadfast under trial and perseveres when tempted; for when he has passed the test and been approved, he will receive the [victor's] crown of life which the Lord has promised to those who love Him.

—James 1:12 AMP

More than that, we rejoice in our sufferings, knowing that suffering produces endurance, and endurance produces character, and character produces hope, and hope does not put us to shame, because God's love has been poured into our hearts through the Holy Spirit who has been given to us.

—Rom. 5:3–5 RSV

And after you have suffered a little while, the God of all grace, who has called you to his eternal glory in Christ, will himself restore, confirm, strengthen, and establish you.

—1 Pet. 5:10

For I consider that the sufferings of this present time are not worth comparing with the glory that is to be revealed to us.

—Rom. 8:18

I have said these things to you, that in me you may have peace. In the world you will have tribulation. But take heart; I have overcome the world.

—John 16:33

He will wipe away every tear from their eyes, and death shall be no more, neither shall there be mourning, nor crying, nor pain anymore, for the former things have passed away.

—Rev. 21:4

Whoever does not bear his own cross and come after me cannot be my disciple.

—Luke 14:27

Activity

Take some time today to read and meditate on the following scriptures:

James 1:2–4

1 Peter 4:12–19

Hebrews 12:11

Hosea 6:1–3

Mark 13:13

Isaiah 43:21

2 Corinthians 4:8–10

Psalm 34:19

Philippians 1:2

And many, many more!

Chapter 24

You versus Yourself, Part 1

The primary scripture reference is Hosea chapter 5. This is intended to be a three-part lesson. I encourage you to do only one part a day, so you can have time to fully understand and absorb all that God has for you here.

Allow me to start this lesson off with what I truly believe is a true statement: You will spend a lot of time in your life battling yourself. Whether you come to know Jesus Christ as Lord and Savior or not, you will constantly encounter you versus yourself. You will win some rounds, but will most likely lose twice as many, because the flesh is always hungry, always wanting comfort, and always wanting its own way and all on one-sided terms.

You will even turn away from all that is good just to win one battle in this fight, but let me tell you what "winning" really means. It means that self gets what it wants, and God gets robbed again.

Today, we will examine chapter 5 of the book of Hosea, and I would like to look at a few important verses just a little bit closer but then spend the majority of today's reading making some very interesting comparisons and contrasts.

But first, here's a summary from the high points of Hosea chapter 4 for purposes of context. In chapter 4 we examined the nation of Israel as a whole, but specifically focused on their priests, which represented their leadership.

Because Israel's leadership had failed them, they rightly fell under some harsh criticism. What's important here is to be aware of the lessons offered to others as opportunities available to us and then make every effort to take them and apply them.

Today, as we dissect Hosea 5, I want to look specifically at you and me. This is by far one of my favorite books in the Bible. I love it because of what God did in my heart as I studied it. He tore me down and rebuilt me brand new in a lot of ways, and I am just so thankful. The story of Hosea is primarily a story about how God can reconcile broken relationships that have been thoroughly trashed by sin. We find that the primary relationship here is between God and Israel and it is severely fractured due to Israel's sin.

Remember that God has always been the faithful covenant keeper, while we, in contrast have always been the faithful covenant breaker.

In Hosea, we also have the marriage relationship between our writer and prophet Hosea and his repeatedly unfaithful wife Gomer, and their relationship too, is severely damaged by sin. God uses the painful dysfunction of a repeatedly unfaithful wife (Gomer) and Hosea's willingness to take her back over and over again as a representation of God's love for us. Israel has "cheated" on God multiple times, but God's incredible love for His people is unable to be extinguished. Even when we choose sin over Him, He takes us back!

And here is something that has probably stood out to me the most in this book: The tremendous pain in God's heart because of Israel repeatedly returning to sin is so clearly visible. Experiencing the reality of this all but broke me completely. Never before in scripture have I seen God so hurt and offended.

It was almost as if I could actually somehow feel some of the hurt God was experiencing at this time. It made the memory of my own sin seem like a sharp knife that I, for a time, kept putting in His back over and over. I knew better, yet I still chose sin. It was one of the most terrible times of realization and reflection I have ever experienced in my life. I could hardly bear how I had hurt God.

Some important themes in Hosea:

- The people He has loved so perfectly and blessed so generously have turned their backs on Him and chosen idols and adultery instead.

- And we also have seen Hosea's pain caused by the depth of his wife's sin, which she has dragged her family into—so deep in fact, that Hosea had to go and buy her back from the sexual bondage she led herself into.
- We have seen our Loving God offer reconciliation in exchange for Israel's repentance, and commanded Hosea to offer the same to Gomer, his wife.
- And for a season, we saw Israel and Gomer accept reconciliation, but it just didn't last because both Israel and Gomer never fully abandoned their destructive and addictive desires, because they loved self more than anything or anyone else.

Q: Have you been going back and forth between God and your sin? Explain.

_____

_____

_____

_____

_____

_____

This is exactly where we find probably the strongest indictment against Israel as charged by God back in chapter 4. He calls them out for rejecting His knowledge and instead choosing ignorance so they could protect their sin.

> *My people are destroyed for lack of knowledge; because you have rejected knowledge, I reject you from being a priest to me. And since you have forgotten the law of your God, I also will forget your children.*
>
> —Hosea 4:6

Remember that choosing ignorance does not relieve us from the responsibility to prior knowledge of something.

Q: It is very convicting to read the words spoken by God in Hosea 4:6: Do you often reject the truth or knowledge of something because it conflicts with your plans or desires? For the Christian, this is extremely important because we have the knowledge of God—think about it:

1. We know who Jesus is, and why He came to the earth.
2. We know about the cross, and what it cost.
3. We know how He has called us to live.
4. So, when we choose to sin anyway, we risk perishing for not reflecting the truth of God's knowledge. Christian, don't think God will not take your physical life if you continue to cheapen His grace by choosing sin and ignorance.
5. How terrible would it be to have God shorten your time here on earth because you loved your sin too much.
6. And what about those who think they are saved and then go ahead and play this dangerous game? If they were never truly in Christ, then they will lose everything!

In contrast to Hosea 4:6, we have a beautiful prayer of King David in Psalm 19; David was also no stranger to choosing sin over righteousness. You see, a heart that truly loves God, like David's did, will always find repentance as the only reasonable course leading back to reconciliation.

Q: Where are you right now in the discipline of your personal repentance? Is it a regular part of your life?

_____

_____

_____

Q: Do you understand the importance of repentance and the role it plays in your relationship with God? Explain.

_____

_____

_____

Friend, this is how good our Great God is—He restores the sincerely repentant heart in an instant because He just loves us that much.

> *The law of the Lord is perfect, reviving the soul; the testimony of the Lord is sure, making wise the simple; the precepts of the Lord are right, rejoicing the heart; the commandment of the Lord is pure, enlightening the eyes; the fear of the Lord is clean, enduring forever; the rules of the Lord are true, and righteous altogether. More to be desired are they than gold, even much fine gold; sweeter also than honey and drippings of the honeycomb. Moreover, by them is your servant warned; in keeping them there is great reward. Who can discern his errors? Declare me innocent from hidden faults. Keep back your servant also from presumptuous sins; let them not have dominion over me! Then I shall be blameless, and innocent of great transgression.*
>
> —Ps. 19:7–13

David is referring to unintentional sins, and he wants God to know that he is intentionally dealing with his own sin by confronting it instead of denying it: *"Let the words of my mouth and the meditation of my heart be acceptable in your sight, O Lord, my rock and my redeemer"* (Ps.19:14).

Now to Hosea 5:

> *Hear this, O priests! Pay attention, O house of Israel! Give ear, O house of the king! For the judgment is for you; for you have been a snare at Mizpah and a net spread upon Tabor. And the revolters have gone deep into slaughter, but I will discipline all of them. I know Ephraim, and Israel is not hidden from me; for now, O Ephraim, you have played the whore; Israel is defiled.*
>
> —Hosea 5:1–3

Some important facts:

1. Ephraim was the largest and most influential tribe in Israel and was often used as a representative of the northern kingdom.
2. It can be reasoned that when the largest and most influential city becomes corrupt, it doesn't take much to corrupt the rest of the nation.

3. Galatians 5:9 says, *"A little yeast works through the whole batch of dough."* Their deeds do not permit them to return to their God. *"For the spirit of whoredom is within them, and they know not the Lord"* (Hosea 5:4).

4. Sin causes spiritual blindness and distorts our reality; it can be like continuing to be thirsty even though you are constantly drinking water—all you can think about is drinking more and more water.

The pride of Israel testifies to his face; Israel and Ephraim shall stumble in his guilt; Judah also shall stumble with them. With their flocks and herds they shall go to seek the Lord, but they will not find Him; He has withdrawn from them. They have dealt faithlessly with the Lord; for they have borne alien children. Now the new moon shall devour them with their fields.

—Hosea 5:5–7

5. So now we see here that Judah has chosen the same destructive sinful course and God will judge them as well.

6. Remember that Israel will fall and be conquered by the Assyrians in 722 BC.

7. Judah will fall in 586 BC to the Babylonians.

8. God's people will be scattered and enslaved once again and will also endure over 500 years without God's voice or guidance.

Blow the horn in Gibeah, the trumpet in Ramah. Sound the alarm at Beth-aven; we follow you O Benjamin! Ephraim shall become a desolation in the day of punishment; among the tribes of Israel I make known what is sure. The princes of Judah have become like those who move the landmark upon them I will pour out my wrath like water. Ephraim is oppressed, crushed in judgment, because he was determined to go after filth. But I am like a moth to Ephraim, and like dry rot to the house of Judah.

When Ephraim saw his sickness, and Judah his wound, then Ephraim went to Assyria, and sent to the great king. But he is not able to cure you or heal your wound.

—Hosea 5:8–13

Notice that Israel is often referred to as "Ephraim" during this time. It reflected this tribe's importance.

- Israel first and then Judah would eventually turn to Assyria for help.
- Remember, there is drought and sickness upon their land as a result of their sin.
- But seeking help from Assyria is definitely not a good thing for them to do—showing weakness to a former enemy will most likely make you very vulnerable to them.
- And that is exactly what happened to Israel!

> *For I will be like a lion to Ephraim, and like a young lion to the house of Judah. I, even I, will tear and go away; I will carry off, and no one shall rescue. I will return again to my place, until they acknowledge their guilt and seek my face, and in their distress earnestly seek me.*
>
> —Hosea 5:14–15

If you have never read the book of Hosea before, let me tell you that you have been missing out on one of the most powerful pieces of scripture in the Bible. It contains lessons I believe we especially need to learn or relearn as a society and as a nation today. Maybe we can see God acting in a similar manner toward us right now—I mean, what is the difference between who we are and the way we are living right now, compared to how Israel was living during the days of Hosea?

I'm not seeing too many differences myself! Our nation has set up many different kinds of idols for the people to worship. We worship professional athletes, musicians, and movie stars. We also worship comfort and pleasure through food, alcohol, drugs, and illicit sexual desires. There seems to be no end to what we are willing to idolize.

Meanwhile God has been put away on a shelf and saved for an hour on Sunday, if people happen to make it to church at all. Instead of turning to God's Holy Word for guidance, we seek out the latest self-help books, demand more doses of psychotropic medications, and tell our problems to doctors and counselors who assure us that no matter how we feel, there is a reason for it, and it's not our fault.

I can only imagine how God must feel: If it's anything like He did in the days of Hosea, we as a nation have sinned terribly and through our selfishness disrespected every single one of His blessings.

But here's the most amazing thing in all this: Just like He responded to Israel in Hosea's day, God today continues to call us back to Him. The question is, are we even listening? It would behoove us to take heed and learn from Israel's mistakes. It's never too late to turn back to God while we still have breath in us.

Could it be that God has given us the lousy leaders our unfaithfulness has proven to deserve? When we elect leaders whose policies defy the Lord or refuse to acknowledge God and His commandments, we have walked onto very dangerous ground before the King of kings. We must remember that He did this with Israel, so why wouldn't He do it to us? Look at what Hosea 8:4 says:

> *They set up kings, but not from Me [therefore without My blessing]; They have appointed princes, but I did not know it. With their silver and their gold they made idols for themselves, That they might be cut off.*
>
> —Hosea 8:4 AMP

My friend, God's hand of discipline when He applies it is a heavy one. When we continue to hurt Him with our sin, what other option does He have left? Sin must be dealt with; the righteousness of His perfect justice demands it.

All throughout the book of Hosea, God had been pleading with the people to return to Him. It seems that God had no choice to withdraw His loving Hand from His people until they came to true repentance, but they were all fat and happy and felt they really didn't need Him at the time.

Here's where I want to compare and contrast Israel and Judah here for a moment:

- Bible history tells us that Israel was conquered and scattered into slavery by the Assyrians in 722 BC. No one to this day really knows what became of the 10 northern tribes.
- And we know God also punished Judah, as they too are conquered in 586 BC.

But remember that God is a covenant keeper. God does not lie, nor does He ever go back on His word! He had promised that the Messiah would come from the tribe of Judah, and so it was to be true.

People ask me all the time, "How can a loving God send someone to hell?" And I always give them the same answer: We are already on our way there because our sin has paved the way and has justly condemned us. Apart from God, sin will kill us. We were all born with a curse on us. And we contribute mightily to the whole mess when we condemn ourselves to hell through our choices.

It's only when Christ draws us to Himself and saves us—when He intervenes—that our direction changes!

God did save a remnant from both Israel and Judah, but many did perish in their sin. God kept His promise and sent us Jesus, but because *"many are called, but [only very] few are chosen,"* the "remnant" of Christians who see God will be just that—a remnant. Too many people love their sin more, so we are the ones who choose separation from God.

Q: How are you living right now? Have you become content with how things are for you, to the point where you may feel that you don't need God at this time?

_____

_____

_____

_____

Q: If you are experiencing a disconnect with God, what do you think it would take for Him to get your attention?

_____

_____

_____

_____

_____

Q: Whether we realize it or not, this life is first "you versus yourself" in a lot of ways. Can you honestly see yourself as the greatest obstacle to living a faith-filled life? Explain.

Chapter 25

You versus Yourself, Part 2

Today, we will be once again taking a good look at you and me and examine ourselves through some compare and contrast examples that I previously worked on in my own heart.

It can be very easy to miss our own self-righteousness. In fact, I believe that we usually try to ignore it on purpose. We try to ignore it because it is one of the things that we use to make ourselves feel better, or at a minimum, to see ourselves better than how we see others.

As you are reading this second part of "You versus Yourself," think about how often you compare yourself to others. If you are really honest with yourself, you tend to think that your neighbor's sin is greater than your sin, and by your estimation, they should always get the full punishment.

Now take a look at the following story in which Jesus discusses this very subject:

> *He also told this parable to some who trusted in themselves that they were righteous, and treated others with contempt:*
>
> *Two men went up into the temple to pray, one a Pharisee and the other a tax collector. The Pharisee, standing by himself, prayed thus: "God, I thank you that I am not like other men, extortioners, unjust, adulterers, or even like this tax*

collector. I fast twice a week; I give tithes of all that I get." But the tax collector, standing far off, would not even lift up his eyes to heaven, but beat his breast, saying, "God, be merciful to me, a sinner!" I tell you, this man went down to his house justified, rather than the other. For everyone who exalts himself will be humbled, but the one who humbles himself will be exalted.

—Luke 18:10–14

Let's examine these two men for a moment.

We have a Pharisee:

1. A proud religious man who knows the law backward and forward.
2. He's the self-proclaimed example of holiness before his fellow Jews.
3. He even fasts twice a week, more than was even required by the law.

And we also have a tax collector:

- It would be unusual to even find a tax collector in the temple, let alone to discover one praying to God.
- But this man knows who he is and what he has done and cannot even raise his eyes upward as he prays.

Consider what we observe about these two men:

1. BOTH men are seeking something from God.
2. One man is talking **to** God, and the other man is talking **with** God. There's a big difference!
3. Both men have a heart condition—but one has a terminal problem, and the other just needs some heart surgery.
4. And both men will receive something unexpected from God.

Q: Which of these men has a heart like you? Is it the Pharisee or the tax collector?

_____

_____

Q: Are you the one who's glad you're not like other sinners, proud of your accomplishments for God, and feeling justified by your own "good works"? Y/N _____

Q: Or are you the one who realizes that you're a sinner, totally incapable of saving yourself, and in desperate need of the healing mercies of Jesus Christ? Y/N _____

So, what did they receive? The Pharisee's confidence in his own righteousness is nothing more than a damning hope, and he will be humbled when he is separated from God at judgment. On the other hand, the fate of the tax collector is known from the words of Jesus's own mouth: *"I tell you, this man went down to his house justified, rather than the other. For everyone who exalts himself will be humbled, but the one who humbles himself will be exalted"* (Luke 18:14).

And what Jesus meant by "justified" is that through this man's humble and sincere repentance, God's perfect righteousness was imputed on his account. He had no hope except from the mercy of God.

Q: Which of these men fit the description of your heart today?

_____

The heart is deceitful above all things, and desperately sick; who can understand it?

—Jer. 17:9

The condition of our hearts will ultimately reveal who we really are. One thing we may not be aware of is that as we go through our daily lives, we are laying out a pattern by how we live. Each day we add a new piece to the pattern. Over time, that pattern can be seen by others. It will be this very pattern that confirms whether our words and our actions match up. It will be this very pattern that reveals the true nature and condition of our hearts.

Q: What type of pattern are you laying down today?

_____

_____

Q: When others see this pattern, will it be one that glorifies God first? Y/N _____

Q: How can you alter or change a bad pattern?

_____

_____

_____

Q: Our patterns usually define our reputation. Can you see that in order to repair a bad reputation, you have to totally change the pattern? Y/N _____

Q: Can you also see that unless the heart is changed, the pattern cannot be changed? Y/N _____

Q: What changes do you think need to be made in your heart?

_____

_____

_____

Finally, I ask you to think back about the Pharisee and the tax collector for a moment: The Pharisee thought he had it all together and that God was totally for him. But according to what Jesus said, we know that was not the case.

The tax collector might have also been well off, but he certainly wasn't comfortable with anything about who he was. In fact, the one thing that was missing in his life, the most important thing, was that he knew he was a sinner and desperately needed to be right with God. I think we can safely assume that the tax collector was willing to do whatever it took to fix this great problem. He was already doing business with his sick heart while he was in prayer in the temple!

So, two men who had a heart condition both came into the temple to "pray," but only one left actually being able to meet with the heart doctor (we call Him the Great Physician).

How about you? Do you need to see the heart doctor?

Take some time to examine the pattern you have been laying over your life's journey for all to see. Take a good, hard, honest look and see whether you might need a visit from the Great Physician to change your heart.

Chapter 26

You versus Yourself, Part 3

Today, we will look at the third and final part of what we have been calling, "You versus Yourself." And just in case you hadn't noticed, both of the first two parts discussed matters of the heart, and then asked you to examine your heart in some form or fashion. Well, that's also what we will be doing today on this final part.

As I mentioned in the chapter titled "The Good Soil," the "soil of our hearts" can and does go through various different changes. Scripture talks about hard hearts, selfish hearts, hearts of stone, hearts of flesh, and David even petitions God and begs Him to *"create in me a clean heart, Oh God, and renew a steadfast [or right] spirit within me"* (Ps. 51:10).

It is important that the believer understands that because of sin, there is something seriously wrong with our hearts. Through the act of saving us, God has made us new creatures, but while in this flesh, we will still have to deal with the sin problem. I believe the more we know about what we are up against, the better we can know how much we need God and then allow Him to move in and through our faith to help us become more than conquerors.

The wisdom and knowledge of God found in His Holy Word is the difference maker our hearts need. But we must constantly dwell in His Word, and allow it to test, teach, guide, and even correct us, and this is where the battle of "you versus yourself" is identified. We must deny ourselves in order that we may truly know Him. What Jesus wants is a genuine relationship with us—to the deepest level we are able to comprehend. Today, we are going to look at another common obstacle that gets in the way of this relationship and how God will show us what it means and just how dangerous it can be.

You will find this statement repeated often throughout our reading today, in one form or another: "The ground is level at the cross for all to come and dwell and find perfect peace." Friend, I want you to know that whatever the soil of your heart is lacking, the cross has exactly what you need. The key will be first identifying what is wrong or what is missing.

Fallow Ground of the Heart versus the Level Ground at the Cross

What is "fallow ground?" Fallow ground is soil that was once fruitful but is now being left dormant or neglected. When we allow ourselves to slip into the habit of not faithfully studying and reading God's Word, the soil of the heart will slowly get sick over time.

- When our heart has fallow ground, we cannot produce anything good because we have unhealthy or stripped bare soil (this happens to our heart when sin or complacency strips it bare). Notice that it is not just sin that can do this, but complacency can do so as well. Likewise, neglecting the soil or allowing ourselves to become too busy with other things can have the same effect.
- The soil that is left without proper care or treatment will not only get hard and rocky, but if it does grow anything, it is usually weeds and thorns. It will not produce anything fruitful unless the soil is first cleansed from the weeds and thorns (which can be defined as bad habits and selfish sins).

In contrast to that, the ground at the foot of the cross is clean, pure, level, and safe.

- There we can find the perfect peace of God as we rest in the surety of hope, which was purchased for us in Christ, through His complete victory over sin and death.
- Even though the soil is rocky and rough, it is perfectly fit for all who come to it in humility and submission.

But what happens when a heart comes to the ground at the foot of the cross and wants to dwell there on their terms, instead of God's? Sometimes these hearts come and want to dig holes: they decide to dig holes because they just can't seem to fully trust God, or think they are not good enough to be saved. They want to be close to God but also want to hide in their struggle, while trying to earn the grace of God through their own works.

This ends up in being a huge mistake. When a heart feels it can't trust God unless it can alter or control the circumstances, that heart eventually ends up overwhelmed by the truth of its own imperfections and insufficiency. They also end up becoming slaves to fear because they really can't feel safe without trust, and they can never really understand why they cannot earn their way into His presence.

Believe it or not, there are even hearts that come to the ground at the foot of the cross and find it unacceptable as is! They decide that it's just not what will work to meet their needs. So, the heart decides to pave it over, making it smooth and comfortable, just the way they want it to be. But this too fails, because that heart becomes frustrated in the effort of trying to force God to conform to their standards, or to at least have their way over His way.

If we are honest with ourselves, we have all come to the ground at the foot of the cross with our own set of conditions. We have all come with our demands, and we have all come with our selfish expectations. And when we have come, it has been with fallow ground for soil in our hearts. We come stumbling in with our weeds and thorns, expecting God to just look the other way and ignore them. It is a very sad day indeed when we think we can tell God how we will be saved and what we expect from His love for us.

Activity

List some of the conditions you have given God in the past regarding your following Him.

_____

_____

_____

Q: Have you repented for making those demands or for pushing your expectations on Him in your relationship? Y/N _____

Finally, there's one last type of heart, that comes to the ground at the foot of the cross. It comes with a head held low, meek, and broken, and in deep need of comfort. Like the others, this heart too has sick soil but knows it cannot be well apart from God and has abandoned all its self-reliant ways. This heart is so desperate and so deeply longing to experience the perfect love of God, that it will accept nothing less.

This heart knows that it needs the grace of God badly and will not relent until it is filled with His presence once and for all.

Q: Which heart type are you? The hole digger? The ground changer? Or are you the God needer? (Circle one.)

Q: Can you now see some areas where your heart is not well? Y/N _____

Q: If yes, what are they?

_____

While you are thinking this over, allow me to move on to our final self-evaluation, which I have found to be very helpful personally:

True Repentance versus Self-Justification

I believe that true repentance is much more than most Christians realize.

1. In our society today, many people are looking for the "quick fix" for anything and everything wrong in their lives.
2. Self-improvement and self-help have become a $10 billion industry in the US alone.
3. We are obsessed with the need for quick weight loss, fast paths to success, and finding surefire super-fast ways to eliminate worry and depression.
4. The Bible has all the answers to these areas of our lives, but many people do not want to take the time to invest in what God has to say about their life problems.

This is especially true with how we repent. When we don't follow through with true repentance, we miss the portion of God's sweet peace that is supposed to come with it. God wants to give us full peace of mind, but when we halfway repent, we leave a ton undone. In fact, improper (or worldly) repentance has zero value. Even if you are able to convince someone you have wronged to trust you again, God's love is still unrequited, because you have not made peace with Him wholly, sincerely, or properly!

"Unrequited" means a **love** that is not returned or rewarded. It is a one-sided experience that can leave us feeling pain, grief, and shame. Essentially, we are robbing God of the love He deserves through sincere repentance, simply because of who He is.

Q: Do you think that God stops loving you when you sin? Y/N _____

Q: By you choosing sin, does this mean that in order to do so, you stop loving God? Only you can answer that question, for sure.

What we are saying here is that true repentance is much more than just saying I'm sorry. When we choose sin over God, we have put our love relationship in jeopardy–not from His perspective, but from ours!

Friend, believe it or not, we are constantly in danger of falling out of love with God, while falling in love with our sin. Sin is just that dangerous. If we truly examine the full and complete biblical definition of repentance, most if not all of us will have to admit that we have been repenting halfway—at best.

Repent/Repentance Defined

In the Greek, "metanoia," from which we get the English word *metamorphosis* means a radical, moral turning from sin (of the whole person) to a new way of life oriented toward God.

Unfortunately, most of us treat repentance in prayer like we are placing an order in a fast-food drive thru:

- "Lord, let me have two 'I'm Sorrys,' and three 'Will you forgive mes?' to go with a side order of "I was wrong."
- Thank you, and that should cover me for last night!
- I believe most of us treat it this way because let's face it, repenting is not an enjoyable act, and we just want to get it over with.
- We often leave repentance incomplete.

- We do this when we admit we're wrong but refuse to own the consequences—that is incomplete repentance. That is telling God and everyone else that you are really not sorry.

But notice what our definition says again: Repentance is not only being sorry and owning all of it (consequences included), but it also requires a complete turning away from that behavior in order to be complete. Don't miss this, my friends: The act of repentance is not finished until we are moving toward God at the same pace that we were once moving away from Him.

I imagine if Israel had repented like this, we wouldn't see them suffer as badly as we have in Hosea chapters 4 and 5.

Two things hinder true repentance: an unhealthy or superficial relationship with Jesus and a self-justifying attitude.

An Unhealthy or Superficial Relationship with Jesus

This people honors me with their lips, but their heart is far from me; in vain do they worship me, teaching as doctrines the commandments of men.

—Matt. 15:8–9

You may be asking, "How does someone have an unhealthy relationship with Jesus?" Well, we make it that way because Jesus sure doesn't. Any relationship that is one-sided is not going to be healthy. I have often imagined how God feels when I have repented, but He saw that in my heart I didn't really mean it.

We can even value the act of repentance more than what God intends to accomplish in us through it. Having this mindset not only just worships the act like the way the Pharisees did their works, but it is also evidence of a complete disconnect between heart and mind. There are so many things that we can say about just how dysfunctional this can be.

It can also be described as having a relationship with Jesus that keeps Him up on a shelf and out of the way of our daily life, so to speak. It's like we put Him behind glass that says, "Break only in case of emergency." This is what is commonly known as a "911" relationship—we only call on Jesus when everything has failed and all is going wrong.

Sadly, a person who relates to Jesus this way may know of Jesus but doesn't desire to truly know Him. Nor does this person want to submit their life to Him; but they still want all the benefits that come with a true relationship with Him. This type of person will even expect blessings and demand forgiveness, as if just knowing His name entitles them to His favor. This is why their so-called prayers are thin, devoid of remorse, and selfish, lacking any true intent of real change.

Q: Is this what your relationship with Jesus looks like? Y/N _____

Q: Would you describe your own repentance as sincere and moving toward God all the time? Y/N _____

Q: Can you say that you know Jesus deeper than what only exists in a "911 relationship"? Y/N _____

Q: Describe one time when you compromised true repentance and how/if you corrected it.

_____

_____

_____

_____

A Self-Justifying Attitude

This can be described as the act or fact of justifying oneself, especially of offering excessive reasons, explanations, excuses, etc., for an act, thought, or the like. When we can find nothing in us but the desire to make excuses and to self-justify our actions, we will struggle terribly to find the path to true repentance.

> *Many a man proclaims his own steadfast love, but a faithful man who can find?*
> *Who can say, "I have made my heart pure; I am clean from my sin"?*
>
> —Prov. 20:6, 9

Against you, you only, have I sinned and done what is evil in your sight, so that you may be justified in your words and blameless in your judgment.

—Ps. 51:4

What many do not realize is that all sin is first committed against God and the goodness and holiness of who He is. Until we accept this truth and embrace it, we will not be able to understand the pure gravity of sin and see the ugliness of it from God's perspective. God hates sin, and He wants us to hate it too, and He doesn't want us to have anything to do with it.

Q: Do you think it's important that we strive to see sin the way God does? Why or why not?

_____

_____

_____

Q: Do you hate your sin more than the sins of others? Y/N _____

Q: Earlier, we discussed the difference between fallow ground and the ground found at the foot of the cross: Do you think the reason that some hearts work hard to build up the ground at the cross to elevate themselves is because they do not realize that they have a self-justifying attitude toward everything they do? Y/N _____

Q: Would you say that a heart that has fallow ground for its soil is a sick heart, semi-sick heart, a semi-well heart, a generally unhealthy heart, or an overall healthy heart? (Circle one.)

Q: Since you now have more information to help see the differences, which heart are you, and what type of ground are you standing on right now?

_____

_____

_____

Q: The condition of your heart will ultimately reveal all: Have you ever been or are you now the self-righteous and prideful one who attempts to use your Christianity as a tool to use God or others? Explain.

_____

_____

_____

Q: Are you the person whose heart has a reverse pride problem—a person who needs to wallow in self-pity, while believing the lie that you must earn God's perfect and saving favor because you just can't seem to comprehend that He will take you as is?

_____

_____

Q: Or maybe you're the type of person who insists on remaking God in an image more acceptable to yourself, even going as far as to omit doctrine and truth that does not fit who you think you are or want to be?

_____

Q: Or maybe you're the type of person who's done with your ways because time and again they just don't work. You need peace and to be complete and are ready for God to have His way with you and your life? Explain.

_____

_____

Q: What have you learned about your own heart during this three-day journey?

_____

Q: What changes if any do you think need to be made, and when are you going to make them?

_____

_____

Chapter 27

Learning to Let God Meet Our Needs

Imagine for a moment what it must have been like in the Garden of Eden before sin. The Bible gives us the impression that there were times when Adam and Eve walked with God Himself, "in the cool of the day." We can see an image of them in our mind's eye, walking together, as complete beings, lacking nothing and in perfect fellowship with the Lord Jesus; there was no pain, no fear, and no sickness.

After the Fall, all the harmony and perfection with God became polluted and changed by sin—and the horrible state of separation from God, our Creator had become a painful reality.

I believe that the results of the Fall "created" what are known as "needs." I believe that part of the curse of sin is the "lack" of many of the beautiful attributes that were a part of the blessed nature we were gifted with in the beginning. The true needs we strive for today in life were in fact once original traits or attributes of the complete first man and woman prior to separation from God by disobedience.

We weren't meant to feel lonely or afraid or to be handicapped with identity issues; the struggle for these basic needs to be met from day one resulted in the explosion of sins such as jealousy, murder, theft, rape, and even madness, to name a few.

Thankfully, the Sovereign God knew all this beforehand and preplanned redemption for His favorite yet severely stubborn creation. But it seems that a big part of our time and energy in this life is still spent trying to meet our needs and unfortunately, we can easily gauge a person's happiness by the level of satisfaction they have with their current level of basic needs.

Below I have chosen four basic "needs" based on my experiences in counseling; nearly every one of my clients expressed the importance and necessity for these needs to be fulfilled in their lives when asked this question: "What would make you truly happy?" Interestingly enough, you can also see how the lack of one need can affect other needs, which can thereby result in the regular disruption of our daily lives. This disruption causes us to take drastic measures to attempt to meet these needs, and this usually leads to poor choices, which can give sin an opportunity to have a place in our lives.

Security

Every person needs to feel safe—whether it is personal security; family, marriage, or relational security; or job/financial security. We put alarms on our houses; buy guns; put passwords on our phones and computers; and go to extremes to protect our finances, spy on our friends, children, our spouses, and even strangers!

By our actions, it is clear that we don't feel safe or secure with anything in our lives. A lack of security comes from a lack of trust; many people I have met don't trust their spouses or even their parents. But this is exactly what the enemy wants.

A person who cannot trust or feel safe is robbed of their peace. These insecurities are very real and are one of the first "needs" we try to meet. Imagine the magnitude of torment a person must feel when their basic need for security is absent or compromised. In all of our relationships, we must be willing to accept a certain level of vulnerability to trust someone enough to seek security with them.

In a marriage, we can easily see the need for security. Husbands and wives must be able to trust that their spouse is keeping the marriage covenant holy and secure by resisting the temptations of adultery. Spouses must also be secure in the fact that they will not be abused either verbally or physically. All this needed security comes at the high cost of making oneself vulnerable to trust, hoping that the need to feel secure doesn't end up becoming the thing you fear or dread because it was either never there to begin with or was easily disregarded or thrown away.

Even to love on human terms is so risky because human love is so imperfect and selfish. In Matthew chapter 5, Jesus is preaching to a large crowd in what has come to be called "The Sermon on the Mount." In verse 4, He says, *"Blessed are those who mourn, for they shall be comforted."*

We can easily understand that Jesus might have been referring to those mourning due to the loss of a loved one or even one who would mourn over his or her own sin. In these two examples we can surely agree that God is the only true and capable comforter from any loss we may experience in this life. We can also see that it is good to mourn over our sin because godly sorrow leads to godly repentance, and the comfort is then given by God through the gift of forgiveness and salvation. I ask you to consider this as well: Jesus could be saying that since loving by human standards is so risky, you will mourn—because loving on human terms will eventually hurt you.

I can hear Him also saying, *"I AM the only One who can comfort you, and My love is perfect and will never hurt you!"* The security we so badly need can never be fully met without strings on human terms or conditions—only God can truly make us secure.

The author of Hebrews knew this truth and revealed it in Hebrews 13:5–6 (NIV):

> *Keep your lives free from the love of money and be content with what you have, because God has said, "Never will I leave you; never will I forsake you." So we say with confidence, "The Lord is my helper; I will not be afraid. What can mere mortals do to me?"*

I am safe and secure only in Jesus Christ.

Q: What areas of your life right now are lacking in real security?

_____

_____

_____

Security in My Identity

Jeremiah 1:5 tells us that He knew us before we were formed in our mother's womb. Ephesians chapter 1 tells us that He chose us to be His before He even laid the foundation of the world. A person who finds themselves in an identity crisis is really caught up in the middle of one of the most distracting and temporarily believable lies that the enemy can create. It can be a lie that consumes a lot of time and resources, such as your mental and physical health, which you often cannot get back.

If you think you will find your identity through your job, your spouse, your kids, or one of your hobbies, you will find that it will not work—none of these things will ever be able to tell you who you are because they have no eternal value.

As much as I love my dear wife, she cannot define me because she did not create me. Before I am anything at all—a pastor, husband, father, son, friend, etc., I am a disciple of Jesus Christ and an adopted child of the Living God, and an heir to the throne of the King of kings. And that my friends, is the most secure and eternal identity ever!

Q: Are you in an identity crisis right now? Y/N _____

Q: What is keeping you from trusting in God to provide your identity? He made you for a purpose—do you believe this?

_____

_____

_____

Significance

Every person needs to feel like they matter—that they were put on this earth for a purpose. For the men or women who choose to walk through this life without Christ, this will never happen.

But people continue to search for significance through their job, education, and personal/worldly accomplishments. The truth is the world has a standard that can never be met. It will always be "what have you done for me lately," and every achievement becomes a mere shadow of the next distant goal that we hope will be the one that finally validates us (in our eyes, and the world's).

There can be no security or peace in a person who feels he or she has no purpose for his existence. The search for significance continues to haunt every athlete, businessperson, doctor, mailman, computer geek, shoe salesman, military commander, and housewife. This search is driven by feeling that we will somehow be incomplete if we do not obtain a certain status either in life or through another person.

Q: In what way does accomplishing a goal or obtaining something build lasting significance?

Q: And if there is something there, some fragment of significance, how long does it last? Be honest—we have all chased something temporary.

How sad and empty is the soul that does not feel valued or important. But my question to everyone (including myself) is this: To whom do we want to be significant? Can we be satisfied with being volunteer of the month, salesman of the year, even world's greatest dad? All these are merely temporary accolades, and they all require you to do something. But what about next month and next year—and how many "world's greatest dads" are there, anyway? I have personally seen at least three other guys wearing a shirt that makes this claim.

Even if we decide to seek our significance through another human being, how long will it be before that person hurts or offends you? Knowing human nature very well, we can say that it won't be too long before something happens and then we find ourselves right back at ground zero with our "value tank," empty, struggling to trust that person or someone new all over again.

I'm not saying you cannot find some value through the love of a spouse or a very close friend; what I am saying is that it's risky, they will eventually hurt you, and it will not last because of our imperfections. There will always going to be a need for "resets" in relationships with human beings. You see, Romans 5:8 tells us *"God shows His love for us in that while we were still sinners, Christ died for us."*

You have been significant in the eyes of God since before what we understand as the beginning (again, read Ephesians 1). While you and I were still sinning away, we mattered to Him. How can you ignore or top that?

He didn't wait for us to acquire a title or earn an award; He loved you before anything ever mattered with no strings attached. Once again, and this cannot be stressed enough, we must learn to focus on and fully value what is eternal. I want to caution you to love God back without strings. Do not pull away from Him because you "don't feel" valued. Your feelings and your faith have a strange relationship in that feelings tend to cloud and often override the facts and when we trust them, feelings usually lead us astray.

God's facts are that He loves and values you, period. There is nothing in this world that can match or even come close or overcome His great love for us. The Apostle John said everything in this world is temporary and already passing away, but the God who loves you and holds you as precious and significant to Him is from everlasting to everlasting.

Here is all the proof we need that we truly matter and exist for a purpose. Philippians 2: 6–11 tells us that our Savior stepped down from His position at the right hand of God the Father, leaving the throne as God to put on the form of a servant, and even die a criminal's death. He then rose and conquered death, restoring all that was lost in the Garden—all for you and me. You and I matter to God!

Satisfaction

This need is one that does the most damage in the short term. We seek to be satisfied in many ways—through relationships, sex, our jobs, food, drugs, and alcohol; every day, we are looking for some sort of satisfaction.

We seem to never be fully satisfied with the way things are in any given moment: Some people are facing situations in life where their satisfaction level is way beyond their reach. People with chronic pain or disabilities often know that their current condition may be as good as it is going to get.

I find it strange that most people (at least in our country) seem to have a lot but still lack satisfaction. How ironic is it for a person to appear so full but actually be so empty inside? Do you see a pattern here yet?

Just as with security and significance, we are always looking to the wrong sources to fulfill our needs. The world tells us we deserve it and therefore we should have it, and if we don't have it, the world provides the ways we can seek it out. And when we try the world's way, we never attain it. Why? Because the world is not made to satisfy us. And we were not made to satisfy ourselves.

I love to use pornography here as the example, because just about every man I have ever counseled (including myself) has looked at porn. So many men (and now more and more women) are becoming more than temporarily comfortable with an addiction (that's right addiction) they foolishly think they control. And since people do find temporary satisfaction in it, they think it's not only okay but healthy! I know all too well what porn has done to me and my relationship with God, and I personally want nothing more to do with it. I am not going to let anything like that come between the Lord and me ever again.

Many men have told me that porn is "safer" than the "emotional investment of a relationship" or the random "hookup" with a stranger. That isn't true in the short term and seeking satisfaction through pornography has been proven to do severe long-term physical, emotional, and spiritual damage. The few examples I am about to give you may be shocking but are true. Recent studies show that porn addiction actually damages the brain by shrinking that part of the brain "which activates when people feel motivated or rewarded," causing it to work less efficiently! Scientists in Berlin who discovered this also believe that people who watch a lot of porn are likely to "need increasingly graphic material to achieve the same sexual stimulation."[1]

Pornography is a lot more dangerous than our society would like to admit. Why? Because it is in high demand, and it is very profitable. But what about the damage it can do, both in the short and long term on our minds? According to an article in Advanced Psychology Partners.com:

> Most people enjoy pornography to satisfy desires, loneliness, curiosity. However, some are not content with more "tame" material and seek out higher highs. A very rare few take

matters into their own hands and find victims to act out their darkest desires and fantasies. Many prolific serial killers, including Bundy, Dahmer, Richard Ramirez, and John Wayne Gacy professed to porn addiction. In fact, Dahmer stated he would prepare to hunt for a victim by reviewing pictures of his previous victims, which he considered his victories. For Bundy, Dahmer and the like, seeing others victimized desensitized them; they began to see their victims as disposable."[2]

In truth, pornography is never able to satisfy our desires. Porn exists in a diluted fantasy world, which poisons and perverts the goodness of sex when it is expressed outside God's design. Most people are left the shame and guilt of a frustrated and unsatisfied heart. Porn is not meant to satisfy—it is only meant to draw you in deeper and deeper, with expectations that never quite get there.

Porn is not the only way we degrade ourselves on our quest for satisfaction in this life; there are so many others. But God does not want us to suffer through life this way; He has already provided a road to real satisfaction, but it must be on His terms.

Q: In what ways right now do you seek satisfaction?

_____

_____

Q: Is it because something is missing? Y/N _____

Q: Are you seeking for satisfaction first and foremost from God? Y/N _____

Q: If no, why not?

_____

_____

_____

So, if apart from God we can never truly be satisfied, then we will have no significance or security in this world and definitely no peace. Do you see how all these needs are connected and can only be met by one Source? Consider this from Psalm 103:5 as David reminds us that it is in fact the Lord Himself *"who satisfies you with good, so that your youth is renewed like the eagle's."*

It does not say anything about brain damage, or dry and empty promises, or even half-full cups or barren tables. On the contrary, David tells us in Psalm 23 that the Lord sets a table for us and blesses us right in the presence of our enemies, and our *"cup overflows."*

How satisfied is the man or woman who seeks their portion from the Lord God's good table? Please, my friends, turn away and leave behind what the world is offering by way of temporary pleasures; they will only leave you wanting more always, or they may just kill you.

> *And the Lord will guide you continually and satisfy your desire in scorched places and make your bones strong; and you shall be like a watered garden, like a spring of water, whose waters do not fail.*
>
> —Isa. 58:11

> *You make known to me the path of life; in Your presence there is fullness and joy; at Your right hand are pleasures evermore.*
>
> —Ps. 16:11

Satisfaction is found in God alone.

Peace

Here's another hard truth: Choosing to live apart from God causes us to strive against Him and if that is the case, there is no peace to be found. How many of us simply long for a quiet place to lay our head or solitary place that provides a temporary reprieve from the challenges and demands of life. I believe we all do.

I also know that most people have some very serious plans as to how they will obtain this peace, and none of these plans include God. It amazes me that the Prince of Peace, the One who promises rest to the weary and relief from our heavy burdens (Matt. 11:28) isn't even in the equation.

Rather than praying for peace from the only One who can truly provide it, we would rather try to "pay" for peace through a vicious and exhausting cycle of hills we force ourselves to climb thinking that we will rest when we have "earned it" and all is put in its proper place. As we subject ourselves to this foolish plan, we never realize that things will never fully be set in their place. We totally miss the fact that God wants us to rest in Him while in the midst of the storms, but that can only be done through His power, not ours, because we don't have the ability to do so.

Once again, can you see a pattern here? No security, no peace. No identity, no peace. No satisfaction, no peace. No Jesus (the Prince of Peace), no peace. Many will die knowing only the hard work and the measure of sweat and stress that it cost. There really won't be any reward when you try to pay for or create your own peace. The pain and suffering we all experience throughout our lives has only one real release—Jesus Christ.

> *You will keep him in perfect peace whose mind is stayed on you, because he trusts you.*
>
> —Isa. 26:3

Friends, choose this day to trust God to be your peace-provider and *"depart from evil, and do good, seek peace and pursue it"* (Ps. 34:14 KJV).

> *Do not be wise in your own eyes; Fear the LORD, and turn away from evil.*
>
> —Prov. 3:7 NASB

Commit this scripture to memory and pray in it daily until you believe it:

> *Don't worry about anything; instead pray about everything. Tell God what you need, and thank Him for all He has done. Then you will experience God's peace, which exceeds anything we can understand. His peace will guard your hearts and minds as you live in Christ Jesus.*
>
> —Phil. 4:6–7 NLT

Five Common Obstacles That Keep Us from Seeking Our Needs through God

Pride

The basic foundation for every sin a man commits is pride. It allows us to deflect responsibility for our thoughts, words, and deeds; it enables us to revel in selfishness and breeds a sense of self-entitlement. Pride says, "I know a better way, my way," and that way is always self-serving. Proverbs 16:18 says, *"Pride goes before destruction and haughtiness before a fall."*

Bad Habits

Bad habits are things we do solely to fulfill the wants of the flesh, which are a result of separation from God.

> *When you follow the desires of your sinful nature, the results are very clear: sexual immorality, impurity, lustful pleasures, idolatry, sorcery, hostility, quarreling, jealousy, outbursts of anger, selfish ambition, dissention, division, envy, drunkenness, wild parties, and other sins like these. Let me tell you again, as I have before, that anyone living that sort of life will not inherit the Kingdom of God.*
>
> —Gal. 5:19–21 NLT

Hard-Heartedness

This is a condition of the heart that is cold, stubborn, and not open to any form of healthy reasoning. It offers an unyielding resistance to God's truth, which then begins to separate the person from God. Hard-heartedness produces spiritual blindness and an unrelenting selfishness.

> *But God shows His anger from heaven against all sinful, wicked people who suppress the truth by their wickedness. They know the truth about God because He has made it obvious to them. For ever since the world was created, people have seen the earth and sky. Through everything God made, they can clearly see His invisible qualities—His eternal power and divine nature. So they have no excuse for not knowing God. Yes, they knew*

God, but would they wouldn't worship Him as God or even give Him thanks. And they began to think up foolish ideas of what God was like. As a result, their minds became dark and confused. Claiming to be wise, they instead became utter fools. And instead of worshipping the glorious, ever-living God, they worshipped idols made to look like mere people and birds and animals and reptiles. So God abandoned them to do whatever shameful things their hearts desired. As a result, they did vile and degrading things with each other's bodies. They traded the truth about God for a lie. So they worshipped and served the things God created instead of the Creator Himself, who is worthy of eternal praise! Amen.

—Rom. 1:18–25 NLT

Unhealthy Thoughts Lead to Faulty Thinking

Unhealthy thoughts easily take over when the way we want things to be is challenged. When we choose to trust in our own understanding, we fall rapidly into a state of faulty thinking. Without divine guidance, all we are left with is what we know. And when compared to what God knows, we know nothing! Failure to study and apply God's Word daily leaves us with no true resource from which to make clear decisions.

Left to our own interpretations we will quickly reject God's truth because it will come into direct conflict with our own version of the facts, which is completely self-serving (see Ephesians 4:17–24).

Trust in the LORD with all your heart and lean not on your own understanding. In all your ways acknowledge Him and He shall direct your paths.

—Prov. 3:5–6 NKJV

Unrestrained Sin

Greg Ogden says, "When a society can no longer be shocked or no longer has a healthy shame, it is able to indulge in every kind of impurity."[3]

The temptation to do what one feels is desirable in the moment can be very strong. When we abandon all moral decency and simply give way to those desires, unrestrained sin is the result. When evil is called good or simply no longer recognized as evil, we will sin carelessly without offense or restraint. Often the temptation for the believer to be accepted by the world is the first stage of abandoning the commands and statutes of the Living God. When given *permission* to have a place in our lives, sin can develop into a seemingly unbreakable pattern. Beware of unrestrained temptations: This manner of sin is always closer to us than we realize. Peter gives this warning: *"Be sober-minded, be alert. Your adversary the devil is prowling around like a roaring lion, looking for anyone he can devour"* (1 Pet. 5:8 CSB).

Your Prayer for Today

Almighty God, I thank you for my life today and all that you have given and forgiven in my life. I submit all my needs to You, for I know that you care for me and will provide for me all that I need. I also ask that You grant me an extra portion of wisdom that I may be able to understand my sin nature and overcome it through Your power. In Jesus's name, Amen.

Chapter 28

Divine Grace Can Make Anyone Brave

As a counselor, one common stumbling block I find in nearly everyone I sit down with is fear. Fear has many "faces," and I think we all would be surprised by the multiple different ways we allow it to exist in our lives.

Fear is a very stubborn spirit and has a unique ability to stick around in our hearts. And because of this, we must realize that our fight against fear will more often than not have a beginning but no end as we progress in our walk as Christians. Simply stated, fear will probably be a lifelong battle in one form or another.

We must be as aware and knowledgeable as possible in this fight so that we know what we must do. God's Word can teach us how to identify fear but also how we should handle it and eventually be victorious over it. Before we take a look at the two types of fear mentioned in the Bible, let me first expand on one of the main reasons fear can so easily overcome us.

I think we can agree that we fear what we cannot control. Human beings both consciously and even subconsciously generally need to be in control. All laws, rules, and regulations are a form of control, and I believe the good and just laws are God-inspired through His common grace to provide a sense of order in our society. For example, technology can fool us into thinking we have more control than we actually do even as we are inundated with programs that monitor, evaluate, inform, calculate, and even regulate. Just think of the control a person feels they have by simply owning a smartphone. So, it is not hard to see that when something happens that is beyond our grasp, we quickly panic. Along with this fear of losing control, we can also experience:

- Fear of the unknown
- Fear of the future
- Fear caused by the wrong view of God
- Fear of what others think or even do
- Fear that creates worries and anxieties about our health and well-being.

Activity

List any of your fears that are not on this list and explain why they have power or influence over you.

All the fears listed above along with many more we experience in this life can be very paralyzing. In fact, most of us struggle with many of these fears every day, but this is not how God wants us to live. For example, Isaiah 41:10 encourages us, *"Do not fear, for I am with you; Do not anxiously look about you, for I am your God. I will strengthen you, surely I will help you, Surely I will uphold you with My righteous right hand"* (NASB 1995).

And Jesus reminds us that our great God even cares for the birds of the air, so how much more will He provide for His children? *"So don't be afraid; you are worth more than many sparrows"* (Matt. 10:31 NIV). Already just these few verses cover many different types of fear. God encourages us not to be afraid of being alone, of being too weak, of not being heard, or even of lacking physical necessities.

What we also see here are examples of His perfect and complete sovereign Hand over all creation; not even a speck of dust is displaced without His foreknowledge of it or His will to allow it to be so.

These encouragements found in His perfect truth continue throughout the Bible, relieving many aspects of fear and bringing us peace and confidence in Him. But if you are not spending consistent time in the scripture, you will most likely not be connected to the comfort and security that only He can provide. Take a moment to answer the question below—be honest with yourself.

Q: When your comfort is compromised, how easy is it for you to become uneasy and even afraid?

Now that we have laid a basic foundation, let's look at the two types of fear mentioned in the Bible: In the Old Testament, the Hebrew word *yare* or *yirah* means being afraid, but it also means to stand in awe of God and who He is, producing a reverential fear of Him. This is a respectful fear that acknowledges God's complete authority in all matters spiritual and moral; this is not merely a "fear" of His power and righteous retribution, but also a wholesome dread of displeasing Him.

"The fear of the LORD is the beginning of wisdom, and the knowledge of the Holy One is insight" (Prov. 9:10). This is a "fear" that banishes the terror that causes us to shrink from His presence, and it influences and affirms an attitude that all circumstances are guided by trust in God.

Many Christians struggle right here because they have the wrong fear of God: It's one thing to tremble in fear because of God's power, but it is something completely different to stand confident in the reverential fear of God, in awe of His awesome power!

Q: Are you living in fear of the justice of God because you fear the consequences of sin? Explain.

Christians who have the proper understanding of fear are confident that even if they must experience the discipline of God because of sin, it will be ministered by Him in a righteous way that will ultimately be to the believer's benefit. This reverential "fear" of God will inspire a constant carefulness in us and will even affect the way we deal with and care for others. All this comes through our complete trust in who He is.

Our submission and obedience also become so much easier as a result. Simply stated, this type of fear is rooted in utter respect and reverence, which cause us to bow before His awesome power and be truly thankful for the incredible love He has for us. The love He so generously pours out on us can overcome any type of fear and cancel out any of fear's harmful effects on our faith.

The second type of fear discussed in the Bible comes from the Greek word *Phobos*, which means a fear that causes flight, or running away, and even to tremble and cower in the corner like a scared animal. This is the type of fear that comes from the enemy. Consider what scripture tells us about this second kind of fear in 2 Timothy 1:7: *"For God gave us a spirit not of fear but of power and love and a sound mind."* Notice that Paul identifies this type of fear as a "spirit" that does not come from God!

Also, the Apostle John tells us in 1 John 4:18 that *"There is no fear in love, but perfect love casts out fear. For fear has to do with punishment, and whoever fears has not been perfected in love."* Unfortunately, this is the type of fear that most of us are very familiar with. This type of fear is the root of all anxiety and is even connected to depression, violence, and other forms of irrational behavior. My friend, these are not characteristics of the saved and regenerated person.

Finally, when I'm battling with fear, I usually go back and read about the lives of men like Joshua for encouragement. I imagine the type of man who Joshua was; he was no doubt a brave man and a fine warrior, and by the time he was chosen to succeed Moses, he was a hardened combat veteran who had seen the worst of men and war up close and personal. Remember, when Israel first went to war, they had nothing to fight with except farming tools, which they had brought with them from Egypt in their exodus from slavery.

The only way Joshua could acquire a weapon (such as a sword) was to kill a man in battle and take that sword from him! This is how all the men of Israel most likely came into possession of their weapons. Yet, even after experiencing all of that, Joshua was afraid when the Lord called him to finish the work Moses started and lead the people into the land that God had promised them. Read Joshua 1:1–9, and I'm sure you will be surprised to find that the Lord had to tell Joshua three times to not be afraid!

Activity

Friends, here's the challenge I want to leave you with this week: Take some time alone with the Lord in prayer; spend some time in reflection and confession to examine your fears and give them over to the Lord.

I suggest that you write them down in your journal and commit them to the Lord each day, trusting that He will bring you peace in them and enable you to put down or release the fear that comes from the enemy. Always remind yourself that fear **does not** come from God and in order for fear to exist in your life, you must receive it from the enemy and give it a place in you.

Pray for faith to believe and trust God, so as to seek the reverent fear that He requires of us, and the fears of the world and our enemy will no longer have any dominance over you.

I speak to you with complete confidence in this because I just lived through it a short time ago; my very life was preserved by our faithful Lord and Savior, and I experienced no fear because I placed all my trust in Him. You can too—if you really and truly want to be free from the "phobos" type of fear.

My prayer for you is that you will and that you continue to seek and discover His amazing love, grace, and mercy. The perfect love that He gives will destroy all fear—just embrace it because He has promised to "*never leave you, nor forsake you*" (Deut. 31:6).

Chapter 29

Nine Basic Steps in Building Significance in Your Wife

Okay, men, this is the place where we will start to build and guide our marriages toward Jesus as we strive to love our wives as Christ would have us to. Remember, your wife's significance is largely dependent on how much she can trust you. Think for a moment of how much our significance depends on our own ability to trust Christ, and you will be able to understand how important it is that we lead our wives in this way.

In the same manner that we have confidence and security in what Jesus has done for us through the cross, your wife will need to trust your love for her in every way in order for you to effectively lead her to the cross. Building "the trust" can begin this way:

1. Your wife's hopes, dreams, desires, fears, and concerns must be as important to you as they are to her, and she must know this. Man, you must make every effort to find interest in the things that are of value to your wife; do not put her hopes, dreams, or concerns below yours. If you can do this, you will be instilling in her the confidence that you truly care. It is a guarantee that she wants to

share yours. This is one of the first pieces of the trust; she does not want to walk through life with you on the same street, but beside you on the same path.

God commands that you love her as much as you love yourself because He knows that no man will neglect caring for himself. Understand that God knows how selfish you and I are, so we must be instructed to turn our love away from ourselves first, and through Christ, love our wives the way God has intended us to.

Q: Are you supporting your wife's dreams?

Q: Does your wife see that you value her hopes, aspirations, and desires?

Q: How are you leading your wife through her fears?

Q: Is your love for yourself still greater than your love for your wife? If so, are you ready to commit to allowing Christ to rearrange your heart's priorities (2 Timothy 1:7, 1 John 4:18, Ephesians 5:28–31)?

---

2. Look your wife in the eye when she speaks to you and actually listen to what she has to say; give her the respect of your full and complete attention. God decided it was good for you not to be alone (Genesis 2:18), so honor Him by honoring your wife and give her the respect and attention she deserves when she desires to share her life and heart with you.

Q: Are you really paying attention to what she has to say?

Q: If she were to be asked, would she say that she feels heard?

Q: What have you learned about her since you committed to communicating with her and listening to her in the manner in which she needs?

_____

_____

Q: How has your relationship changed through this process? Please explain in detail.

_____

_____

3. Express your love to her daily in a nonsexual way. Your wife will joyfully respond to regular nonsexual touch and acts of kindness, and this will build in her confidence and security, knowing you love her for her complete self, not just sexually.

   As men we often think that we are expressing love through sex, as this is our primary desire and preferred method of expression. Not so with women. Most women need to know they are fully and completely loved first, and through this, they will be able to better respond to us and give themselves sexually, as another expression of their love.

   This is where we build another piece of trust; loving your wife completely also ensures her that you won't be taken sexually by another woman.

   Q: Are you regularly expressing your love in nonsexual ways? If so, how has this deepened your love for each other and changed your intimacy?

_____

_____

   Q: Are you confident that your wife feels loved for her whole self, not only her "sexual parts"?

_____

_____

NINE BASIC STEPS IN BUILDING SIGNIFICANCE IN YOUR WIFE

4. Your wife must see your love for your children and your desire to be their mentor, protector, and spiritual leader.

   One huge characteristic that children need in their father is discipline along with mercy and forgiveness. It is also very important that your wife sees you love her children. This is another piece of the trust because her investment and attachment to your children is different from yours because she carried them in her body.

   Equally important, regular love, respect, and attention from a husband to his wife are major parts of security in the heart of a child. Understand that the way you love and care for your wife will be the way your son will love his future wife, and it will also establish the behavior patterns your daughter will look for and tolerate in her future husband.

   Collateral damage: Unfortunately, children are often the reason women will stay in bad marriages.

   Q: Do your children consistently see your love for their mother?

   _____

   _____

   Q: Are you regularly teaching your children about Jesus and the freedom of His life-saving gospel?

   _____

   _____

   Q: Are you teaching them mercy, forgiveness, love, and living a life of good conscience before God daily? Please explain in detail.

   _____

   _____

5. Pray for your wife daily asking that Jesus be her first love, not you (Revelation 2:4).

   Plead with God daily to help you reveal Christ in her life and remember that He is the centerpiece and lynchpin in a godly, healthy marriage. Learning to love her selflessly (which can be so hard because we are selfish) is showing her a reflection of Jesus Christ.

Q: Are you daily lifting your wife up and praying for protection over her heart and asking Jesus to strengthen her faith in Him?

_____

_____

_____

Q: Are you loving and leading her to the cross in humility on a daily basis?

_____

_____

_____

Q: What does loving this way mean to you? Please explain.

_____

_____

_____

6. Keep your word with your wife on everything: Let your yes be yes, and your no be no (Matthew 5:37).

   This means that you follow through with what you say and do to your best ability as a man. Do not promise things you do not intend to fulfill and be sure she knows how much you value keeping your word to her. Answer your cell when she calls no matter what you are doing and make it a point to contact her the minute plans change and be prepared to tell others no when you know you need to be home. This is also a huge piece of the trust.

   Q: On average, how honest are you with your wife?

   _____

   Q: What piece of the truth have you been compromising on? Please explain.

   _____

   _____

   _____

Q: How honest do you expect her to be with you?

_____

_____

_____

7. Strive to keep your life ordered and simple.

   God completely understands that married life has many commitments and responsibilities, but it also has many, many distractions. As leaders of our families, we must strive to remove things (and even people) that distract us from our daily devotion and service to God and the proper care of our wife and family (1 Corinthians 7:32–35).

   This is the proper order: God, wife, children.

   Q: What steps have you taken to simplify your life and protect your family time?

   _____

   _____

   _____

   Q: What steps have you taken to ensure that God is first in your life and in the lives of your family, regardless of your responsibilities or commitments? Please explain in detail.

   _____

   _____

   _____

8. Speak to your wife in ways that build her up, not tear her down (Ephesians 4:29–32).

   God commands that we always use words that honor both Him and others. Regardless of the situation, our language should be such that it gives grace to all who hear.

   Speaking to your wife with love, respect, and honor (especially in front of your children) will strengthen her self-respect, and she will in turn love you greater and deeper.

Q: So, how do you talk to your wife?

_____

_____

_____

_____

Q: Do you treat her with the respect as your equal and helpmate (Genesis 2:18), or do you treat her like a servant or someone less knowledgeable and weaker than you?

_____

_____

_____

_____

Q: Are you nice to her only when you want something from her (like sex, for example)? Please explain.

_____

_____

_____

_____

9. Learn to submit to your wife's needs.
   Sit down with your wife and ask her what is important to her and what she needs from you and then make it your duty to meet those needs daily.
   This is one of the most basic ways we can love our wives and one of the most important means by which we express their value to us.
   Write her needs down and pray over them, asking God to empower you to understand them and meet them. Remember what's at stake here; this is the life partner God have given to you as a gift from Him. Submitting to your wife's needs means that it is your job to meet these needs for the betterment of her overall mental, physical, and spiritual health.

Q: This is very important. Have you had this conversation with your wife yet? It is important that you do follow the suggestions in Item 9 and that your wife knows it is a priority for you to strive to love and serve her in this manner. Explain in detail how this is challenging you.

_____

_____

_____

_____

_____

_____

Chapter 30

You Are What You Think

What do you suppose people would think of you if they were able to know your thoughts? What if, for example, other people were able to discern all your lustful thoughts or know all your false statements? Kind of scary to think about, right? One thing is for sure, if that were possible, we would probably be a lot more disciplined with what we allow to float around inside our minds.

Pastor Oswald Chambers wrote, "Our battles are first won or lost in the secret places of our will in God's presence, never in full view of the world."[1] I believe Chambers is saying that the essence of who we really are is on full display for God alone, and He sees every one of our struggles, including the war of our thoughts. And it is clear to me that this is where we must first do battle with the sin nature that still resides in us.

God sees it all, and we should be well aware that we create and entertain thousands if not millions of thoughts every day, and if we were truly honest, we have to admit that the majority of our thoughts are not godly. But it is in our nature to both produce and express selfish thoughts. Now, I am not using our fallen nature as an excuse; I just mention it so we can understand that everyone is subject to an unholy pattern of thinking.

Here's why I can confidently say that we are what we think: because the Living God is able to read and know all of our thoughts. In fact, He even knows the intent behind every single one of them!

How's Your Heart?

The Bible tells us several times that the human heart is broken and corrupt, and it is right here where we find the source of the issue: The human heart has been polluted by sin and is completely given over to selfish rebellion against God. Jeremiah 17:9–10 confirms this, and God tells us what He intends to do about it: *"The heart is more deceitful than anything else, and incurable—who can understand it? I, the LORD, examine the mind, I test the heart to give to each according to his way according to what his actions deserve"* (CSB).

First, notice that our hearts have been officially designated as more deceitful than anything else, and left unto itself, it is in an incurable condition. Next, God tells us that He examines our minds—now, I just had to pause for a moment to try to comprehend the reality of that! It should give us great pause every time we process unholy thoughts and remind us that the Lord is way ahead of us and is already in the process of examining them. Remember that He even sees our intent behind each thought.

As our internal process progresses further along, we can agree that our minds will produce thoughts that are often lived out and expressed through our words and our actions. You see, God says there will be an accountability for these thoughts because our thoughts are alive enough to destroy us: They don't have to become words or actions to truly be dangerous.

Jesus proves this to us right here in Matthew 5:21–22 and again in verses 27–28:

> *You have heard that it was said to our ancestors, Do not murder, and whoever murders will be subject to judgment. But I tell you, everyone who is angry with his brother or sister will be subject to judgment. . . . You have heard that it was said, Do not commit adultery. But I tell you, everyone who looks at a woman lustfully has already committed adultery with her in his heart* (CSB).

Why is Jesus making such a big deal about what goes on inside our head? Aren't our thoughts our own? Who are they hurting if they just remain as thoughts? In reality, these bad thoughts separate us from God in and through their unholiness and filth. God has commanded us to be holy as He is holy. God does not have thoughts like these; in fact, He never has, and He doesn't want us to, either. His Holy Word has told us exactly what we should be training ourselves to think about:

> *Finally brothers and sisters, whatever is true, whatever is honorable, whatever is just, whatever is pure, whatever is lovely, whatever is commendable—if there is any moral excellence and if there is anything praiseworthy—dwell on [think on] these things.*
> —Phil. 4:8 CSB

God Is Not Inactive When Our Hearts Are Bad

I believe that it is clear enough to conclude from the Jeremiah 17 passage above that God loves us so much that He does not intend to leave our corrupt heart in this condition: He will either redeem it through the forgiveness of the cross, or He will judge it in all its rigid, self-destructive stubbornness. This is what is meant in Jeremiah 17:10 when He says, *"I, the Lord, examine the mind, I test the heart to give to each according to his way according to what his actions deserve."*

His judgement is merely another expression of His love—for the saved Christian, judgment is a beautiful thing. This judgment results in God's acceptance and approval of the repentant person because their sin has been paid in full through the atoning blood of Christ on the cross. This means that a saved Christian will not be condemned by his or her thoughts, or by any other form of sin.

But for the unsaved, it is another story completely: The lost soul has nothing worthy enough to offer God as payment for their sin, so they must pay for it themselves. But they will never be able to because even that person's own life given as payment will not be enough. Not only is the unsaved person faced with an unpayable debt problem but added to that will be eternal suffering and separation from God Himself and everything in His perfect paradise.

Q: Now, how much do you think you should be aware of your thoughts?

_____

_____

Q: How much do you think you have to lose by not checking them and disciplining what you think about? Everything, or nothing?

_____

_____

False Fronts and Many Faces

Another part of the problem is that we are really good at putting up false fronts. We are capable of wearing many false faces, so people can only see who and what we want them to see. Rarely, if ever, do we show others who we really are. It just seems way too risky. And let's face it, in our own minds, who we really are just isn't exciting enough or appealing enough for us to show others, so we have to make things up.

How much thought do you suppose goes into the fabricating of a false front? I personally believe it takes a lot, because I have done it. Each false front has to have exciting appeal and a believable backstory to support it.

Now imagine feeling that you need to create multiple versions of that garbage. If you want a thought process that will take you further away from God, then this will be perfect for you.

Q: Are you aware that you put up false fronts? Y/N _____

Q: How many different faces do you wear in just one day?

_____

How sad do you think it is for God to see the real intent behind our lies? I'm certain He grieves the fact that you are too afraid to be who He made you to be, or that you don't think His work in creating you was good enough.

It is hard for us to show people our flaws: It's hard for us to reveal how we really think because we are so concerned about constantly having worldly acceptance. If given the opportunity, your pride will not allow or accept any situation that isn't going to make you look like gold in the eyes of other people. This is yet another reason why having godly discipline in place to help us form better thoughts along with having the courage to throw the bad ones out is so important.

The truth is that Jesus didn't create us to only be concerned with satisfying ourselves. Believe it or not, your lustful thoughts will not make any of your relationships better. Neither will your jealous, angry, or bitter thoughts. He created us to pour out into others in love and selfless service, not to set up false fronts for the wrong approval and be nothing but takers and hoarders, thereby building up only ourselves. That's why He said that it is not what goes into a man that makes him unclean, but instead what comes out of him (Matt. 15:11).

And what should come out of us are words and actions that are built on a foundation of righteous and unselfish thoughts—thoughts that first seek to glorify the Living God.

None of your false fronts will gain you anything that is eternal. Instead, you will waste time that you do not have to spare playing a game that you will most certainly lose. What time will do though is reveal that you really are what you think and then all those unholy and so called "private thoughts" will become the public record in your condemnation.

Thoughts Become Words and Actions

My friends, it is not a bad thing to realize that you are what you think, if you are constantly working toward the right kind of thoughts.

Think about this for a moment: Every word you speak starts out as a thought—the thought has meaning and context, and in order to express these thoughts, we decide to do so through the use of words. In the same way, each one of our actions also begins as a thought, and like our words, there is intent and purpose behind the exercise of these actions.

Now consider this: God intends for the foundation of our thoughts to be built upon His Holy Word. Here are some great examples:

> How can a young man keep his way pure? By keeping your word.
> I have sought you with all my heart; don't let me wander from
> your commands. I have treasured your word in my heart so that
> I may not sin against you.
>
> —Ps. 119:9–11

In verse 11 *"your word"* referred to here in Hebrew means, "anything God has spoken, commanded or promised." It is on this word that David the author intends to build the foundation of his thoughts—if all his thoughts are about the spoken, commanded, or promised word of God, this will ensure his way stays pure. David even asks God to help keep him from wandering from it. This is a beautiful request and one I'm sure God was happy to honor in response to David asking.

But even more important, it isn't just God's word that David is pursuing. In verse 10, he says that with his whole heart he is seeking God Himself!

Q: What is priority one on your needs list? What are you after the most in this life?

_____

_____

Q: Have you hidden God's word in your heart so that you will not sin against Him? Y/N _____

Q: Is God's word a priority in your life right now? Y/N _____

Next, Psalm 19:14 says, *"May the words of my mouth and the meditation of my heart be acceptable to you, LORD, my rock and my Redeemer"* (CSB). Each time, the psalmist makes reference to the importance of the heart and the mouth being in sync with one another. Since the heart in scripture is primarily referred to as the ruling center of the whole person and the spring of all desires, your heart would not be right if your thoughts were not right.

Can you see just how important this is?

Who Is Your Personal Witness Serving?

I believe one of the most important areas in our lives is our personal witness. With that very important fact in mind, the truth is that your words reflect your thoughts and when you speak, your thoughts are put on display. How we love, respect, honor, and value God is placed in view for all to see daily in the way we outwardly express ourselves.

Maybe you are one of those Christians who has no problem talking about sports or politics; you make your thoughts well known to all you come into contact with. You have shown those around you how much you love, respect, honor, or value sports and/or politics. You regularly make a great case for your favorite team or an important political matter, but you have shared exactly zero about Jesus. And in all of this, you still call yourself a Christian—friend, who or what are you really representing? Answer these questions in reference to your witness:

Q: Are you right now speaking in a way that would bless every ear that hears you? Y/N _____

Q: Are your words glorifying God and in so doing speaking life to those around you who are lost? Y/N _____

Q: Or are you storing up the gospel in your heart just for yourself? Y/N _____

Can we really call the gospel the "Good News" if it isn't being preached or heard? In Luke 2:10, the angel of the Lord appeared to the shepherds in the field and told them, *"Fear not, for behold, I bring you good news of great joy that will be for all the people."* Just as the Lord God had given an important message for His angel to give to the shepherds, so He has given us this same message.

This important question still remains: In your thoughts, have you made the gospel to be a priority for both the words you speak and the actions that are constantly on display in front of others?

You Really Are What You Think

Finally, we end this lesson by looking at the main truth of this personal reflection:

> *For as he thinks in his heart, so is he [in behavior—one who manipulates]. He says to you, "Eat and drink," Yet his heart is not with you [but it is begrudging the cost].*
>
> —Prov. 27:3 AMP

I presented this verse to you in the amplified translation so I would not have to type a whole page trying to explain it! What we can take away from this verse first is that a person may say one thing with his or her mouth but be in a totally different place in their heart. Simply put, their thoughts have another agenda or position, which is different from what they are telling you with their words.

So, something just isn't lining up—who this person is claiming to be on the inside doesn't match what is being presented on the outside. Now, the Pharisees were very good at this; they had an appearance of holiness on the outside, yet Jesus clearly saw their hypocrisy within.

Interestingly enough, the word *hypocrite* in the Greek language means, "actor." Many people, including the Pharisees, were playing a role that did not match who they really were in their hearts. They had no true humility or devout allegiance to God, and their words and their actions would eventually reveal their true identity.

We spoke earlier about how we are so good at wearing many faces. I'm closing with this because it is something that I see so very often these days in people during counseling. The many faces come from the fact that the person does not have their identity rooted in Christ and therefore do not have any idea of who they are really made to be, so they search and search for approval of the world and others, constantly changing faces until one works for a while. And when that one fails, they just take it off and put on another.

The problem here is that not only does this do spiritual and emotional damage to themselves, but they also hurt others when their pretense is proven to be a lie. And then they find that the lies run deeper into other areas of their relationship, and pretty soon, the victim realizes that they are broken by the deception and also realize that they have been used.

This does the most damage is when the person wears a false face while also claiming to be a Christian. God's credibility and reputation is damaged because the lies shatter all forms of trust. How could any truly enlightened believer ever trust a phony Pharisee again after meeting the real deal named Jesus Christ?

You can do that same damage to someone if you choose to come into someone's life claiming to be something or someone that you are not.

Finally, how does a person so easily put on all these false faces? Their mind is not built upon the solid foundation of the Word of God, so their thoughts are not solid, but instead are fabrications of what they need to feel good about themselves or to obtain what they are after.

Truly, you are in fact what you think. And all that we are, good or bad, will one day be exposed most likely by us ourselves.

> *How happy are those whose way is blameless, who walk according to the LORD's instruction! Happy are those who keep his decrees and seek him with all their heart. They do nothing wrong; they walk in his ways.*
>
> —Ps. 119:1–3 CSB

Let's agree to pursue a renewed mind, one that is built upon the foundation of God and His Holy Word. Then we can move forward in this life with true happiness, confidence, and contentment as we reveal who we really are to others through how we live.

> *Do not be conformed to this age, but be transformed by the renewing of your mind, so that you may discern what is the good, pleasing, and perfect will of God.*
>
> —Rom. 12:2 CSB

PART 4

Being a disciple means living a grace-filled, spirit-led, Christ-committed life. A disciple is born to live transformed.

—Pastor Nick Maddox, BT Church

Chapter 31

Living in the Belly of Our Choices

As we take in the Lord's Word together, every time you see Jonah's name or Solomon's name, I want you to substitute your name in its place. I spoke to a man recently that I knew from my previous occupation, and he asked me what I was preaching on. I told him we had just started the book of Jonah.

His response was, "Oh, isn't that the story about the guy who was swallowed up by a big fish?"

I said, "Yes, it is."

And he then asked, "So, what's so important about that story? What could possibly be relevant for us today?"

I said, "Well, there was a lot that was relevant for the time these events occurred, because all of it really happened. And it is also relevant for us today; even Jesus emphasized the relevance of Jonah's call when He made a point to tell the Pharisees and Sadducees that they will be judged for their unbelief by the generation of Ninevites who repented through the message preached by Jonah and through the mercy of the Living God."

You see, Nineveh was a city of several thousand people. What we see written in the book of Jonah and what we will be studying together was probably the largest revival in the OT! So yes, this is a very relevant series of events—in fact, very important ones for us as Christians. Maybe you have asked yourself, "What does Jonah and his life have to do with me?" It's a great question, and I believe we have a very appropriate answer.

You are going to hear me reference this same theme throughout the book of Jonah because this is what we have in common with him and every other human being in the Bible—with Jesus being the only exception:

Jonah's sin was intentional: He chose to disobey God and in doing so chose to leave His presence. Jonah didn't like a thing about his calling because he didn't like a thing about the Ninevites. He couldn't have cared less if God judged them. After all, Nineveh was a hated enemy of Israel. But what God wanted to teach Jonah and everyone involved in this story and beyond, was that no one is out of the reach of His forgiveness, if they would sincerely repent.

So, Jonah chose to disobey God and go his own way. Now contrast Jonah's attitude with Jesus's attitude—Jesus chose to do exactly what God called Him to do, even if it wasn't comfortable or convenient, and we know that most of His mission on earth was not easy.

> *For you were called to this, because Christ also suffered for you, leaving you an example, that you should follow in His steps. He did not commit sin, and no deceit was found in His mouth; when He was insulted, He did not insult in return; when He suffered, He did not threaten but entrusted Himself to the one who judges justly.*
>
> —1 Pet. 2:21–23 CSB

Q: How have you responded to the call of God?

_____

_____

_____

Q: If He were to call you to do something outside your comfort zone, what would you say to Him?

_____

_____

_____

_____

Oftentimes, when God calls us we try to rearrange the conditions or the circumstances of the call to be something we feel more suited to. It may be something as simple as God prompting you to go visit a sick brother or sister, but instead of following through with what God wanted, you decide to change the plan and call the person instead. Now, it doesn't seem to be that big of a deal, right? You looked in on the person, and you feel good about yourself, so you think God should also be happy. Unfortunately, that is not what God wanted; He wanted the personal impact of your physical presence to be there with that sick neighbor; He wanted a deeper connection to be made.

Instead, you pulled a Jonah, and changed the original plan to better suit what you were willing to do. But how is it that we even think we can do that? I mean this is God who is calling us and commanding that we go forth as His ambassador. Does an ambassador have the authority to change the King's will? Certainly not. It would be absolutely sinful to even try. But we too often respond and act like Jonah.

Q: When God calls you to do something, do you often change His plans to make the mission more acceptable or convenient for you? Explain.

_____

_____

_____

_____

_____

OK, maybe now you are saying, "You are really reaching here, Pastor Mike. How do I know whether God wanted me to show up in person rather than just make a call? How am I supposed to know exactly what God wants me to do?"

Those are great questions, so here's my answer: God will always prompt our heart to do something particular. What we immediately do subconsciously is rewrite the plan in order to make it easier for us to accomplish. If God were to ask you to check on a certain person, we can probably say we would have two choices: go and visit or just make a call. You will seriously have to ask yourself what would Jesus do? Let me simply say this: Always be ready to go the extra mile and do exactly what God asks you to do. Don't give your own considerations a chance to even have a say in the matter. What do you think God was intending to accomplish when He asked Jonah to go and preach repentance to Nineveh? Since Nineveh was a large city, did God expect Jonah to only reach out to half the people? No, God's plans are perfect. He was glorified in the repentance of the Ninevites, they were blessed by His forgiveness, and Jonah was supposed to learn to love all people the way God does. Unfortunately, Jonah's heart wasn't quite to that point.

We are just like Jonah. We have our own preferences, and they include people. Deep inside, we already know who we will forgive, who we won't, who we will pursue, and who we will abandon. But that is not how God wants us to be. We will see Jonah's obstinate attitude more than once in this story and each time, it would behoove us to draw you back and examine the intentionality of our own choices—because as I have said before, most of our sin is in fact intentional.

Now let me give you an example from the life of Solomon, who next to Christ, was the wisest man to ever walk the earth.

- Here's a man that the Bible tells us had it all.
- He sat on a throne made of pure ivory that was covered in layered gold.
- He had over 40,000 horses (liken them to cars of today).
- He possessed more wealth and comfort and authority than anyone ever has.
- Solomon had 700 wives and 300 concubines! Why? Because as king, he did what he wanted. But you can be sure that God did not

condone this. It's like looking at porn today. Imagine how many men or women we have sex with in our hearts and minds when we look at porn.

- There was not one sexual pleasure that Solomon did not know.

He had it all, he tried it all, and experienced it all, yet in his heart he could not find true satisfaction, and this totally confounded his mind. The more he indulged, the less satisfied he became. Then his lustful heart became his downfall.

> *King Solomon loved many foreign women in addition to Pharaoh's daughter: Moabite, Ammonite, Edomite, Sidonian, and Hittite women from the nations about which the Lord had told the Israelites, "You must not intermarry with them, and they must not intermarry with you, because they will turn your heart away to follow their gods." To these women Solomon was deeply attached in love. He had seven hundred wives who were princesses and three hundred who were concubines, and they turned his heart away. When Solomon was old, his wives turned his heart away to follow other gods. He was not wholeheartedly devoted to the Lord his God, as his father David had been. Solomon followed Ashtoreth, the goddess of the Sidonians, and Milcom, the abhorrent idol of the Ammonites. Solomon did what was evil in the Lord's sight, and unlike his father David, he did not remain loyal to the Lord.*
>
> —1 Kings 11:1–6 CSB

After everything God gave Solomon, the lust of the flesh caused him to turn from God to worship Ashtoreth, the goddess of sex. Solomon turned his back on God, and not only lost his kingdom, but he lost his place in God's Kingdom. Solomon died a dejected, sick, old man. But the question we need to ask is: Did all that wisdom, wealth, and power make Solomon happy? The answer is no, it did not.

> *So I became great and surpassed all who were before me in Jerusalem; my wisdom also remained with me. All that my eyes desired,*

I did not deny them. I did not refuse myself any pleasure, for I took pleasure in all my struggles. This was my reward for all my struggles. When I considered all that I had accomplished and what I had labored to achieve, I found everything to be futile and a pursuit of the wind. There was nothing to be gained under the sun.

—Eccles. 2:9–11 CSB

Rejoice, young person, while you are young, and let your heart be glad in the days of your youth. And walk in the ways of your heart and in the desire of your eyes; but know that for all of these things God will bring you to judgment. Remove sorrow from your heart, and put away pain from your flesh, because youth and the prime of life are fleeting.

—Eccles. 11:9–10

You may be asking yourself, "OK, Pastor Mike, all this about Solomon is very interesting, but what does it have to do with us and the story of Jonah?" We have the example of Solomon and his father, David, and all the other human beings mentioned in scripture; that means we should learn from how they lived, how they triumphed and be most cautious as well as alertly aware of how terribly they failed.

My sin, your sin, is often intentional and if left unchecked, it will eventually kill us. And it can permanently separate us from God.

Today, I want to challenge your mindset, your pattern of thinking, and how you process your choices and decisions. I want us to start thinking about how we can attack sin not only when it first presents itself to our minds, but I also want us to focus today on how we can subdue sin preemptively—before it takes hold in us!

Fact: We are pattern-oriented creatures. But what does that mean? It means we follow the same thought and action patterns throughout our lives. And if our lives are ruled by sin, then it is easy to conclude it is most certainly a pattern that will lead to death. When you became a Christian, the pattern of sin was broken, and a new pattern came into existence. Godly desires took over.

Q: Does that mean there is no sin in your life? Y/N _____

Q: Have you allowed godly desires to take over? Y/N _____

The answer to the first question is no, because your unredeemed flesh is still here. But the more you pursue righteous affections, the less you will sin. Only you and God know the answer to the second question because only you and God truly know your heart.

Sin as a life pattern is incompatible with salvation. That's because to experience salvation is to be saved from something, and that something is sin. If a person could continue to sin after being saved from sin, that would mean that salvation is ineffective.

If we honestly accept that sin in us is intentional and that it is a deadly pattern that will eventually kill us, we must learn to attack each sin at its birthplace in our hearts and minds. We also have to be honest with ourselves and ask an extremely hard question: "Am I really saved?"

Please check your heart as you sit there and read this today; none of us here are guaranteed any other time like right now to get our hearts and minds right with God.

Life is not something you control, so that means that if God is knocking on your heart right now, then right now is when you should respond. Tomorrow or even the next ten minutes are never guaranteed. The beautiful thing about all of this is that even if our sin is intentional, God's forgiveness is promised to all who repent. I suggest you memorize 1 John 1:9 and be quick to repent when you do fail.

So back to our story.

You may be asking: Why did God do all of this? Why did He call Jonah?

Why does He want to offer repentance to the Ninevites, who were an enemy of His chosen people? Why does God want us to love and serve this city, our city?

- We are God's chosen and called ambassadors!
- We (you and I) are His light and salt!
- We (the church) are the means He has chosen to make Himself known to the world!

Why does God want us to tell people about Him where we live right now? Because He loves them; He loves them all.

Why did the Lord go after Jonah after he refused to be obedient and fled the presence of God? Because He loved him.

Are you seeing a pattern here yet? I will even go as far as to say that God's love is predictable. It's predictable because it is so dependable.

But, if you delay in repenting and submitting to God's Holy authority, you may catch yourself saying, "Well, God went after Jonah, right?" Yes, He did.

But that doesn't mean He will chase after you when you run from Him or call your name more than once, dear friend. Scripture confirms that if you prove to God that you love your sin more than you love Him, He may just turn you over to it. (Read Romans chapter 1.)

Let me ask you this: How many men and women since Jonah's time has God chosen not to pursue after they turned their back on His saving call? I believe if we knew that number, we would be both alarmed and even depressed. I personally don't believe that God chooses people for hell. People have no problem making that choice for themselves.

But God does expect us to respond to the cross of Christ with a decision. As Joshua so aptly stated:

> *"But if it doesn't please you to worship the* LORD, *choose for yourselves today: Which will you worship—the gods your ancestors worshiped beyond the Euphrates River or the gods of the Amorites in whose land you are living? As for me and my family, we will worship the Lord."*
>
> —Josh. 24:15

Understand this: To be called to do God's work is what can protect, enrich, and bless you. To be called to God's work is what can save you!

Does God actually need us?

We know that our God is holy, eternal, almighty, and totally self-sufficient. For what reason(s) would He needs us, if any? He does not need any created being, but we do need Him.

All of creation is dependent on the life that God alone sustains:

> *He makes grass grow for the cattle, . . . All creatures look to you to give them their food at the proper time. . . . When you take away their breath, they die and return to the dust.*
>
> —Ps. 104:14, 27, 29 NIV

God, on the other hand, is not dependent on anything or anyone. He suffers no lack, He knows no limitation, and He experiences no deficiency. He is the great *"I AM THAT I AM"* of Exodus 3:14 with no qualification or exception. If He needed anything to stay alive or to feel complete, then He would not be God.

So, God does **not** need us.

But, amazingly, He loves us passionately, and in His goodness, He wants us to live with Him forever. So, 2,000 years ago, God Himself put on skin, came to Earth, and gave His very life to atone for our sin and prove His deep love for us. He paid the ultimate price to reconcile us to Himself, and nobody pays that high a price for something they don't want or value.

Q: Do you understand the depth of love that the Living God has for you? Y/N _____

He has already given you the best He has—His Only Son. And His Son took the beating that you and I deserved; then He bore the cross, hanging there like a common criminal, murdered for you! Knowing all of this—

Why do you run from Him?

And why would you expect Him to chase you?

A Closer Look at Jonah

> *"Come on!" the sailors said to each other. "Let's cast lots. Then we'll know who is to blame for this trouble we're in." So they cast lots, and the lot singled out Jonah. Then they said to him, "Tell us who is to blame for this trouble we're in. What is your business, and where are you from? What is your country, and what people are you from?" He answered them, "I'm a Hebrew. I worship the Lord, the God of the heavens, who made the sea and the dry land."*
>
> —Jon. 1:7–9 CSB

Jonah's First Bad Choice

Jonah's first bad choice was his intentional disobedience to the call of the Living God. In verses 7–9, Jonah's first confession—you can almost hear his

273

tone—is very melancholy and matter of fact. He immediately confesses who he is a Hebrew and, at the same time, he acknowledges who God is, while making it clear that it's his fault that the storm had come upon them.

Even a believer who is in a state of rebellion can give glory to God if he will only tell the truth about God. The sad and tragic part here is that Jonah's life contradicted his knowledge of God. Jonah knows that he deliberately disobeyed God; he knows God is pursuing Him, and yet he still seems kind of apathetic about it.

I know that if I were in Jonah's shoes and I knew this was all my fault, the thought of being tossed over the side into the sea would not sit well with me! Have you ever seen the movie *Jaws*? I don't think the idea of being a snack for a big fish is something I would want to experience. Being in the sea is definitely out of our element.

I'm certain Jonah had no idea what God was going to do next, and this is the same place where we often find ourselves when we admit and accept our disobedience. My friends, please remember that Jonah's sin was intentional: He chose to disobey God and in doing so chose to leave God's presence.

What happens when we're separated from the presence of God? My answer is that it could be anything goes.

Q: What have you intentionally chosen that has caused you to be separated from the Living God?

_____

_____

_____

Q: Are you ready to dwell in the belly of your choices? Y/N _____

This is a question I like to ask myself once in a while, because it always gets me recentered:

Q: What is the source of all your wisdom, knowledge, and understanding?

_____

_____

_____

The Effects of Suppressing the Truth of God

- To get what we want, we are often OK with rejecting God, suppressing God, distorting God, re-creating God in our own image and to our own liking. It should be no surprise that the final outcomes of our choices are often much worse than we would expect.

  Think back to the example I used earlier in this chapter: God calls you to reach out to a sick brother or sister. You decide how you will make that happen in the most convenient manner for you possible. I think suppressing the truth of God could also mean that we replace God's intent with our own intent based on what we are or are not willing to do.

- This is what Jonah did and this is what you and I do nearly every day until we either die in our sin or finally submit and obediently come under the authority of the King of kings!

- If you are separated from Christ right now, I'm sorry to say that you chose it, and you probably find yourself running to sin on a regular basis!

- But when we come to Christ, the bondage to sin is broken, and all the chains we put on ourselves are gone! Listen to this my friend: when we return to God, all the running is over—it's done. Doesn't that sound beautiful? I say return because God never moves— you and I move away from Him by going our own way.

- While we are here on earth we are stuck in this imperfect body and must wrestle with sin and the declining physical state of the body. But we Christians have the gift of the Holy Spirit living in us in all power. Instead of running to sin, we now only stumble into sin from time to time, and not anything like we used to!

Here are three more questions I regular contemplate:

Q: When you choose to run from Jesus, who, then, do you run to?

_____

Q: Who can really help you?

_____

Q: Who actually loves you without any strings attached in this life and will accept you just as you are?

In the past I ran to alcohol or was caught up in the vicious trap of my own anger. The funny thing is, others have told me the same. When we don't run to Jesus but instead run to something or someone else, it's like getting cut with a really sharp knife. You don't know you have been cut until the air hits the open wound, and by then you have already lost a lot of blood.

Maybe right now in one form or another, you are in the midst of going your own way. God is not in the picture and if He is, you have Him in a very limited role depending on the needs of your situation.

Q: During times like this, have you ever had a random thought about the reality of hell just pop into your head? Y/N _____

Q: Does hell ever cross your mind when you intentionally disobey God? Y/N _____

Q: I would guess for most people the answer is no—but what about you, Christian? Y/N _____

So, we have been cut, and we are running: How much longer until we bleed out? Everything in this life has a beginning and an end, and that includes us.

Back to Jonah

So far in chapter 1, it doesn't seem like anything was bothering Jonah too much. In fact, by the way he is acting, I think Jonah would have rather perished in the ocean than go to Nineveh and preach the blessing of repentance.

In order to enable ourselves to intentionally sin, we must remove anything that will prick our conscience or put what we desire out of our reach: I believe that most of what we do is intentional—rarely can we say, "Man, I don't know what came over me when I decided to steal money from work!" "I don't know how I found myself on a porn site last night for two hours." "Well, I didn't intend on getting drunk last night!"

Sometimes, we try to justify our sin: "I had to tell her a lie because the truth would have been too hurtful for her to receive."

We make these conscious and subconscious decisions hundreds if not thousands of times each day and most of our choices are selfish and flesh driven—not Holy Spirit driven!

> *For though they knew God, they did not glorify Him as God or show gratitude. Instead, their thinking became worthless, and their senseless hearts were darkened. Claiming to be wise, they became fools and exchanged the glory of the immortal God for images resembling mortal man, birds, four-footed animals, and reptiles. Therefore God delivered them over in the desires of their hearts to sexual impurity, so that their bodies were degraded among themselves. They exchanged the truth of God for a lie, and worshiped and served what has been created instead of the Creator, who is praised forever. Amen.*
> —Rom. 1:21–25 CSB

My friends, what I am saying is that the biggest obstacle to willfully and intentionally committing sin is the truth of God! Since God is the source of all truth, when we choose our own way or rely on our own understanding, then we really are against Him, right?

- The truth of God is often too hard for us to accept!
- The truth of God is often too convicting!
- The truth of God doesn't ask for change, it **demands** change!
- The truth must be removed from the situation in order for us to proceed forward.
- Understand that very few of us sin out of sheer ignorance.

But way too often, the truth is ignored, disregarded, questioned, or rationalized away, or more often than not, it is traded for the lie we need, just as the Apostle Paul described in scripture.

Do you remember the question I asked you earlier about hell? Contrary to popular belief, hell is a real place! It is the place of:

- Everlasting torment and punishment. (Revelation 14:10–11)
- Aguish, pain, agony, and despair. (Matthew 8:12)

- Eternal separation from God. (2 Thessalonians 1:7–9)
- Final destination for the devil, his angels, and all who have denied and disobeyed the Living God. (Matthew 25:41, Revelation 21:8)
- Where the Lake of Everlasting Fire and brimstone is located. (Revelation 20:10, 14–15)
- The place of never-ending doom, death, and destruction. (Mark 9:3–48)

The Sailors Respond to Jonah's Testimony

In Jonah 1:10, the sailors respond: *"Then the men were seized by a great fear and said to him, 'What is this you've done?'"* Here's how this question would be asked of Jonah today: "Why have you done this?" or "Why have you done this to us?"

Even an unbeliever who knows some truth about God can rightly rebuke a Christian who is resisting God. The men on the boat knew he was fleeing from the Lord's presence because he had told them. So, they asked him:

> *"What should we do to you so that the sea will calm down for us?"*
> *For the sea was getting worse and worse. He answered them, "Pick*
> *me up and throw me into the sea so that it will calm down for you,*
> *for I know that I'm to blame for this great storm that is against you."*
>
> —Jon. 1:11–12 CSB

Why would Jonah ask them to do this? Maybe he did this because he knew that anything was better than his continual resistance against and running from God. But needless to say, we are all in this great struggle against God—fighting for self, first . . . always.

> *For the flesh sets its desire against the Spirit, and the Spirit*
> *against the flesh; for these are in opposition to one another, so*
> *that you may not do the things that you please.*
>
> —Gal. 5:17 NASB 1995

Maybe Jonah was tired of running from God, or maybe Jonah wanted to die; either way, he was fully aware of his disobedience to God, as he dealt with this great conflict within himself.

How many of you have had the courage to say that this catastrophe, this terrible situation, this horrible storm in our lives is my fault: Toss me overboard, and it will cease—get away from me for a while, I'm toxic, I'm not a good influence or the best example right now? How many of you have had the strength and courage to do this? And I mean do this without setting yourself up as the victim. Without saying, "Oh poor me, I'm so terrible; feel sorry for me."

"Nevertheless, the men rowed hard to get back to dry land, but they couldn't because the sea was raging against them more and more" (Jon. 1:13 CSB). Much like us, the sailors tried their best, used all their resources to solve the problem at hand, but instead their problem just got worse. Jonah had given them the solution—it was the God solution! Once again, God was looking for the response of obedience, since Jonah had told them the truth about the situation.

Q: How many times have you ignored God's truth and instead searched for a solution to a problem or situation from your own knowledge and understanding, abilities, and resources?

And then you find that you fail and fail miserably—many today still do this and are still too proud to repent to God and seek His help. Your pride will one day kill you, my friend.

> *So they called out to the LORD: "Please, LORD, don't let us perish because of this man's life, and don't charge us with innocent blood! For you, LORD, have done just as you pleased." Then they picked up Jonah and threw him into the sea, and the sea stopped its raging.*
>
> —Jon. 1:14–15 CSB

Do you see what just happened here? Obviously the sailors were concerned about themselves, but they were more concerned about the life of one man (Jonah), than Jonah was about the entire city of Nineveh! Verse 16 tells us that *"The men were seized by great fear of the Lord, and they offered a sacrifice to the LORD and made vows."*

The sailors were transformed from fearing the storm, to fearing the Living God, just like the disciples did in Matthew 4. Think about this for a moment: They were enemies of God until the day Jonah stepped on their boat. God used Jonah's sin for His Glory and the greater good of all who were on that boat!

They witnessed a miracle: God revealed His great power to them, and they responded by worshiping Him and making vows to Him. Remember, divine intervention (miracles) is one of the ways God makes Himself known to us. Verse 17 tells us that *"The Lord appointed a great fish to swallow Jonah, and Jonah was in the belly of the fish three days and three nights."*

God uses the great fish as His tool of correction and refinement: It sounds like Jonah was probably sinking deep down into the water when the great fish swallowed him up. Simply speaking here—Jonah was in great trouble.

Jonah finds himself living in the belly of his own choices. I will tell you that if you think the storm was bad, where he lands is much worse. You will see that Jonah will liken being in the belly of the whale to being in the grave.

Being in the belly of the whale is no different than any other place of correction that God will either assign or allow us to enter into. This is often where we find the truth of the gospel and the power it has to break the bondage of sin.

- Freedom dwells in, comes from, and is poured out for all through the Good News of the Cross.
- You can suppress the truth, but if you do, do not expect to find true freedom.
- You can try to run from it like Jonah did, but you will never be able to fully escape its far-reaching power:

The justice and mercy of God flows from the purity and truth of the good news!

> As He was saying these things, many believed in Him. Then Jesus said to the Jews who had believed Him, "If you continue in My word, you really are My disciples. You will know the truth, and the truth will set you free." "We are descendants

of Abraham," they answered Him, "and we have never been enslaved to anyone. How can You say, 'You will become free'?" Jesus responded, "Truly I tell you, everyone who commits sin is a slave of sin. A slave does not remain in the household forever, but a son does remain forever. So if the Son sets you free, you really will be free."

—John 8:30–36 CSB

So let me ask you these questions today:

Q: If you are suppressing the truth, will you allow this to continue? Y/N _____

Q: Will you continue to reject God, suppress God, distort God, and re-create God in your own image and to your own liking? Y/N _____

Q: Will you turn away from God by rejecting the demands of His truth on your life? Y/N _____

Q: And if you are running away from God now, will you continue to run, and for how long?

_____

Q: Where will you run to and to whom?

_____

_____

Please don't wait for God to summon a great big fish or some other huge obstacle to totally swallow you up or consume you—please know that all that isn't necessary. Turn to Christ and submit to Him and trust Him today.

Activity

Write a prayer today to God on the notes page provided here and make a point to focus on two important things: first, a prayer of thanksgiving for all He has done for you and next, a prayer of repentance for all you are in need of now. Please believe me, you need this. Let the Living God hear from your heart today.

Chapter 32

A Radically Changed Life— from Levi to Matthew

The Call of Levi (Mark 2:13–17)

The story of the call of Levi (Matthew) in the gospels is clear evidence of how God expects us to respond when His call comes upon our lives. Just as Christ did not hesitate in responding to our need for redemption and reconciliation, so should we move with an urgency that expresses our true love and devotion to Him. How we respond to the call and commands of Christ in our lives will ultimately be the most revealing evidence of the true nature and condition of our heart.

> *Jesus went out again beside the sea. The whole crowd was coming to Him, and He was teaching them. Then, passing by, He saw Levi the son of Alphaeus sitting at the toll booth, and He said to him, "Follow Me," and he got up and followed him.*
> —Mark 2:13–14 CSB

A simple call—words of invitation. What Levi just heard would change his life for eternity. We will discuss this more later. Next, we see Jesus hanging out with sinners: Time for a party: "*While he was reclining at the table in Levi's house, many tax collectors and sinners were eating with Jesus and his disciples, for there were many who were following him"* (Mark 2:15 CSB).

Notice that the Pharisees don't ask Jesus; instead, they choose to ask His disciples what is going on:

> *When the scribes who were Pharisees saw that He was eating with sinners and tax collectors, they asked His disciples, "Why does He eat with tax collectors and sinners?" When Jesus heard this, He told them, "It is not those who are well who need a doctor, but those who are sick. I didn't come to call the righteous, but sinners."*
>
> —Mark 2:16–17 CSB

We should concentrate on two main points as we examine the call of Matthew. We must seek to:

1. Live with an attitude of **desperation** for Christ—we must seek Him with a desperation that is built on a passion like no other in our lives.
2. Live with an attitude of **expectation** from Christ—we should always expect God to respond to our attitude of desperation toward Him, knowing that he who seeks Him is guaranteed to find Him.

Mark 2:13 says, *"Then Jesus went out again beside the sea. The whole crowd was coming to Him, and He taught them."* We start by finding our Lord right where He is expected to be: He is about the work and mission of His Father. Verse 14 adds this detail: *"Then, moving on, he saw Levi the son of Alphaeus sitting at the tax office, and He said to him, 'Follow Me!' So he got up and followed Him."*

Who Was Levi?

When we first encounter Levi in chapter 2, we find that he was a greedy tax collector that the Lord would redeem and transform into the humble disciple Matthew. And we believe that it was Jesus who most likely changed his name to Matthew, which means "gift of God." His original name is taken from the priestly tribe of Levi, who were called for service in the temple. However, Levi's occupation would have banned him from the temple and caused him to be hated by his fellow Jews. Tax collectors were considered the scum of the earth and a disgrace to their own families.

Think about this for a moment—the religious system of Jesus's time was so broken that the people who needed to receive comfort and healing from the Word of God the most—the lepers, paralytics, and tax collectors weren't allowed in the temple, yet the evil spirits roamed in and out at will (Mark 1:21–27).

This is an indictment of the church of today: We build all these beautiful structures and huge elaborate buildings, and then we set up a strict set of rules defining who will and will not be allowed to walk through the front doors! In many churches today, legalism is the "measuring stick" as well as the "beat stick" used to judge others—Christians and non-Christians alike.

Instead of putting all our faith and confidence in the power of the Living God and allowing His Perfect and Holy Word to change the hearts of people, we choose to discriminate against those who don't "look like Christians" or those whose sin in our eyes is either too horrible or too exposed.

To me, God has called the church to be the aid station on the battlefield. It was meant to be a place where the wounded and broken can come and gather together, and through worship and the Word, find strength and healing among others who are in the same shape they are. In my mind it can't be allowed to be anything else. God's house is for worship, teaching, fellowship, and healing.

I believe a judging type of attitude reflects a critical spirit in us, and we should always be on the lookout to keep our own judgments in check. This can be another way of inviting the enemy "in."

When you don't have the desire or courage to make the investment in those who are truly lost, when you are not leading through the conviction of the perfect and righteous love of Christ, which is the true discerner of hearts, then you will end up attracting and even unknowingly inviting the self-righteous and the selfish. You will get those people who are false or hollow in their walk.

And even worse, you may even be opening the doors to wolves whose only intention is to devour and destroy the church from the inside. God's Holy Spirit will not dwell in a church that is built upon corrupt hearts or one that allows or tolerates the presence of those types of people.

And this is exactly how the enemy was able to walk freely into the temple of God in Mark 1. The religious leadership was self-serving and evil, and when the gatekeepers (pastors, church leaders) are legalistic, lost, and corrupt people, then there is nothing to stop the enemy from walking in and contaminating God's house.

How Does One Become a Tax Collector?

When Rome conquered a nation or a territory, they would use a tax system as one of the ways to generate income for Rome and as one of the ways to control the conquered people. In the case of Judea, Romans would offer tax franchises to the highest Jewish bidders, and they would buy them and become tax collectors, who would then hire their own set of thugs to help them collect from their fellow countrymen.

This was a smart system: It gave the Romans a political advantage by not having to get directly involved in the tax collecting process. They would just hire some enterprising locals to do it for them. It was also smart because one way to keep a conquered people in check is to find a way to keep them divided against each other.

Citizens were required to pay taxes for 1 percent of each man's annual income, import and export goods, taxes on crops, wine, olive oil, and fruit; there was a sales tax and a property tax. In fact, tax collectors could even walk up to a man and tax him for what he was carrying in the street!

Since Levi's tax office was in Capernaum and close to the sea, he may have not only known the fishermen who were following Jesus, but he may have even collected a fish toll or tax from them. Imagine Peter, James, and John who were fishermen having to pay a tax to Levi for the fish they caught!

I want you to also imagine the look on their faces the day that Jesus walks in the door with Levi and introduces him as one of the brethren!

"Ill-Gotten Gain"

Taxes were inflated by the tax collectors so they could take a cut for themselves and pass on the rest to the Roman officials for whom they worked, who then would most likely take their cut, and the rest would go to Caesar to fund the Roman army and the needs of the empire.

It is likely that Levi had heard of Jesus—most likely everyone in the area had. His miraculous works and penetrating words were spreading like wildfire across the valley into and out of the towns and cities.

Capernaum is believed to have been a small community (about 600 to 800 people in the first century), so Levi probably knew someone who had either witnessed a miracle performed by Jesus or who had been healed by one of His miracles. This explains Levi's radical obedience and dramatic response to Jesus's simple but powerful call in Mark 1:14: *"And He said to him, 'Follow Me!' So [immediately] he got up and followed Him."*

Truth

When Christ calls there is only one answer. We don't choose Him, He chooses us! John 6:44 says, *"No one can come to me unless the Father who sent me draws him."*

Accepting the call of Christ means accepting to suffer. Matthew not only walked away from a lot of wealth, but by leaving his tax collector office, he also put his life in danger from the Romans for whom he had collected the taxes. Being a tax collector wasn't a job a person just walked away from.

Levi (Matthew) was chosen as an example against those who thought "much" of themselves: Jesus purposely chose people who were simple, lowly, outcasts, forgotten, and overlooked in order to mock the wisdom of the world. What I love the most about Levi is that he didn't try to hold on to any of his wealth or comfort—when it came to following Jesus, his decision was obvious, and I'm certain that the people who knew him were completely convinced that his conversion was genuine.

> *We do, however, speak a wisdom among the mature, but not a wisdom of this age, or of the rulers of this age, who are [doomed to pass away or are] coming to nothing.*
>
> —1 Cor. 2:6

> *Now we have not received the spirit of the world, but the Spirit who comes from God, so that we may understand what has been freely given to us by God. We also speak these things, not in words taught by human wisdom, but in those taught by the*

Spirit, explaining spiritual things to spiritual people. But the person without the Spirit does not receive what comes from God's Spirit, because it is foolishness to him; he is not able to understand it since it is evaluated spiritually.

—2 Cor. 2:12–14 CSB

The wisdom of God is far beyond the reach of the selfish, invisible to the eyes of the lost, and unimaginable to the minds of the worldly. When God opens the spiritual eyes of the believer, he or she sees beyond the limits of their temporary existence and, through real hope, finds identity and purpose. We find that our plan and purpose were written long ago. I like to believe that these realities overwhelmed Matthew once he discovered them, just as they did me when I discovered the truth. It was then in that moment that I first began to really live.

Levi found himself living with an attitude of desperation for Christ: John Calvin said, "In the great readiness and eagerness of Matthew to obey, we see the Divine power of the Word of Christ."[1] Mark 2:15 says, *"While He was reclining at the table in Levi's house, many tax collectors and sinners were also guests with Jesus and his disciples, because there were many who were following him."*

Matthew invites Jesus to his "family table" for dinner. Mark calls it a "banquet" because of the extravagance of the fine food and the rest of the spread; but it certainly wouldn't be considered a fancy party because of the guests! Many fellow tax collectors were there, and most likely even other folks of questionable character—notice that verse 15 identifies "tax collectors and sinners" among the guest.

But this was Matthew's proclamation of his new life as a Christ follower, he was celebrating. Notice that Matthew immediately invited Jesus into his world. Christ came because it is only through Him that we can be rescued and redeemed from the stain of sin and the corruption of the world. Think about it, my friend: Isn't it amazing where Jesus will go and what He will do to save us? It's a "come as you are" situation because whatever needs to be changed or made new is His job. Isn't that awesome? Romans 5:8 states it this way: *"But God shows His love for us in that while we were still sinners, Christ died for us."* The Bible says that God came and got you.

It is good for us to remember where we were when Jesus came and pulled us out. Do you remember what He brought you out of? Man, I sure do. I can just imagine Jesus in that moment, reclining—hanging out, comfortable. The Creator of the world, comfortable in this environment, with these people!

Q: How does it make you feel to know that Christ called you, came to you, and accepted you while you were caught up, entangled in, and trapped in your sin?

But no self-proclaimed righteous man of the time (Pharisee) would ever "lower" himself to be in the presence of their company. At that party there was probably a lot of coarse language, crude joking, and gluttony—remember, these people were not all cleaned up yet. All the religious leaders could do was watch, get angry, accuse, and complain.

I've known some pretty good people in my life by my estimation. I say good because I knew they were at least better than me; at least, they weren't caught up in the garbage I was. The sad thing was that they viewed people with a different social status as "lesser than." That always served as a reminder to me that just being good wasn't going to be good enough.

You don't need an official title to act self-righteous. The Pharisees were supposed to care for the lost, but they didn't. They were supposed to minister to the lost, but they didn't. They were supposed to share the love of God, but they didn't do that, either.

They had no concern for the real problem in the lives of Matthew and his friends—the religious elite didn't care about their dying, sin-stained hearts, or that they were completely separated from the Living God. They only seemed to care about what they did or didn't do, and whether they did so by **their** rules.

Q: How do you respond when you encounter a lost soul?

Q: Do you respond by sharing the healing love of the gospel, or do you just look away, accuse, gossip, and complain?

_____

_____

And we should not be surprised or stunned when nonbelievers curse, cheat, lie, get drunk, and so on. How should we expect unsaved people to act? The same way we lived and acted prior to our submission to Christ: Sinners sin; it's what they do. So why was Jesus there?

The scribes asked the same question in Mark 2:16: "*When the scribes of the Pharisees saw that He was eating with sinners and tax collectors, they asked His disciples, 'Why does He eat with tax collectors and sinners?'*" This point cannot be stressed enough: "*When Jesus heard this, He told them, 'Those who are well don't need a doctor, but the sick do need one. I didn't come to call the righteous, but sinners'*" (Mark 2:17).

Like Jesus, we are called to bring the life-saving news of the gospel to sinners:

> *I wrote to you in a letter not to associate with sexually immoral people. I did not mean the immoral people of this world or the greedy and swindlers or idolaters; otherwise you would have to leave the world. But actually, I wrote you not to associate with anyone who claims to be a brother or sister and is sexually immoral or greedy, an idolater or verbally abusive, a drunkard or a swindler. Do not even eat with such a person. For what business is it of mine to judge outsiders? Don't you judge those who are inside? God judges outsiders. Remove the evil person from among you.*
>
> —1 Cor. 5:9–13 CSB

OK, wait a minute here; Paul has given us some important instructions. If anyone who claims to be a brother or sister in Christ chooses to continue in sin after being confronted, Paul says to remove the evil person from among you. These are powerful instructions: Notice that he says we are to "judge" those who are in the church.

What the Apostle Paul is saying here is that we are allowed to be "fruit inspectors"—it is OK to lovingly "inspect" the fruit (the works and the lifestyle) of fellow believers. This is called holding each other accountable.

Now back to Jesus and the party at Matthew's house. If you want to share the gospel with lost people, you're going to have to be around lost people. And they usually come with a lot of baggage, use bad language, and have addictions and issues—just like we once did. Some of us still have issues. Who will come and help you? I'm sure you are hoping someone will.

- We must be careful not to get entangled in the ways (sin) of the world; we must remain separated from it, while determining through faith to be a light to it.
- "Be Holy as I am Holy." Holy means to be set apart—completely separated and 100 percent distinguishable from anything stained, tainted, or unclean; fully and completely set apart from sin!
- First John 2:25: *"Do not love the world or the things of the world. If anyone loves the world, the love of the Father is not in him."*

Remember the story of the paralytic at the beginning of this chapter—his heart condition (sin condition) was in greater need than his physical condition, but Jesus brought healing and restoration to both.

> *When he entered Capernaum again after some days, it was reported that he was at home. So many people gathered together that there was no more room, not even in the doorway, and He was speaking the word to them. They came to him bringing a paralytic, carried by four of them. Since they were not able to bring him to] Jesus because of the crowd, they removed the roof above him, and after digging through it, they lowered the mat on which the paralytic was lying. Seeing their faith, Jesus told the paralytic, "Son, your sins are forgiven."*
>
> *But some of the scribes were sitting there, questioning in their hearts: "Why does he speak like this? He's blaspheming! Who can forgive sins but God alone?"*
>
> *Right away Jesus perceived in his Spirit that they were thinking like this within themselves and said to them, "Why*

are you thinking these things in your hearts? Which is easier: to say to the paralytic, 'Your sins are forgiven,' or to say, 'Get up, take your mat, and walk'? But so that you may know that the Son of Man has authority on earth to forgive sins"—He told the paralytic—"I tell you: get up, take your mat, and go home."

Immediately he got up, took the mat, and went out in front of everyone. As a result, they were all astounded and gave glory to God, saying, "We have never seen anything like this!"

—Mark 2:1–12 CSB

Matthew had to make a choice, and Christ was requiring him to make it immediately—Jesus didn't expect Matthew to wait and think it over. He said to Matthew, *"Follow me."* [NOW]. The Bible tells us that Matthew's response was in fact immediate and despite what he knew it would cost him, Matthew chose to believe that Jesus was worth it. If we wait to count the cost of what may be lost in the temporary, we may lose our chance to rest in the safety of the eternal.

Jesus did not hesitate in His own call to obedience (Philippians 2:5–11): Had He done so we would not be able to possess what His blood has purchased for us.

Q: But why do we delay in our submission to Christ?

_____

_____

Most often, it's because we do not want to give up control; we don't want to surrender living how we want to live. We have this strange dichotomy in us: we want all the blessings of Christ, but we also occasionally want our alcohol or porn. We think nothing of the lies we tell every day because we have become professional rationalizers. We hold lust in our eyes and in our hearts and think no one knows what we are looking at or thinking. My friends, true obedience has no relationship with worldly compromise!

And remember this—whatever you do gain—comfort, pleasure, money, prestige, and popularity—it all only lasts for a season and then it is gone forever. It's like that steak dinner you were anticipating—after you eat it all, you rarely remember the taste or the satisfaction of it once you get hungry again. And think about this: What did you have to give up in the process?

Consider for a moment the "test" known as Goldman's dilemma:[2] The dilemma is a question posed to elite athletes by physician, osteopath, and publicist Robert Goldman. He asked whether they would take a drug that would guarantee them overwhelming success in sports but cause them to die after five years. In his research, as in previous research by Mirkin, approximately half the athletes responded that they would take the drug.

What we need to be asking ourselves right now:

1. What are you seeking today and what are you willing to leave behind if Christ were to call you?
2. Eternal investments will reap eternal dividends: How do your current investments measure up to this?
3. Is all that you are counting on or investing in only attainable or valuable in the temporary?
4. God sent His Only Son to die the death you could not die and pay the debt you would never be able to pay. Are you living a life right now, as evidenced by your current investments, that leaves no doubt that you are both mindful and thankful for all that Christ delivered you from?

For "whoever calls on the name of the Lord [in prayer] will be saved." But how will people call on Him in whom they have not believed? And how will they believe in Him of whom they have not heard? And how will they hear without a preacher [messenger]? And how will they preach unless they are commissioned and sent [for that purpose]? Just as it is written and forever remains written, "How beautiful are the feet of those who bring good news of good things!" But they did not all pay attention to the good news [of salvation]; for Isaiah says, "Lord, who has believed our report?" So faith comes from hearing [what is told], and what is heard comes by the [preaching of the] message concerning Christ.

—Rom. 10:13–17 AMP

We know that sometime after his conversion. the Holy Spirit would inspire the words of Matthew and he would write the gospel account that bears his name. Bible historians also say that Matthew would then go on to preach the gospel in Persia and Ethiopia, and some reports say he would be stabbed to death while in Ethiopia.[3]

Whatever Matthew's final outcome may have been, one thing is for certain: His life was radically changed the moment Jesus met him that day at his tax collector booth. We know that Matthew, like the rest of the apostles, walked differently after knowing Jesus. We know that they literally changed their lives and then gave their lives—all for Jesus. Their lives glorified the One who changed their eternal address forever.

I don't know about you, but that is the kind of change I want. I want a radical transformation that gives my life real purpose. I want to be concerned about eternity. I want to be concerned about other people's eternity, too.

I want the answer to eternal life. I want to know the One responsible for it. I want to know what real love is and I want to know **WHO** real love is.

And I want you to know that I have found Him.

His name is Jesus, and He is the **answer** to all of this.

He has changed my life **radically** in every way possible.

So, what about you?

Well, here's some adjustments that need to be made in your life right now:

- STOP isolating yourself from God.
- Quit ignoring His call—answer it **immediately** and submit to it **fully**.
- Examine the investments you have made in your life. Are they worth anything in eternity?
- Choose, decide, and resolve today to be obedient to the commands and statutes of the Living God.
- Then move forward with a heart full of thanksgiving; and be confident in the fact that God will not leave you—ever.

Finally, when God moves radically in your life, make sure you move with Him, not against Him or without Him!

And through this book, that is exactly what we will do together!

Chapter 33

What Now?

In 2020, the nasty little bug known as the coronavirus or COVID-19 certainly captured the world's attention. This "unseen enemy" has killed thousands, struck fear into the hearts of millions, and literally taken our nation's economy apart—and for the most part it is still going. Life as we once knew it might never be the same again.

As a result, we have had to become familiar with a slew of new terms, phrases, and habits that have resulted in some new realities, such as, the requirement to practice "social distancing." We have five-star restaurants delivering food to your door now, and we see signs saying, "You must wear a mask to enter here," and you hear a lot of people comment that "this is the new normal."

The times we are living in are certainly unprecedented, to say the least, with the future now looking more uncertain than ever. It's not hard for our hearts to be overwhelmed with fear, and that fear can and does grow quickly to where it can eventually become a huge part of our lives, affecting every part of our day-to-day routine, disrupting once-in-a-lifetime moments and robbing us of any peace we have been trying to hold on to.

At some point you have probably said to yourself, "OK, I have been locked down in my house for the past 120+ days, I have been washing the skin off of my hands, sanitizing everything I own over and over, I haven't seen friends or extended family in weeks or months, and my job has either furloughed me, or let me go all together." All this has people asking, "OK, what now?"

You might even think the scarier question may be, what's next?, but I can tell you with great confidence that it's not.

In fact, I believe that the right question instead is, "God, what do You want me to do next? What will You next use to change me and draw this fallen world to Yourself?" Yet people are still more concerned with the now than they are with what God is going to use next to help us mature. And even though we have a vaccine, there's still no "silver bullet" or cure in sight, and it seems like we could be facing this pandemic situation for an unknown period of time.

Another question that seems to be even more urgent even for Christians is—where's God in the midst of all this? I have heard this question a lot. People ask me, "Pastor, is this the end of the world?" Even believers are struggling right now despite the fact that the Bible clearly speaks of seriously disturbing catastrophes and events as foretold by the prophets to take place in the last days.

It should be clear that the question of "what now" isn't even the right question for us to be asking. Do we **not** believe in the sovereignty of our Mighty God? But this is the problem when God's people do not know His Word—instead, people prefer to get their marching orders for life from some form of social media or the crazy neighbor down the block. I wonder: Have we become just like the satiated and complacent people of Israel that the prophet Hosea encountered?

Unfortunately, I would have to say yes. God's words pierced their hearts then, and it still pierces our hearts with His truth today, **if** we care enough to listen:

> *My people are destroyed for lack of knowledge. Because you have rejected knowledge, I will reject you from serving as my priest. Since you have forgotten the law of your God, I will also forget your sons.*
>
> —Hosea 4:6 CSB

What God is saying here is this is what happens to us when His Holy Word is either neglected or ignored. This is what happens when we ignore the truth, lift up the lie, and claim to be civilized because we have learned "new and more efficient ways" to travel, to communicate, and to end what have now been labeled as "useless or inconvenient lives." Suddenly, the unborn aren't the only ones on the endangered list—the elderly are targets, too.

But unless a crisis comes to our own front door, we are totally OK with being curious for a moment and taking a quick look, like people do as they drive by a car accident, and then lose interest as we drive away. Well, the crisis is at the door, and because people do not know God as they should, they choose to live in fear instead.

We are selfish people, and it can be very easy to live carefree when everything is going exactly as we want it to—even if it is offensive to God. Next, we lose sight of what matters, and it can then be very easy to neglect our relationship with Christ even though He's the very source of everything good in this life we are enjoying.

And then when life turns on a dime and suddenly becomes hard, how we react is so important. Since nothing in this world can fully satisfy our hungry hearts except relationship with Christ, in our neglect of Him, we bounce from one empty pleasure or comfort to another, because that's how we chose to react to difficult situations.

You may be saying, "Wait a minute; am I supposed to feel bad about how I am reacting to this pandemic?" No, but I'm hoping these words bother us enough to examine the way we have reacted to all this. We have given fear power and authority over us and as a result, we have fallen away from our dedication to our relationship with Christ. I think if we can be honest, we will admit that we have been there and know that there is truth in these words.

There is no doubt that fear is a very real evil affliction, and the people who should be the example in how to respond, Christian people, seem to be falling apart just like everyone else right now. How does this happen? Usually, this is what happens when professing Christians weren't living faithful, disciplined lives in Christ when there was no pandemic!

And it is through the practice of an undisciplined, careless attitude and lazy living that the curse of fear can become a very real and paralyzing force in our hearts and lives.

Fear can quickly undo all that we have learned in our walk with Christ and send us back to square one because we lost one thing—our trust in the Living God in all things. But thankfully, it does not end for us here.

Fear—the Great Disabler of Holiness

If you have a hard time believing that anyone in the Bible who loved God also battled against the curse of fear, then you should probably reread Joshua chapter 1 very carefully. Joshua was a guy that I would definitely call a man's man. He was hardened by the years of slavery while in Egypt and then he became battle-hardened as a military commander.

You wouldn't think that there would be too much that would frighten him or cause him to pull back in fear, but in chapter 1 of his story, we clearly see something different. What's really interesting about this chapter is that it starts off with Joshua and God having a conversation, and God is laying down some important instructions, and He starts off by saying, *"Moses My servant is dead"* (Josh. 1:2).

Those are some heavy words for anyone to hear, and I'm sure especially for the man whom God has chosen to take Moses's place—and that man was Joshua. But just how do we know that Joshua was afraid? Here's what the scripture says in Joshua 1:6–9 (CSB):

> *Be strong and courageous, for you will distribute the land I swore to their ancestors to give them as an inheritance. Above all, be strong and very courageous to observe carefully the whole instruction my servant Moses commanded you. Do not turn from it to the right or the left, so that you will have success wherever you go. This book of instruction must not depart from your mouth; you are to meditate on it day and night so that you may carefully observe everything written in it. For then you will prosper and succeed in whatever you do. Haven't I commanded you: be strong and courageous? Do not be afraid or discouraged, for the Lord your God is with you wherever you go.*

God gave Joshua specific instructions, and then notice what comes next: After being told in verse 6 to be strong and courageous, he is told again in verse 7 to *"Above all, be strong and very courageous."* It's clear so far that God says that in order to do what the Lord has commanded him, Joshua must be strong and courageous. Look what happens next in verse 9 where the Lord says: *"Haven't I commanded you: be strong and courageous? Do not be afraid or discouraged, for the Lord your God is with you wherever you go."*

I can only imagine what was going through Joshua's mind as God was instructing him:

- I'm not Moses, I can't do this!
- The people will not listen to me.
- I have no idea how to lead them.
- Who am I that I should be chosen to do this?

And finally, I truly believe that Joshua said directly to the Lord, "I'm afraid I will fail." We see God tell Joshua three times in the beginning of Joshua 1 to be strong and courageous, which means do not be afraid. God even gave Joshua the promise of His presence: The Lord your God is with you wherever you go, but he was still shaking in his sandals.

It appears that Joshua was having a hard time accepting the immense responsibilities of his new job, and he had become fearful. After all, what God was asking of him was a huge task, but Joshua's fear may be rooted in the fact that he thought he had to do all this by his own power, not by the Lord's. Perhaps he didn't yet realize that he could in fact do all things God asked of him through the Lord's strength, and that he would not have to rely solely on his own strength.

We have all been told the same thing—I can do all things through Christ who strengthens me, and it is in fact the absolute truth. But what we must remember is that this gift of overcoming, perseverance, and strength pertains to the will of God, not the plans or ideas of men.

And as Christians, we all have been given this very same promise: God is always with us. So, the question still remains: Why is it so difficult to trust God right from the start? Why is believing that God is all that the Bible says He is so difficult for Christians to accept? Why did Jesus have to perform so many miracles? Shouldn't one miracle have been enough for the fickle human heart to accept and believe? Obviously not.

If you think you might have done better at recognizing Jesus and obeying Him than the apostles did, you had better think again. Even after the power of the resurrection was displayed, people still clung to their doubt, and you would have too. The evidence is found in the time Peter tried to walk on water—once he took his eyes off Jesus, he quickly began to sink.

We take our eyes off Him all the time. This is why we struggle so badly with fear. What this proves is that trust is something that we must learn to submit to. We must decide that we either fully trust Him, or we do not. So, it ends up becoming our basic inability to trust God that keeps the fear alive in our lives.

We will discuss the issue of trust more later on.

God Demands We Seek to Be Holy

What we often miss when we read this is that He is not asking us to or suggesting we should—He has commanded it. But our pursuit of holiness will always be hindered or even halted if we continue to give way to our fears. When we are afraid, we tend to act irrationally.

When we find ourselves under extreme pressure, human beings usually resort to one of two coping methods: We end up either in fight mode or flight mode. Since both are commonly extreme reactions, we rarely make positive or productive choices when we are in fight or flight mode.

It's All about Us

How many times have you told someone this is my problem; I will deal with it? And how many times have you failed to find resolution on your own, and then found yourself so embarrassed because your efforts only made everything worse?

In the desperate need for self-preservation, we flee. We know it is not uncommon at all for a person to try to escape or run away from the problem; we know this is true because we have all done it and will most likely do it again and again.

Unfortunately, when we decide to fight, our idea of fighting usually means that the engagement must be on our terms and within our resources—this means we also try to choose the place and time we will fight, and even how we will fight. But in reality, as in any true battle, we rarely get to choose the battlefield on which we fight; we don't get to say "go" to start it, and we cannot say "stop" when we want to quit.

The hard truth is that life's trials, challenges, and difficult situations and circumstances are not subject to any of our set of rules. Years ago, I read *The Art of War*, which was written by Sun Tzu, a six-century BC Chinese military strategist and philosopher. A well-known quote from his book was one that stood out to me and has had a big impact on me ever since the first time I read it, and it goes like this: "Hence the saying: If you know the enemy and know yourself, your victory will not stand in doubt: If you know Heaven and know Earth, you may make your victory complete."[1] It can also be translated as:

> Know your enemy; know yourself. And your victory will not be threatened. Know the terrain. Know the weather and your victory will be complete.

If you are like me, you may tend to view spiritual warfare as an ongoing military campaign, and as Sun Tzu said, it has all the usual players:

- There's the enemy (Satan and his minions).
- There's you and me (soldiers for Christ).
- There's the terrain or battlefield (your life, your heart, your marriage, etc.).
- Let's not forget that God is in this fight, and if we will let Him be God in a given situation, He will fight for us!
- And then there's the weather (the circumstances and events that evolve around the fight that can and do change at any time).

Q: Ask yourself this: When you have decided to fight, how often was the environment for the fight of your choosing? (If you are like me certainly not often enough if even ever!)

What usually happens is that I find myself thrust onto a battlefield that I did not choose to fight on and in a fight I have no ability to win on my own—and that's pretty much how a trial or difficult situation in this life is usually set up. Here's a couple of examples: Let's say you are fighting for your marriage (such as contending with the discovery of adultery in your marriage) or battling some form of addiction (e.g., porn, drugs, alcohol, or even food). These things often crash in on us or come to a head when we are not prepared to face them.

So, it is safe to say that the ground on which you find yourself taking your stand definitely isn't one you would choose. (No one would choose to have to deal with adultery or an addiction if they didn't have to.)

Now, we know through life experience that the weather can change at any time. Using the example of fighting for your marriage, things may seem to be working toward a possible reconciliation when you suddenly discover that your spouse had a child with their lover—or just as bad, you discover that your beloved child isn't even yours! It's like your partly cloudy suddenly became a raging hailstorm! We need to realize that the weather can and will change at any time in our circumstances.

Lies will eventually get exposed, unholy plans are uncovered, and unhealthy practices are revealed. Even what you or someone else thought were your own private moments suddenly aren't so private anymore. The truth is God sees all our moments—both public and private. God is also the One who exposes all our moments and in His time eventually brings everything into the light. God may be the author of the fight you are in right now.

Q: How do you feel about that?

_____

_____

But believe it or not God does this for our own good—it often hurts, it's painful, and it can be embarrassing, but God will not let us live in a lie.

Q: Has God had to expose something unhealthy in your life, or has He changed the weather suddenly in a situation in your life recently? Explain.

_____

_____

_____

_____

Oftentimes, our response to God's work of exposing us takes the opposite effect because we do not have the courage to accept our faults and own our sin, and once we realize this, the fear in us begins to gain some serious ground. Right here is where the fear we allowed in and the fear we ourselves have chosen to accept begin to do some very serious damage in us.

Q: Let me ask you this: Do we choose to hide inside among our fears because we feel that the pursuit of holiness is just too hard and too much work, or is it that we just fail too often at trying to achieve it?

Q: Does God's command to be holy even matter to us at all?

Something seems to be causing us to regularly quit prematurely almost every time. Instead of embracing the truth of the light, our personal concern for our own perceived well-being and reputation becomes too much to compromise and instead, we either choose fear or allow it to take a huge foothold in us. We may even fear being pulled out of our comfort zone, even though that's the worst place we could be at that moment.

So, we choose to rebel and hold on to our selfishness because it just feels better. And here's the strange part: In the selfish hole we are clinging to, fear is just beating the stuffing out of us, and we are angry at God for that. Trusting God isn't even an option at that point. Trusting Him would mean letting go of the fear (and in the process losing any control we thought we had), stopping the destructive behavior, repenting, and simply waiting for God—but we will have nothing to do with that.

Waiting is usually out of the question for us—so we self-destruct. Even though we know that God answers all prayers one of three ways (yes, no, or wait), we would rather hear no, than wait. So, we seek out something else to help us deal with the discomfort that the fear is causing.

Q: How do you feel about having to wait for something?

Q: If everything we believe about God is perfect and righteous, why do we have such a hard time waiting for Him?

302

Take a few moments to evaluate your recent behavior: Have you demonstrated that you can fully trust God? If not, we need to ask ourselves whether this is how I really feel about God's command to be holy?

If you are like me, you have chosen self over holiness more often than not. And the sad thing is, when we go this route, we totally miss the fact that when we seek God's holiness, we find a measure of His perfect peace.

So exactly how does fear disable our holiness? When we choose fear:

1. We eventually **stop** praying.

   Oftentimes, fear disrupts our thoughts so thoroughly that we cannot slow down and focus on a true heartfelt connection with God through prayer. Because we are unable to concentrate, we convince ourselves through guilt that we aren't able to give God our best, so we give Him nothing instead. Since fear and guilt are so connected, we become convinced that we are not even good enough to pray, so we just don't anymore.

2. We repent, but we **do not change**.

   Believe it or not fear can actually suppress or keep us from owning our sin. Fear is certainly related to guilt, and when we are overcome by it, true repentance rarely happens because we are often waiting for the circumstances to change before we actually do. But just being sorry isn't enough—God expects us to turn away from the bad behavior and move toward holiness. Instead we often try to make deals with God, like. "If you can just get me out of this mess, Lord, I promise I will never do that again." This is not repentance.

3. Fear **poisons** faith.

   If allowed to linger in us long enough, fear will eventually poison our faith. Belief in the sacred and holy mysteries of God and His unknown qualities becomes easier to question and to doubt. Gone is the simple fact that God is all that the Bible says He is. We fear God either won't help us, can't help us, or just doesn't care, so we believe the fear, and our faith becomes poisoned. With fear as our heart's director, the hope that comes from true faith is also diminished; in fact, hope will actually grow cold or disappear altogether. What is there for a person to hope for or have faith in if God can be questioned or doubted? When this is allowed to happen, that person is no longer able to see anything but fear in every situation.

4. Fear **destroys** our ability to love and be loved.

Since fear will eventually warp the true appearance of everything, it only makes sense that fear will force us to only focus on other people's flaws and imperfections. Fear teaches a person to eventually expect the worst and can even make a person's love paranoid and untrusting. Instead of selfless love, the fearful person becomes extremely selfish and cynical. What is really sad is that when a person is governed by fear, they will often subconsciously seek a love that pities instead of one that respects.

5. Fear **insults** the Holy Spirit.

Accepting fear and allowing it to dwell in us means that we trust it more than we trust the Holy Spirit. It then becomes the fear that we listen to, not the Spirit of the Living God. We insult Him by choosing the constant torment of fear over the love, protection, and guidance of the Comforter. The Apostle Paul tells us in Ephesians 4:30, *"And don't grieve God's Holy Spirit. You were sealed by Him for the day of redemption"* (CSB). He tells us not to do this because we can. We need to wake up and be aware of this. When we choose fear, we insult the One who has sealed us and will one day deliver our spirit to the throne of God.

Consider these important points that we must strive to remember:

1. Fear is **not** from God. Second Timothy 1:7 teaches that *"God did not give us a spirit of fear, but one of power, love, and sound judgment"* (CSB).

- Notice that the Bible says fear is also identified as a spirit and does not come from Him.
- This clearly tells us that fear is something that is unholy. Why? Because fear does not come from God because He **is** holy.
- Now notice the things God does give us—His power, His love, and sound judgment by strengthening our mind!

He gives us the ability to choose self-control. Choosing fear is a sin. That is the reality, my friends. The words of the psalmist must become our constant cry in our battle against the torment of fear: Psalm 56:3–4 says, *"When I am afraid I will trust in you. In God, whose word I praise, in God I trust; I will not be afraid. What can mere mortals do to me?"* (CSB)

2. All fear is a choice in our lives.

- I'm not saying that when we come to Christ that you won't experience fear, but when it exists in us (meaning we allow it to linger), it's because we allowed it in.
- There are 365 commands in the Bible against fear, so God is telling you that you have been commanded to resist it.
- Christ Himself was tempted with fear in the garden the night before he was murdered. Sweating great drops of blood from the anxiety of the reality of the cross, He chose obedience instead of giving into fear. In Luke 22:42, Jesus prays, *"Father, if you are willing, take this cup away from me—nevertheless, not my will, but yours, be done."* It is never God's will that we choose fear, but understand that God will use it to draw us to Himself.
  Let's talk some more about trust.

3. Why is it so hard to trust God?
   In counseling, I have heard two reasons given quite often: God being unseen, and He works on His own timetable, not ours. But just to know that we are so shallow that we need to have the source of our trust meet with us on our terms and abide by our schedule should clearly show us just how selfish we are.
   Q: What do we as believers really have to be afraid of?

I purposely put a line here for you to answer this question, hoping that your answer will contain one word: *nothing.*
God's Holy Spirit is in us and promises to protect us, teach us, guide us, and comfort us. Death has been transformed from a damning curse into a simple transition. Eternity is secure and will one day be our forever home! *"There is no fear in love; instead,*

perfect love drives out fear, because fear involves punishment. So the one who fears is not complete in love. We love because He first loved us." (1 John 4:18–19 CSB).

a. Here's the hard truth: Trusting God is actually a testing of your faith.

Sadly, we don't want to submit to this test, and I think I know why— because we know we will fail. We fear failure; we do not want to fail at anything.

When it comes to trusting God, that seems to be something we eventually submit to—but only after everything we have tried has failed and all our personal resources have been exhausted. And by then, we have a lot more damage to account for and oftentimes, we have not just hurt ourselves but others as well.

How do we step out in faith and trust that God's ways are better and more apt to work out than ours?

Instead of giving way to fear and allowing it to lead us deeper into disparity and further from God, how do we allow the situation to make our faith grow stronger?

b. The answer first of all is to allow God's truth to overcome your doubts. God's Holy Word is the true light that can cast out every fearful shadow that lies upon our heart. His truth is something that cannot be denied and when we submit to it, we can be overcome by it.

In Romans 12:21, Paul exhorts us strongly: *"Do not be conquered by evil, but conquer evil with good"* (CSB).

As I mentioned at the beginning, throughout scripture, we see the men and women of God experience a crisis of belief. Fear was a part of the lives of some of the strongest believers in the Bible, and it was something that had to be confronted.

Q: Is the Bible a part of your life every day? Y/N _____

Q: Do you just read it, or do you allow its truth to penetrate your soul?

Let your prayer be that of the psalmist:

How can a young man keep his way pure? By keeping your word. I have sought you with all my heart; don't let me wander from your commands. I have treasured your word in my heart so that I may not sin against you. Lord, may you be blessed; teach me your statutes. With my lips I proclaim all the judgments from your mouth. I rejoice in the way revealed by your decrees as much as in all riches. I will meditate on your precepts and think about your ways. I will delight in your statutes; I will not forget your word.

—Ps. 119:9–16 CSB

Next we need to ask God to help us trust in Him more and more each day—following Him, doing what is right, and leaving the results in His hands.

There will never be anything for us to fear when we are able to place our trust fully in Him. Fears will come and go, and each time we put fear to flight, we will grow stronger and stronger. Each stride with Christ will make us more and more courageous in Him.

Let's toss out the question of "what now?" and replace it with this prayerful question instead: "Father, what will be the **next way** that You will use or allow in my life in order that I may be made more and more into the image of Your Precious Son?"

Chapter 34

Hope in Christ Alone—the Anchor for Your Soul

In a self-proclaimed hopeless society and a seemingly hopeless time, people all over the world are aching for a real, true, and lasting hope. As in ages past, people constantly search for hope through the temporary pleasures and desires of a temporary world: All who travel this path (and they are many) have looked inside themselves and found a whole lot of nothing.

When I talk to people about what they hope for in this life, I get a myriad of answers, most of which only describe things that have no eternal value. Even though they are looking for something that will really stick or something that has real staying power and can build even more hope, the selfishness and narrow-mindedness of the human heart continues to lead them toward the shallow and temporary.

I constantly encounter a lot of "wishful thinking" or comments like this: "If I had only done this or said that." "Why did this/that happen to me? I was hoping it would turn out different," or "I wish had had one more chance to do this or that." Even people who consider themselves Christians are wasting a lot of time looking for momentary satisfaction; they are holding out hope for things that they think will satisfy, but they are still blind to the fact that not everything in this world holds its value; everything has an expiration date.

Sometimes, I am blown away by how nearsighted the modern day "believer" is; but shallow faith combined with the love of self has always produced the same results. A lot of people I asked said they hope that acquiring the "right level" of education will allow them to land their "dream job." Some hope that the right person in their lives will be the difference maker, while some hope that the right title, personal accomplishment, or accolade is what is missing.

Many hope and dream for a comfortable life but don't realize that they lack the drive and desire to work hard for it, and even if they did, there is still a risk because there are no guarantees. Relationally, we jump from one temporary "commitment" to another, treating people the way we try on shoes in a shoe store—one pair after another, one partner after another.

There is no realization or consideration for the destructive nature of this kind of behavior and as a result, the ability to actually make any relationship grow past the physical and the superficial becomes almost impossible today. Traditional marriage and the moral values ordained by God are labeled as "out of style" and "inconvenient." What I do hear pretty often is, "We just want to live together." According to 2014 statistics on relationships, researchers concluded that couples who lived together before they tied the knot saw a 33 percent higher rate of divorce than those who waited to live together until after they were married.[1]

When we enter into relationships outside of God's proper order, they just don't work. Even the hope of finding fulfillment in being a parent is a great thing, but it cannot fill the God-shaped "hope hole" in your soul. How can we have real hope when what we seek continues to give us results like this?

Well, when we as a society insist on doing things apart from God or outside the order He has designed for us, we should really expect nothing less. Another startling statistic is the rising rate of single-parent families in our country: the US government census bureau records that between 1960 and 2016, the percentage of children living in families with two parents decreased from 88 percent to 69 percent,[2] and that number is still dropping.

The desire to allow God to not only build our hopes for us and then fulfill them through a lifelong relationship with Christ is not the desires of the hearts of most people today. It is absolutely crushing to realize that the "many who are called, and the few who are chosen," will be people who claim to know Christ but find no hope in the gospel and even worse are not looking for hope in the gospel!

Maybe you are asking right now why I am telling you this. Because the way that the world is suggesting we seek, plan, dream, work, and engage in relationships today t isn't working at all. People are placing their hope in everything but God, and even though they continue to find that the people, ideas, and things they were counting on always fall short, they continue to chase the same empty promises of the world—just from a different angle each time. To me, this represents nothing more than a pattern of insanity and self-destruction.

So, what does the Bible tell us about hope? Is it really there for us to have and build our lives around and look forward to? Let's look at hope as defined and described in both the Old and New Testaments:

1. Definition of *hope* in Hebrew: "*Yachal*," meaning "trust."
2. Definition of *hope* in Greek: "Elpis," meaning "to expect or anticipate with pleasure." This kind of hope is an absolute guarantee, without a doubt. Bible scholars call it a "confident expectancy."

May your faithful love rest on us, Lord, for we put our hope in you.
—Ps. 33:22 CSB

Israel, put your hope in the Lord. For there is faithful love with the Lord, and with him is redemption in abundance.
—Ps. 130:7 CSB

For we have heard of your faith in Christ Jesus and of the love you have for all the saints because of the hope reserved for you in heaven. You have already heard about this hope in the word of truth, the gospel.
—Col. 1:4–5 CSB

Paul, a servant of God and an apostle of Jesus Christ, for the faith of God's elect and their knowledge of the truth that leads to godliness, in the hope of eternal life that God, who cannot lie, promised before time began.
—Titus 1:1–2 CSB

We can also see both the "*yachal*" and the "*elpis*" in Psalm 23:6, "*Surely goodness and mercy shall follow all the days of my life, and I shall dwell in the house of the LORD forever.*" It is evident here that the Holy Spirit had revealed the coming guaranteed hope of Christ to David when he was writing Psalm 23.

We can also see the hope found in complete forgiveness in Psalm 32:1–2: "*How joyful is the one whose transgression is forgiven, whose sin is covered! How joyful is a person whom the LORD does not charge with iniquity and in whose spirit is no deceit!*" (CSB) Here David describes the blessings imparted by God to a man who has been forgiven of his willful sins (transgression), his premeditated sins (iniquity), and the covering of the sin we all have been born into (original sin). Hope that is found in forgiveness is real and can only be received through faith in Christ.

3. Hope does not come from an individual's desires or wishes but from God, who is Himself the believer's hope: "*My hope is in you*" (Ps. 39:7).

4. Genuine hope is not wishful thinking, but a firm assurance about things that are unseen and still in the future (Rom. 8:24–25; Heb. 11:1, 7).

5. Biblical hope distinguishes the Christian from the unbeliever, who has no hope. Hope by the world's definition and standard is uncontrollable and is merely an expectation of what might or might not happen; it is a great unknown, and never in a person's grasp.

6. Christian hope is not a feeling, but an absolute. We must remember that our mind and our body will dismiss it because we don't "feel" it, especially during trails and the hard times of life.

What effect does our faith have on our belief in the hope of Christ? Read Matthew 9:27–31 and Hebrews 11:1.

a. In 1 Corinthians 13:9–13, Paul expresses the attitude of what a mature believer in Christ should be: leaving behind the childish ways and things of the past (verses 9–10), and also expresses the expectation (hope) of the knowledge and understanding of all to come (verse 12). Verse 13 says we are to abide in (live in a constant state of) faith, hope, and love (daily until we are called home).

b. Lack of faith affects our ability to have real hope and gives birth to:
Fear: Luke 12:4–6, 1 John 4:18, and 2 Timothy 1:7
Anxiety: Proverbs 12:25
Worry: Matthew 6:33–34

c. Simple disobedience will affect your faith:
- Ephesians 4:29 (the way you talk).
- Colossians 3:5, Matthew 5:27-28 (what you think about and desire).
- Matthew 6:5–6 (what you do—both publicly and privately).

Take some time to examine what you hope for, but more importantly, make sure you have the right source for the hope you have.

Q: Would you say that you are a hopeful or hopeless type of person?

_____

Q: Is your hope found in Christ or in someone/something else?

_____

Q: Are your hopes building toward eternity, or are you still stuck in hoping for things that will eventually expire?

_____

_____

_____

Chapter 35

It's Time to Endure

If you live in South Texas, you know that you have to learn to endure the summer season the same way you had to learn how to endure the spring season. Actually, we only have one season here in South Texas—hot! It is true that a lot of life is spent making adjustments and learning to adapt. Many of us have already had to learn how to adapt to much harder things than just the weather. In fact, some of us are going through a rough season right now.

For some, there are seasons of difficult personal relationships. They can occur in a marriage or in relationships with children, parents, siblings, and in-laws. As a counselor, I get a front-row seat to the hurt, pain, separation, or even loss. It can be very hard to endure, and sadly some people are never fully able to handle it. Maybe you or someone you love is in a season of sickness and suffering or is experiencing a difficult financial season. All you see in front of you are fear and uncertainty as the responsibilities of life hang heavy on you.

One thing that makes every season even longer than it should is the interference of our humanity in the middle of everything. Our fallen nature and daily battles with the flesh only serve to make everything we endure all that much more difficult. Oftentimes, it seems we just don't get a break, no matter what we try or who we call. These seasons, for many of us, can appear to be hell on earth. So, what does the Bible have to say about all this?:

> There is an occasion [or a season] for everything, and a time for every activity under heaven: a time to give birth and a time to die; a time to plant and a time to uproot; a time to kill and a time to heal; a time to tear down and a time to build; a time to weep and a time to laugh; a time to mourn and a time to dance; a time to throw stones and a time to gather stones; a time to embrace and a time to avoid embracing; a time to search and a time to count as lost; a time to keep and a time to throw away; a time to tear and a time to sew; a time to be silent and a time to speak; a time to love and a time to hate; a time for war and a time for peace.
>
> What does the worker gain from his struggles? I have seen the task that God has given the children of Adam to keep them occupied. He has made everything appropriate in its time. He has also put eternity in their hearts, but no one can discover the work God has done from beginning to end. I know that there is nothing better for them than to rejoice and enjoy the good life. It is also the gift of God whenever anyone eats, drinks, and enjoys all his efforts. I know that everything God does will last forever; there is no adding to it or taking from it. God works so that people will be in awe of him. Whatever is, has already been, and whatever will be, already is. However, God seeks justice for the persecuted.
>
> I also observed under the sun: there is wickedness at the place of judgment and there is wickedness at the place of righteousness. I said to myself, "God will judge the righteous and the wicked, since there is a time for every activity and every work." I said to myself, "This happens so that God may test the children of Adam and they may see for themselves that they are like animals." For the fate of the children of Adam and the fate of animals is the same. As one dies, so dies the other; they all have the same breath. People have no advantage over animals since everything is futile. All are going to the same place; all come from dust, and

all return to dust. Who knows if the spirits of the children of Adam go upward and the spirits of animals go downward to the earth? I have seen that there is nothing better than for a person to enjoy his activities because that is his reward. For who can enable him to see what will happen after he dies?

—Eccles. 3:1–22 CSB

One aspect about the Bible that I really appreciate is its relatability to the human condition. In multiple places throughout scripture, we see clear pictures of people contemplating both life and death as well as having a deep association with suffering. To me, that's about as real as it gets. With that being said, I want us to focus on a word that we hear often in scripture; depending on which translation you use, it will be presented as "being steadfast," or "to endure," or "enduring."

What does it mean to be steadfast or enduring? The biblical definition of endurance can be stated as "the continuing commitment to Christ in the face of difficulty." It was born through hostility, persecution, and death of the saints of God and even the Lord Jesus Himself: The endurance of Christians in the face of persecution and temptation is noted throughout the entire Bible. The simple truth is that the Christian life requires a commitment, and that commitment requires endurance. Just as the choice to sin is ours, so is the choice to endure.

It seems kind of crazy to have to endure so much if we can never be totally satisfied, especially if it's never going to last, or never fully going to work out—at least not in this life. It really sounds like a lot of trouble, doesn't it? The Apostle Peter tells us why enduring is important in 2 Peter 1:3–11.

2 Peter 1:3–11

- Verse 3: "*His divine power has given us everything required for life and godliness through the knowledge of him who called us by His own glory and goodness.*"

   What Peter is telling us is that God has already given us everything we need to live a godly life. In fact, if you have the Holy Spirit in you, then you have all you need. In Him is where you can find and receive godly wisdom, knowledge, and discernment. These are qualities that are lacking in the unsaved, worldly person. Sure, they may have knowledge, but it is worldly knowledge, or they do not possess the wisdom to apply it. I do not know too many unsaved men who have discernment, for if they did they wouldn't be running headlong into sin.

- Verse 4: *"By these, He has given us very great and precious promises, so that through them you may share in the divine nature, escaping the corruption that is in the world because of evil desire."*

    These are the promises of abundant and eternal life. A life submitted **to** Christ, and a life that is found **in** Christ would experience abundance no matter what happens. We actually can be the recipients of abundant peace, joy, contentment, etc. Sharing in the divine nature refers to being a new creation in Christ, and to one day receiving a glorified body, finally escaping the corruption of both this world and of physical death, which comes with it.

- Verse 5: *"For this very reason, make every effort to supplement your faith with goodness, goodness with knowledge, knowledge with self control, self control with endurance, endurance with godliness, godliness with brotherly affection, and brotherly affection with love."*

    The command to "make every effort" is not a suggestion—you must give it all you've got. Add these fruits to your faith: self-control, endurance, and godliness are all listed next to each other because there is an important connection. The Christian commitment to endure comes from being founded on godliness and self-control. I believe godly endurance enables us to keep our eyes on a goal, and that goal is to live a life that glorifies God.

- Verse 8: *"For if you possess these qualities in increasing measure, they will keep you from being useless or unfaithful in the knowledge of our Lord Jesus Christ."*

    "If you possess these qualities in increasing measure" means choosing to express these spiritual qualities righteously and that is what causes them to increase in you. But this is certainly not accomplished through our own strength or abilities—it is done through the Holy Spirit in us. And Peter tells us that not having them

can make you useless or unfruitful in the knowledge of our Lord Jesus. For the committed Christian being "unfruitful" shouldn't even be seen as an option. These attributes of righteousness should be something that we are constantly seeking to own as we grow closer and closer to Jesus.

- Verses 9–10: *"The person who lacks these things is blind and shortsighted and has forgotten the cleansing from his past sins. Therefore, brothers and sisters, make every effort to confirm your calling and election, because if you do these things you will never stumble."*

    Lacking these spiritual qualities leads to spiritual blindness and can make a person unable to discern his spiritual condition. I believe I would rather lose my physical sight than to be shackled once again with spiritual blindness. When we ignore or refuse to pursue spiritual qualities, we can develop amnesia toward what was accomplished at the cross. How scary is that? Eternal security is a Holy Spirit–revealed fact, and the person who pursues these qualities is secure in their salvation and is producing fruit that confirms this. This Christian will also be less apt to stumbling into fear, despair, or doubt.

Peter closes out this important block of instruction with a promise from the Living God in verse 11: *"For in this way, entry into the eternal kingdom of our Lord and Savior Jesus Christ will be richly provided for you."*

Our lives have in fact been created for a purpose, but because of sin, each of us is only given a designated period of time to live—but that does not cancel our God-given purpose. The easiest way to make sense out of this is by understanding that we are all "on the clock," so to speak. Time is ticking away on the here and now, and this temporary season we know as life may be a lot closer to being over than we realize.

> *Your eyes saw me when I was formless; all my days were written in Your book and planned before a single one of them began.*
>
> —Ps. 139:16 CSB

God has our number of days laid out and sealed in heaven. In this life, we have an arrival date as well as a departure date, and those tickets have already been purchased. But despite what sin has done to us, God has both a preplanned journey and a mission for us that we must be sure not to miss. The truth is that His plan can be missed and already has been missed by millions since the beginning of time. Remember that our choices have no effect on God's plans, but they can certainly make our journey a lot harder than it has to be.

In fact, God knows us so intimately that He even knows when our choices will delay us as well as when we will stray from our true journey. And because He knows our stubbornness, I believe He has preplanned for each of us to learn how to endure, as well.

> *Lord, you have searched me and known me. You know when I sit down and when I stand up; you understand my thoughts from far away. You observe my travels and my rest; you are aware of all my ways. Before a word is on my tongue, you know all about it, Lord. You have encircled me; you have placed your hand on me. This wondrous knowledge is beyond me. It is lofty; I am unable to reach it.*
>
> —Ps. 139:1–6 CSB

Our "season of opportunity" to endure and live a life that gives God glory is upon us right now!

Q: Do you desire to deeply know the God who already knows you intimately in every way? Y/N _____

2 Timothy 2:3–13

- Verse 3: *Share in the suffering as a good soldier of Christ Jesus.*

    As a Christian, you are a holy soldier and are engaged in a daily spiritual battle. I believe that Paul calls us "a good soldier in Christ" because our commander (Jesus) who we are fighting for is righteous, and our cause is just, and this life is a good fight meant to be fought in faith. And we are not fighting this battle alone—we are called to help each other endure, and that means we share in their suffering and help others endure the hardships of life.

Consider Ecclesiastes 4:9–12: *"Two are better than one because they have a good reward for their efforts. For if either falls, his companion can lift him up; but pity the one who falls without another to lift him up. Also, if two lie down together, they can keep warm; but how can one person alone keep warm? And if someone overpowers one person, two can resist him. A cord of three strands is not easily broken"* (CSB).

Too many of us choose to go at this life alone. I don't know anyone who would want to die alone, so who would really want to live totally alone? Do you know why I believe this? Because the terrible loneliness that Jesus experienced on the cross was the worst ever, and that has always stuck out to me. I am certain that He does not want that for anyone.

How terrible it must have been for Him to experience abandonment from the Father, while He was dying on the cross. But the sin of the world was laid on Him, and God cannot have anything to do with sin, so He had to separate from Jesus. I believe that Jesus endured that loneliness so no one would ever have to.

This may be a controversial thing to say, and this is certainly a big statement: But I do not see rewards in heaven for the self-imposed loners, rogues, and isolationists. Here Solomon tells us that life in all circumstances is much better with companionship. Whether we like it or not, God made us to be "people persons." Remember that someone He sent to you loved you enough to share the gospel with you. The gospel does not spread if it is not shared with people by people.

- Verses 4–7: *"No one who is serving as a soldier gets entangled in the concerns of civilian life; he seeks to please the commanding officer. Also, if anyone competes as an athlete, he is not crowned unless he competes according to the rules. The hardworking farmer ought to be the first to get a share of the crops. Consider what I say, for the Lord will give you understanding in everything."*

A good soldier stays on mission, fights to stay focused, and avoids distractions. The athlete and the farmer both receive a reward for the hard work they put into the goals of their labor. No athlete or farmer will receive a reward without dedication to the hard work, and that dedication is bonded with endurance.

- Verses 8–9: "*Remember Jesus Christ, risen from the dead and descended from David, according to my gospel, for which I suffer to the point of being bound like a criminal. But the word of God is not bound.*"

  Paul commands that we remember Jesus as the perfect example of endurance in all forms. Paul also reminds us that even though he is in chains, the Word of God is never tied down or restrained. But even in chains Paul endured—the proof is found in the fact that seven of his 13 letters we have in the New Testament were written from prison. Now that is endurance!

- Verse 10: "*This is why I endure all things for the elect: so that they also may obtain salvation, which is in Christ Jesus, with eternal glory.*"

  No matter what, Paul is determined to endure so he can be an example for fellow believers.

- Verses 11–13. "*This saying is trustworthy: For if we died with him, we will also live with him; if we endure, we will also reign with him; if we deny him, he will also deny us; if we are faithless, he remains faithful, for he cannot deny himself.*"

  I love what Paul says here (my paraphrase): "If you believe anything I have said, then you can surely believe this—trust my words: Those of us who died with Him, well guess what, we are guaranteed to live with Him! But be warned: If we choose to deny Him, He will deny us. But even if we struggle in being faithful, He will remain faithful, because that is just who He is, and He cannot go against Himself."

It's time for Christian men and women to endure.

What Are We Called to Endure?

- Sin and our flesh
- All the trials and tribulations of this life
- Whatever God calls us to or assigns us to do
- Waiting, when we are called to wait

Q: How have you responded to what God has called you to endure?

_____

_____

Q: Or have you been picking and choosing only what you want to endure, or are you willing to endure no matter what He sets before you?

_____

_____

Why Are We Called to Endure?

- To live a life that first glorifies God
- To confirm or affirm our conversion and calling to the faith
- To produce godly fruits and works
- To encourage fellow believers
- Because we are commanded to

Q: Do you understand that an important reason why we endure is so we can express Christ likeness? Y/N _____

Q: When it has been time to endure, have you pushed back and asked God "why" too many times? Y/N _____

Q: Do you think God owes you an answer? Y/N _____

How Are We Called to Endure?

I have been crucified with Christ, and I no longer live, but Christ lives in me. The life I now live in the body, I live by faith in the Son of God, Who loved me and gave Himself for me.

—Gal. 2:20 CSB

By dying to self (Luke 9:23)

- By daily relying on the power of the Living God
- By daily seeking to grow in knowledge and faith
- Being mindful of forgiving others
- Being quick to repent
- With patience
- With joy

Blessed is the one who endures trials, because when he has stood the test he will receive the crown of life that God has promised to those who love him.

—James 1:12 CSB

The crown is for all believers, but is especially dear to those who endure sufferings, who bravely confront persecution for Jesus, even to the point of death. James tells us that this crown is for those who love God even in the flood, the storm, the sickness, or to the death.

Q: How do you express your love for God?

_____

_____

_____

_____

_____

Jesus says, *"If you love me, you will keep my commandments"* (John 14:15). How can we do this? The answer is so simple: By choosing to faithfully endure!

Chapter 36

You Have a Divine Appointment for a Fight

As we continue to dig deeper into the discipline of our calling as Christians, here is a question to think about: When was the last time you picked a fight? When was the last time you found the courage within you to stand up for what was right—for what you believe in, no matter what the cost? This is the very type of fight you have to pick every day **if** you truly want to follow Jesus.

I'm not talking about going out and hurting people, settling old scores, or even anything remotely resembling the type of violence that dwells in the hearts of evil people. The type of senseless aggression that exists in this fallen world is rooted in fear, and this is not what we are about—we do not accept it, nor do we empower it.

There are good fights, and there are bad ones, too. Mankind has primarily been fighting for the wrong reasons for a very long time.

We know that since the beginning of time, human history has recorded generation after generation fighting and killing each other for land, power, wealth, greed, and much more, and even much less. All worldly fighting has been at best only for temporary gains.

Today, blood continues to be spilled, the innocent continue to die, empty political promises and lies continue to be spewed, money and wealth continue to change hands, and borders continue to be moved or compromised. Sadly, no matter how "civilized" we think we have become, nothing has really changed.

But what I am talking about here, is fighting for something that has more value than anything temporary here on earth—and it's a fight I don't think we can avoid. I'm talking about the fight for your soul.

We War Not Against Flesh and Blood

The real fight I am calling you to today is for our eternity. The Bible tells us clearly that, *"though we walk in the flesh, we are not waging war according to the flesh. For the weapons of our warfare are not of the flesh but have divine power to destroy strongholds"* (2 Cor. 10:3–4).

The Apostle Paul is telling us here that the greater and more important battle goes beyond the physical realm of flesh and blood, concrete and stone and is in fact a spiritual one; it is a war that will most certainly have eternal consequences for all of us. Paul also tells us that even our weapons are not of this world, but are in fact divine, with the power to tear down and destroy mighty spiritual strongholds.

We all have strongholds in us that need to be torn down. Many of us have strongholds of addiction, lust, fear, greed, bitterness, jealousy, gossip, anger, even thoughts of murder and suicide. It is against these very strongholds and many more that the Lord Himself is calling us to stand up to and pick a fight; it's a fight for holiness, and without it we will not see God.

Are you ready, willing, and able to answer His call to arms?

Gearing Up for Battle

You can be certain that our Great God would never call His beloved saints to battle without equipping them with all we need to be victorious.

Let's take a look first at the call to battle and then one of the ways He has equipped us for victory—and it is guaranteed to be an eternal one, if we can just find the courage to endure and the faith to believe and trust Him. It begins here in Ephesians 6:10–20, which we will break down together.

In the Chapter 6 of his letter to the church at Ephesus, Paul proclaims the following, beginning in verses 10–11: *"Finally, be strong in the Lord and in the strength of his might. Put on the whole armor of God, that you may be able to stand against the schemes of the devil."*

Paul makes it very clear that we must rely completely on the strength of God's power and His great might (in Greek, "of one who has the strength of soul to sustain the attacks of Satan") as our requirement for victory; we must access this great power through trust and faith in Christ.

Along with that, there is never a time that it is safe to ignore, abandon, or compromise His biblical truth as Proverbs 28:9 tells us: *"If one turns away his ear from hearing the law, even his prayer is an abomination."*

It's clear that the power of His biblical truth is required for our victory. We must learn to lean on the Living Word, Jesus Christ. And remember, Jesus is the only way, the only truth, and the only life, and no one can come to the Father except through Him (John 14:6, my emphasis and addition of "only").

Knowing the Enemy

Continuing with Ephesians 6:12, Paul again reminds us who we are really dealing with as he explains, *"For we do not wrestle against flesh and blood, but against the rulers, against the authorities, against the cosmic powers over this present darkness, against the spiritual forces of evil in the heavenly places."*

Just as he had instructed the Corinthian church, he faithfully conveyed the same message to the Ephesians, making no excuses and not holding back anything regarding the identity, true nature, and characteristics of our enemy. If this scripture is frightening even to the believer, how much more so to the unbeliever who is not guaranteed the companionship and protection of the Holy Spirit!

It makes me very sad to consider the stubborn ignorance of the average nonbeliever, who walks around daily getting beat up by forces they cannot see or hear, let alone even possibly comprehend. We all have friends and loved ones who right now are living as zombies: They are nothing more than dead spirits being carried around in a dying body. Many of them are on the endless search for peace and contentment in this life, but apart from Christ, there is none to be found.

Even Jesus Himself made a point to identify the true fight (spiritual warfare), when He told us *"not to be afraid of those who can kill the body but cannot kill the soul. Rather, be afraid of the One who can destroy both body and soul in hell"* (Matt. 10:28 NIV).

The soul that searches for satisfaction only by way of the temporary things of this world will discover what it truly means to be afraid through the horrible pain of separation from God. His righteous punishment and an eternal death sentence are to be expected for all who choose to live a life of rebellion. The lost will then know the fear of the Living God and the power of His perfect justice. This is a sad truth, but it is the truth nonetheless, and it has to be said. The world has no problem lying to us about the open grave that is found at the end of the fleeting pleasures of this life, so we should have no problem laying out the truth about the terrible fate of a life that is to come for someone who has purposely lived for self.

Putting on the Uniform

In Ephesians 6:13–18, Paul describes in detail the armor of the Christian warrior and here's where the Lord requires us to go to work.

Verse 13 says, *"Therefore, take up the whole armor of God, that you may be able to withstand in the evil day, and having done all, to stand firm"* (NASB). Notice first that Paul says we must put on the **whole** armor of God— half or part of the uniform will not be sufficient enough to stand. The word *stand* is one we will lean on heavily in this exegesis (exegesis is the critical explanation or interpretation of a text). It is important for us to know that to "stand" is a requirement of the Christian warrior. But the Christian warrior must also understand that it is not possible to do so without submitting to God's supreme power and authority in order to do it.

Yet you must have courage to believe that in Christ you can stand, no matter what the enemy throws at you. *"I can do all things through Christ who strengthens me"* (Phil. 4:13 NKJV).

- Stand means to plant your feet firmly on the foundation of your faith which is built on the undeniable truth of Christ and who He is.
- Stand means to not waiver or buckle under pressure, because you are keeping your eyes fixed on King Jesus, *"the author and finisher of our faith,"* who *"because of the joy awaiting Him, He endured the*

cross, disregarding its shame. Now He is seated in the place of honor beside God's throne" (Heb. 12:2 NKJV).

Stand, my friends, and one day you will see His face and His place of glory with your own eyes. In Ephesians 6:14–15, Paul tells us once again that we must:

Stand therefore, having fastened on the belt of truth, and having put on the breastplate of righteousness, and, as shoes for your feet, having put on the readiness (in Greek, preparation, the act of preparing the condition of a person, to make ready), given by the gospel of peace.

Let's begin to examine the armor of God together. Here in these two verses Paul gives us the first of six pieces of the armor:

1. **The belt of truth**

    This was the first piece of protective armor a Roman soldier would put on, because it was designed to fit closely to the body as any good belt was designed to do. It might also include an armor-plated apron attached to it that was meant to protect very vulnerable parts of the body such as the lower abdomen and the groin.

    The belt would also surround and secure other pieces of the uniform, so they would not get in the way during battle. The belt here is meant to emphasize that we keep God's truth close while always being ready *"to preach the word of God. Be prepared in season and out of season* [in times of both convenience and inconvenience, in good times and in bad times]; *to correct, rebuke and encourage—with great patience and careful instruction"* (2 Tim. 4:2 NIV; amplified).

    The belt is the foundation of the armor, and it is formed and fashioned in the truth of the gospel.

    Q: Have you fastened the belt of God's perfect truth around you, securing all the areas of your life in the undeniable facts, which are recorded for us in the Bible? Y/N _____

    Q: Can you say that you trust and believe God's word completely? Y/N _____

Let's now look at the remaining pieces of the "whole armor of God" and break down their significance as well.

2. **The breastplate of righteousness (verse 14)**

   In Roman times, a breastplate was obviously worn to protect the vital organs such as the heart, lungs, and the organs of the upper abdomen. It was made in one of three ways:

   - As a solid piece of thin metal (about 1 mm thick) that would be shaped to the torso of the wearer.
   - Or it may have been made of several bands of metal connected by a series of leather straps.
   - As a type of chainmail that was made by linking small metal rings together until they formed a vest.

   Paul's reference to the breastplate was for a man to guard his heart by *"putting on"* the righteousness of Christ, who promises to protect those who truly love Him, for *"the Lord is faithful. He will establish you and guard you against the evil one"* (2 Thess. 3:3).

   In Proverbs 4:23, scripture also commands us to *"Guard your heart above all else, for it is the source of life"* (CSB).

   In the latter part of Isaiah 59, the Lord speaks through the prophet telling of judgment and redemption coming through the Messiah, and He would come with a breastplate of righteousness on His chest and a helmet of salvation on His head (verses 16–21)!

   To truly desire to live like Christ will naturally cover you with a breastplate of His righteousness!

   Q: What does righteousness mean to you?

   _____

   Q: Are you conscious about protecting your heart? Y/N _____

3. **Feet prepared with the Gospel of Peace (verse 15)**

   Roman soldiers wore thick leather shoes and boots that had nails in the soles of them to help the soldiers grip the ground well in combat.

   Likewise, the gospel of peace is the good news of Jesus Christ, and the man or woman who has their feet prepared with the gospel of peace will be able to stand firm and not slip in the times of trial and will not be prone to run to trouble.

"Therefore my beloved brothers, be steadfast, immovable, always abounding in the work of the Lord, knowing that in the Lord your labor is not in vain" (1 Cor. 15:58).

And let's not forget this beautiful encouragement to the church at Thessalonica: *"For now we live, if you are standing fast in the Lord"* (1 Thess. 3:8).

Q: Are you known as a peacemaker and peace giver, or are you a war maker and peace taker?

Now we move on to verse 16, where we find another critical piece of the armor.

4. **The shield of faith**

"In all circumstances take up the shield of faith, with which you can extinguish all the flaming darts of the evil one."

The Roman soldier was known for his large, imposing shield, which generally was reported to be about 2.5 ft. by 4.5 ft., weighing 18–20 pounds; it was able to protect his entire body. The shield was both an offensive and defensive weapon as well as an instrument used to carry wounded fellow soldiers from the battlefield.

Notice that the Bible says, "in all circumstances"—a good Roman soldier would not get caught without his shield while on the field of battle; likewise, no soldier for Christ should be caught without his or hers, either! That means that whatever comes against us in this life must be met head-on first and foremost by our "shield" of faith.

It is obvious how the shield can be likened to our faith, and how its attributes are as necessary to our faith as its many uses were essential to the welfare of the Roman soldier.

The definition of our faith can be described as a basic and unshakable trust in God, and our continual trust in God's Word despite the circumstances; faith is necessary to "shield" us from all types of temptation (flaming darts) and sin.

In Psalm 91:1–2 David tells us, *"He who dwells in the shelter of the Most High will abide in the shadow of the Almighty. I will say to the* Lord, *my refuge and my fortress, my God, in whom I trust."*

But our faith can be an offensive weapon too, as we are called to be true and bold witnesses to the gospel, no matter what the situation or the cost. In Luke 9:23, Jesus clearly defines the requirements for being a disciple (as first denying yourself and then picking up your cross daily); this is not an easy task to do and most certainly requires faith.

In fact, in Luke 9:24 Jesus says it may even cost you your life to follow Him, but only a life to be lost in this world, with a promise of a new and eternal one, to those who are faithful: *"For whoever would save his life will lose it, but whoever loses his life for my sake will save it."*

Q: Are you prepared to go on the offense for the cause of the cross? Y/N _____

Q: Are you prepared to lay seed for the gospel that one day may require you to lay down your life? Y/N _____

Q: In order for our faith to "shield" us in times of need, we must care for it through proper daily maintenance of prayer and Bible study: What does your daily routine look like, and what condition would you say your "shield" is in? Is it battle-worthy?

_____

_____

_____

_____

_____

5. **The helmet of salvation (verse 17)**

   "And take up the helmet of salvation, and the sword of the Spirit, which is the Word of God."

   The Roman soldier's helmet was usually made from a combination of metals; it weighed somewhere between 6 and 8 pounds! Now, that is a heavy piece of equipment! Having been a soldier myself, I cannot imagine having to wear something that heavy on my head. The average Kevlar helmet that a US soldier wears today weighs just under three pounds, and we think that is too much!

Obviously, the helmet was designed to protect the head, which has always been a major target in all forms of combat, whether it be close quarters combat during the times of the Romans, or the target of a headshot from a distant sniper hidden far away today.

Just as the metal helmet was designed to protect its wearer's head from the enemy's blows, the spiritual helmet protects the Christian from the enemy's attempt to strike a blow that could "steal away" the assurance of salvation from the believer.

In the military, I learned that my mind would always quit before my body would, so it was important to protect my mind. Satan and his minions know this, too!

I believe that the peace that God gives to a person who is secure in their salvation is like a bulletproof helmet that protects us from the lies of the devil. The devil desires that we waver in that security, and his plan is to eventually strip us of our faith in all of God's promises. We can keep salvation "close" to us, so to speak, by regularly renewing our mind.

We need to discipline ourselves to seek protection by renewing the mind (Romans 12:2) daily, even hourly, even moment by moment—as much as is needed or required in order to stay faithful.

Putting on the helmet of salvation is as much like us filling our mind and heart with God's Word as it is allowing His Holy Spirit to intercede for us by trusting Him, for it is written, *"Therefore He is able to save completely those who come to God through Him (Jesus), because He always lives to intercede for them"* (Heb. 7:25 NIV).

Q: Christ would never save you and then just let you go: The assurance of salvation is critical to our overall spiritual health. Are you secure in yours? Explain.

_____

_____

And the peace of God, which surpasses all understanding, will guard your hearts and your minds in Christ Jesus.

—Phil. 4:7

Q: Can you say right now that you are safe from a headshot? Is the metal of your helmet being reinforced by the daily renewing of your mind? Explain.

_____

_____

_____

_____

The final piece of our armor is known as the sword of the Spirit.

6. The sword of the Spirit

Just like our shield, the sword of the Spirit requires a similar discipline. The Roman soldier's sword was a little more than two feet long and made of pure iron; it was feared across the civilized world because every nation that fell to Rome bled by its blade. Known as the "short sword," the "civilized" world would never be the same because of it.

But as daunting as this man-made "Roman ambassador" was, it will always pale in comparison to the one true "rapier" that is *"Sharper than any double-edged sword, it penetrates even to dividing soul and spirit, joints and marrow; it judges the thoughts and attitudes of the heart"* (Hebrews 4:12 NIV). I'm talking about the Holy Sword of the Spirit, and it's a weapon that no true Christian warrior can fight without.

The sword of the Spirit is not only the gospel (the Good News of our Savior), but it is also the Bible, the Holy Word of God, which no one, not even the fallen ones, can stand against. Christ used the sword (the Holy Word of God) to rebuke the devil when He was tempted in the desert in Matthew 4:1–10, 11. Satan left Jesus because he was unable to overcome the Holy Word of God.

It is up to us to seek to truly know the Word of God and take it into our hearts deeply, while at the same time seeking to master its wisdom, so we can effectively wield this sword, as sharp as it is, in an obedient and precise manner. The amazing thing about the Sword of the Spirit is that the more you know it, the easier it is to use, both on the offensive as well as on the defensive.

Q: Are you seeking to be a master swordsman? Are you using God's Word to lift others up and proclaim the good news to the lost? Explain.

Q: Is there one verse in particular that you feel has shaped your life or that you draw a lot of inspiration from? Write the verse out here and explain how/why it has had an impact on you:

Activity

Now agree to memorize two more verses that you love.

Finally, in Ephesians 6:18–20 the Apostle Paul almost pleads with us to be *"praying at all times in the Spirit, with all prayer and supplication,"* continuing with the same tone of seriousness as he spoke in his detailed description of the whole armor of God.

My dear friends, I hope you realize that this is not a joke or matter to be taken lightly. The armor of God is not merely a metaphor, or some sort of symbolic representation—it is real "equipment," which is critical to the health and welfare of our spiritual lives. Paul wrote this letter to Ephesus while in prison in Rome, and I firmly believe that he meant every word of it.

Even while in chains, he urged us *"to keep alert with all perseverance, making supplication for all the saints,"* and also for asked for prayer for himself, *"that words may be given"* to him to *"boldly proclaim the mystery of the gospel"* because he knew his work was not yet done.

The Apostle Paul, who in the next verse refers to himself *"as an ambassador in chains,"* was always ready to pick another righteous fight, because he was a true Christian warrior.

The next question is, are you ready to put on the whole armor of God, and pick a righteous fight? If you consider yourself a true Christian, and I hope you are, I'm certain a fight has already been divinely appointed for you.

You have all the true weapons of war—the whole Armor of God. Now suit up and join the fight!

Q: What are you fighting for or against today?

_____

_____

Q: Are you fighting for holiness in your life, or for something else more selfish?

_____

_____

Q: Do you truly know who your real enemy is? I guarantee that he most certainly knows you!

_____

_____

Q: Who or what are you taking a stand for today?

_____

_____

Q: Are you standing for the Living God, or are you just concerned about standing for you?

_____

_____

Chapter 37

Sex and the Gospel

It's time for some straightforward talk about sex and what the Bible has to say about it. Sadly, few people possess a biblical perspective of sex and therefore, most fail to honor God in how sex is supposed to be viewed, accepted, and expressed.

What most Christians miss is that sex is a gift from God, and it is designed to bless not only the expression of love from man to woman but to also draw them both closer to God. Since sex is meant to only be experienced in the covenant of marriage, it is holy and can also be seen as an act of worship. In a godly, healthy marriage, sex is viewed as "another component" of the marriage covenant, not the only component. God designed the marriage covenant to build "oneness" between a man and a woman in every way. The Bible confirms this in Genesis 2:24: *"This is why a man leaves his father and mother and bonds with his wife, and they become one flesh"* (CSB).

This means that a marriage in the proper alignment with God will also include a strong and growing friendship, a healthy parenting partnership, and a oneness in every other area of a human relationship. No relationship can exist and stay healthy on sex alone: God did not design it that way. One of the many beautiful truths of marriage is that a couple's sexual relationship can be enhanced as the marriage progresses if the friendship component and the spiritual connection to God are healthy and thriving. The more a couple grows in their faithful dedication together in Jesus, the more God will bless the marriage as a whole.

We need to cover three main points today:

1. The biblical definition of sex.
2. What God says about sex.
3. Why His commands about sex are so important.

As we proceed throughout our study, here is one thing that I want us to continue to be mindful of, as it will really help us to keep topics like this in the proper perspective:

> *And whatever you do, in word or in deed, do everything in the name of the Lord Jesus, giving thanks to God the Father through Him.*
>
> Col. 3:17 CSB

We were all created for one primary purpose, and that is to live a life that gives God glory. That means we must honor him with our sex life also. In our counseling sessions, we get a lot of questions about sex, and they are usually the same questions regardless of age or gender:

- "Is sex dirty? Why do I like it so much?"
- "My wife has to have sex with me, right? She has to submit to me."
- "Is porn OK in marriage as long as we look at it together?"
- "Isn't sex my right as a person?"
- "Isn't my sex life my own business?"

We will get around to answering these questions soon, but first, let's look at some numbers. As of 2016, here are some startling statistics:[1]

- In the US, 19.7 million new sexually transmitted infections occur each year.
- More than half of all people will have an STD/STI at some point in their lifetime.
- Each year, 1 out of every 4 teens contracts an STD/STI.

- By the age of 25, 1 in 2 sexually active persons will contract an STD/STI.
- In the US, 50 million adults currently have genital herpes. Up to 776,000 new infections occur each year. By 2025 40 percent of all men and half of all women could be infected.
- In the US, 1 out of 20 people will be infected with Hepatitis B at some time in their lives, and half of those instances will have been transmitted sexually.
- An average of 50,000 new cases of AIDs occur each year in the US, and more than 1.2 million cases already exist in the US.
- STDs among adults in the 45–65 age range is skyrocketing (tripling over the last decade), with steady increases in the 19–24 and 25–34 age ranges. Medicine, people living longer, divorce, online hookups, etc.
- In the US, over 600,000 abortions are performed each year: This averages out to about 180 abortions to each live birth. (average of 85% are unmarried sex without commitment or consequences)

My friends, please understand that these statistics are the consequences when we engage in sex outside the marriage covenant.

Biblical Definition of Sex

Sex is a gift from God that is designed by Him to only be experienced by a man and a woman through the covenant of marriage. He gave it to us as a means of glorifying him as we fulfill its design through procreation (Genesis 1:28).

It is a critical component to intimacy, comfort, and companionship (a special bond and friendship that just does not develop without Jesus), and physical pleasure, which we see beautifully expressed throughout Song of Solomon.

And **yes**, the physical pleasure part of sex is important to God or else it would not be part of the covenant.

- Sex is an act of worship. Sex is as much spiritual as it is physical. We will expand on this point shortly.

- Sex is only meant for, and can only properly be expressed before God, in the marriage covenant. Hebrews 13:4 says, *"Marriage should be honored by all, and the marriage bed kept pure, for God will judge the adulterer and all the sexually immoral"* (NIV).
- **All** sex outside marriage is sin (Fornication).

What God Says about Sex

Sex is designed **only** for the married man and the married woman: *"But because of the temptation to sexual immorality, each man should have his own wife, and each woman should have her own husband"* (1 Cor. 7:2). Later in this chapter, the Apostle Paul says that it is better to marry than to burn in your lust and lack of self-control. It is a fact that very few people can fend off lust, especially apart from Christ.

God hates sexual immorality. This word comes from the Greek word *porneia* where we get the English word *pornography*, which stems from the concept of "selling off" as in the "selling off of our sexual purity." We can include fornication (sex outside marriage), whoredom, idolatry, adultery, and homosexuality, as all are sexually immoral acts before God and clearly against His commandments. It is fact that 8 out of 10 men in church admit they have a porn problem, and the other 2 are liars!

Q: The Bible says that our bodies are temples of the Holy Spirit, and that He lives in us. When we choose to look at porn, do we then invite Him to join us?

That is kind of a trick question. but it is meant to make you think about who we are supposed to be when we call ourselves a Christian.

> *Do you not know that your bodies are members of Christ? Shall I then take the members of Christ and make them members of a prostitute? Never! Or do you not know that he who is joined to a prostitute becomes one body with her? For, as it is written, "The two will become one flesh."*
>
> —1 Cor. 6:15–20

Once again, sex is meant only for the marriage covenant and its members: Jesus, husband, and wife, and it must not be defiled by unholy lusts.

> *But he who is joined to the Lord becomes one spirit with Him. Flee from sexual immorality* [run from it—computers, TV, movies, etc.]. *Every other sin a person commits is outside the body, but the sexually immoral person sins against his own body. Or do you not know that your body is a temple of the Holy Spirit within you, whom you have from God? You are not your own, for you were bought with a price. So glorify God in your body.*
>
> —1 Cor. 6:17–20 (amplified)

I find it interesting that God tells us in James 4:7 to *"Therefore, submit to God. Resist the devil, and he will flee from you"* (CSB), but God tells here in 1 Corinthians 6:18 and also in 2 Timothy 2:22 to flee from youthful lusts. This should give us a great indicator of just how strong sexual sin can be.

Sexual sin is the only sin we commit against all involved—God, self, and others. We must understand that our bodies are **not** ours to do with as we please: *"You are not your own, for you were bought at a price. So glorify God with your body"* (1 Cor. 6:19b–20).

Our bodies belong to God as scripture so says. In fact, every part of you—body, mind, and spirit—was purchased with the most expensive and valuable currency ever—the blood of Jesus Christ! My friend, I promise you we all will be held accountable for how we have taken care of our body.

Sex in marriage requires mutual submission to God first, and then to each other:

> *I appeal to you therefore, brothers, by the mercies of God, [by realizing the great mercies we have received] to present your bodies as a living sacrifice, holy and acceptable to God, which is your spiritual worship.*
>
> —Rom. 12:1–2

Remember that sex is an act of spiritual worship, a gift given to us from God, and sanctioned **only** for the marriage bed, or the marriage living room, etc. Therefore:

> *Do not be conformed to this world* [we can clearly see through the statistics mentioned earlier that there are tremendous consequences for "conforming to the world's way" or doing sex "your way": the results can be disease, death, and even separation from God], *but be transformed by the renewal of your mind, that by testing you may discern what is the will of God, what is good and acceptable and perfect.*
>
> —Rom. 12:2 (amplified)

God has promised that through the knowledge of scripture, He will reveal to you what is truly good. Here's a verse I still use regularly when I need to renew my mind: *"I have made a covenant [agreement] with my eyes; How then could I gaze [lustfully] at a virgin [or beautiful woman]?* (Job 31:1 AMP) Let's recap what was just said above:

- Submitting your bodies in obedience to God during sex is an act of spiritual worship.
- Do not conform to the world's standards for sex; they bring separation from God, disease, and death.
- Be able to renew your mind through the memorization of scripture.

Here's something else from God that ensures the freedom we need with each other in marriage:

> *For the wife does not have authority over her own body, but the husband does. Likewise the husband does not have authority over his own body, but the wife does. Do not deprive one another, except perhaps by agreement for a limited time, that you may devote yourselves to prayer; but then come together again, so that Satan may not tempt you because of your lack of self-control.*
>
> —1 Cor. 7:4–5

Now, you may have just read this and said to yourself, "Wait a minute, Pastor Mike. I don't see anything about freedom here!" Well, here's how this works: Neither the husband nor the wife holds the exclusive rights to their body. Instead, God wants them to give themselves freely to one another! And we are not to withhold sex as some sort of punishment or tactic to manipulate.

Instead, God teaches us another example of the beautiful act of mutual submission. And then Paul says this: The only time God wants us to put sex on hold is specifically for a time of prayer and fasting. An "intermission" in your marriage like this will keep you focused on Christ and will actually deepen and strengthen your intimacy. Of course, if one partner is ill or exhausted, the other should understand. Remember that God wants mutual submission. It is supposed to be both a joy and a pleasure for a married couple to give themselves freely to one another.

Why Honoring God's Commandments Regarding Sex Is Important to Him

Sex was designed as a gift from God and meant only for the marriage covenant; "one flesh" signifies the unifying of not only our bodies but of our hearts and lives. The act of becoming one creates a new entity—a family.

Genesis 2:24 says, *"Therefore a man shall leave his father and his mother and hold fast to his wife, and they shall become one flesh."* This idea is repeated in Hebrews 13:4. Notice that Genesis 2:24 does not say anything about children, brothers, sisters, or mothers-in-law. The family is first created when the man and the woman consummate the marriage through sex.

God's commandments regarding sex are for our benefit and protection. Not only do we get the gift of sexual intimacy, but by honoring it, we are not subject to the consequences—separation, disease, and death.

As a pastor I get this question a lot: "What's the big deal? Why do we have to wait for marriage to have sex?"

> *Put to death therefore what is earthly in you: sexual immorality, impurity, passion, evil desire, and covetousness, which is idolatry. On account of these the wrath of God is coming. In these you too once walked, when you were living in them.*
>
> —Col. 3:5–7

My friend, to God it is a big deal because our way is not holy. Our ways outside the commandments of God are **all** sinful. All they can offer

341

is some temporary satisfaction at the risk of a lifetime of separation from the Living God. Separation from God means that those who end up that way find themselves in hell. And what about the suffering sexual sin can produce in our lives now? The consequences of some sexual sin have no cure physically at this time (AIDs and herpes, for example). That could end up being a wound you carry for the rest of your natural life.

God does not want us to treat people the way we shop for shoes: going out and trying on several different pairs of shoes until we find the ones we think we like. Eventually, we throw them away and go out in search of a new pair. We are not to use people like that. Imagine what would happen if we simply honored God with our sex lives and submitted them to His commandments: We would be so free, and so, so blessed! Sexually transmitted diseases would eventually vanish from the face of the earth if we could just honor, respect, and be obedient to God's laws. One partner for each person for life would guarantee that—that's God's promise.

> Now the works of the flesh are evident: sexual immorality, impurity, sensuality, idolatry, sorcery, enmity, strife, jealousy, fits of anger, rivalries, dissensions, divisions, envy, drunkenness, orgies, and things like these. I warn you, as I warned you before, that those who do such things will not inherit the kingdom of God.
>
> —Gal. 5:19–21

Activity

This might be hard to do but it is necessary. Take a spiritual inventory of your sex life so far. You may or may not want to write some things down. If you decide to, I suggest that you keep it private between you and God.

As I have said before, writing things down with our own hand tends to make them more real. We need to understand how real and really hurtful our sexual sin actually is to God. He is always the first casualty of every sin we commit. Write a prayer of repentance to God. Make sure it contains these five things:

- Confession.
- Repentance.
- Praise.

- Thanksgiving.
- Commitment to righteousness.

Q: Have you honored God with your body? Y/N _____

Q: Have you met with God personally and confessed all impure thoughts and acts? Y/N _____

Q: Have you taken the necessary steps to ensure that you are able to pursue purity? Y/N _____

Explain (e.g., removed all access to porn, etc.)

_____

_____

_____

Q: What is the greatest struggle you are having right now with your flesh?

_____

_____

_____

God wants you to know that even if you have a past that is stained by sexual sin and even if you are caught up in it right now, the gospel of Jesus Christ is fully forgiving and completely healing. God can and will set you free and restore you to Him. All we have to do is sincerely seek Him.

The Lord invites us graciously in Isaiah 1:18: "*Come now, let us reason together, says the LORD: though your sins are like scarlet, they shall be as white as snow; though they are red like crimson, they shall become like wool.*" What I love the most about this passage is that it's as if God comes to us and says, "Let's talk this over. We can work it out together. I can do that for you."

First John 1:9 speaks of repentance and forgiveness, and **if** we confess our sins, we are made new through God's forgiveness. The Greek word for repentance, *metanoya*, is where we get the word *metamorphosis*. This means there can be a real transformation. Sincere confession and repentance can and will change your heart and the entire direction of your life—and that "turn" will be toward Jesus. If you follow Him, He will surely lead you home.

Christian counseling is an extremely effective tool that can help you in your battle against your flesh. It can be a great strength builder and source of accountability. Have you considered seeking counseling at all? Y/N _____

Finally, in the gospel of Jesus Christ is found all the true freedom we will ever need. Let the Good News of Jesus change your life. The gospel is:

- A full reflection of God's love.
- Fully redemptive.
- The way of salvation.
- Totally merciful.
- Fulfillment of God's plan.
- Timeless.
- Life-changing.
- The best news you will ever hear.
- The source of true freedom.
- Very personal.
- The perfect truth.
- Completely caring.
- A road map to eternity.

Chapter 38

Fifteen Straightforward Questions about Your Marriage

Marriage is a holy covenant ordained by God, and it is designed to be recognized and received as a cherished and valuable gift, and it must be lived out in a way that gives glory to God.

Your marriage will require a lifetime of work, sacrifice, and commitment. You will not be able to lead, protect, or honor your marriage if you try to do it apart from Christ: It is His creation, and He must be the key ingredient in it.

As you approach these questions, please be honest with yourself, so you will be able to clearly identify the areas where you are lacking. When you are finished, ask God for guidance and help so you can live them out in your marriage.

1. Start by asking yourself this question: Why should my husband/wife be in love with me?

———————————————————————————

———————————————————————————

———————————————————————————

2. Should your marriage be only about your happiness, or should it be about our happiness? Please explain.

_____

_____

_____

3. What do you think your husband/wife wants from you?

_____

_____

_____

4. What do you think your husband/wife needs from you the most?

_____

_____

_____

5. What is the main thing (or one thing) that you know is a problem, but you do your best to avoid approaching it or discussing it?

_____

_____

_____

6. Do you (still) make promises you do not intend (or never intended) to keep? Please explain.

_____

_____

_____

_____

_____

7. How have your empty promises hurt your husband/wife? Your marriage?

_____

_____

_____

8. How would you define a "Christ-centered friendship?"

_____

_____

_____

9. Do you desire to have a "Christ-centered friendship" in your marriage? If yes, what will that take? If no, why not?

_____

_____

_____

10. Are you aware and mindful of all the "little things" he/she needs from you?

_____

11. Have you taken notice of any/all of the little things he/she already does for you and your family? Do you thank him/her regularly? Do you thank him/her at all?

_____

_____

_____

12. Do you pray over your husband/wife regularly? At all?

_____

_____

13. Are you as dedicated to being a servant to your husband/wife as you are committed to being his/her lover?

_____

_____

_____

14. Do you consider your family the primary ministry in your life? Why or why not?

_____

_____

_____

15. Have you dedicated your life to daily prayer and relationship with God through His Holy Word?

_____

_____

_____

"Christ-centered friendship": A Christ-centered friendship can be defined as an essential commitment in a marriage that will require submission by both parties in order that as each individual relationship grows in Christ, so does the marriage. It essentially puts the marriage in a constant "work in process" state, with Jesus as its "Master Builder."

Scripture References: Ephesians 4:17–32, 5:22–33; 1 Peter 3:1–7; 1 Corinthians 7

Chapter 39

Divorce and the Gospel

Today, we will look at the very controversial and often debated topic of divorce and what the gospel of Jesus Christ has to say about it.

To say that divorce is not a pleasant thing is most certainly an understatement. After all, it is by definition "the legal dissolution of a marriage." But divorce is unfortunately a lot more than a marriage just ceasing to exist. Divorce is probably the most destructive force to ever come upon the family: both the short-term and long-term effects can change the hearts and minds of all involved—most likely for their entire lifetime. I believe that when a marriage is only viewed as something created by men, built up by men, or sustained by men, then you can expect it to eventually fail. Simply stated, divorce is what happens when God has been removed from the picture. Let me ask you this: What gives us the right to try to have any authority over what God has created? Mankind's ignorant and prideful boldness has messed up a lot of things that were given to us by God as a gift and a blessing—and in my opinion marriage is at the top of this list.

Even Christians today are running to the divorce lawyers in record numbers. It seems that the very vows that each believer willfully took before God and a crowd of witnesses didn't really matter or mean what they originally said they did. Today, marriage is too often treated like getting a meal in the drive-thru line at a fast-food restaurant with a mistake in it. Because you didn't want pickles, you send the entire meal back. Does that sound right? No, remove the pickles.

In other words, fight for your marriage. Fight for it first out of love and honor for God and then for each other. No one marries the perfect person because they do not exist. Believe it or not, God wants to use your spouse to help change you, so that means that you are not the one who is perfect, and neither is your spouse. This also means that you do the necessary things prior to getting married to help ensure that marriage is the right step and with the right person. Here's a few recommendations I have added from what I personally include in counseling when someone comes to me to asks about marriage:

1. Seek out premarital counseling.
2. Stay in relationship with Jesus: Be devoted to personal Bible study, prayer, and worship. Trust that God has the best in mind for you. This also means you must be okay with waiting for His timing.
3. Stay sexually pure and honor God with your body.
4. Date to mate: This means that "playing the field" is not an option.
5. Only pursue someone who is like-minded in the faith with you. Unequally yoked couples do not last.

Now let's take a look at some stats on divorce—where the reality of it all comes into view.

Statistics on Divorce

- The US national average of divorce averages roughly about half.[1]
- 67% of second marriages end in divorce.
- 74% of third marriages end in divorce.
- 42 million Americans have been married more than once.
- The US has the sixth highest divorce rate in the world (Russia is #1).[2]
- There are nine divorces in the time it takes for a couple to recite their wedding vows (two minutes).
- Forty-three percent of children in the United States are being raised without their fathers.

- It is estimated that divorce rates in 2020 climbed to a new high due to COVID-19, but true numbers will not be known until sometime in late 2021.
- "A staggering 81 percent of divorce lawyers routinely use social media evidence in divorce cases, most particularly: a spouse's actual social media communications, the time and place of those communications, and the person's state of mind while on social media. This means that if you have been carrying on an online affair with an old flame—or anyone else for that matter—the social media evidence of that online affair may be presented in court during your divorce."[3]
- Is Facebook, Twitter, Instagram a threat to your marriage? The answer is yes!
- "If you're an evangelical Christian adult who has been married, there's a 26 percent likelihood that you've been divorced—compared to a 28 percent chance for Catholics and a 38 percent chance for non-Christians."[4]

Sampling of Quotes on Divorce

Quotes like the following reflect what the world thinks about divorce:
- "Divorce is the start point for a brand-new life. Don't lose the chance to redesign it upon your dreams."—Rossana Condoleo[5]
- "Divorce isn't such a tragedy. A tragedy is staying in an unhappy marriage, teaching your children the wrong things about love. Nobody ever died of divorce."—Jennifer Weiner[6]
- Here's a thought—instead, how about teaching your children how to fight for what is valuable; how about teaching forgiveness, compromise, and unconditional love?
- "Ah yes, divorce . . . from the Latin word meaning to rip out a man's genitals through his wallet."—Robin Williams[7]
- "Marriage is grand. Divorce is twenty grand."—Jay Leno[8]
  "Stephen Hawking is getting a divorce. That's scary. If the smartest guy in the world can't figure out women, we're screwed."—Jay Leno
- *If Marriage Means You Fell in Love, Does Divorce Mean to Climb Out?*

This is a title of a book currently on sale on Amazon; the blurb below describes how this book is intended to be used:

"This funny divorce Planner or Journal is the ideal gift for People who were divorced or plan to do a divorce. Great for Ex-Wives or Ex-Husbands to, sketch, write memories and thoughts take notes or doodle of their new Life. This journal can also be useful to write down your good or bad memories or just to plan your new life."[9]

What truly makes me sad is how our society has trivialized divorce. It's almost as common an experience as going to the dentist for an unattended sore tooth—neither one is something you would look forward to, but both probably happen more than they should.

Marriage Is a Covenant, Not a Contract

- **Contract:** A contract is a legally binding agreement between two or more parties with specific terms in which there is a promise to do something in return for a valuable benefit. Of course, a contract will also specify what will happen if either party does not uphold their part of the agreement. So, if you do this or don't do that, then I can do this or that. For example, buying a car is done on a contract.
- **Covenant:** In strong contrast to contracts, a covenant is a binding agreement between two parties where both parties (God and man) agree to uphold their end of the agreement regardless of what the other party does or does not do. God is the creator of marriage. Marriage is the one earthly relationship that most closely resembles the covenant God has with His people. God is a God of covenant, and the Bible is a covenant document. "Testament" is actually Latin for covenant; the Old and New Testaments are Old and New Covenants.

What Does God Say about Marriage and Divorce?

And Pharisees came up to him and tested him by asking, "Is it lawful to divorce one's wife for any cause?" He answered, "Have you not read that He who created them from the beginning made them male and female, and said, 'Therefore a man shall leave his father and his mother and hold fast to his wife, and the two shall become one flesh'? So they are no longer two but one flesh. What therefore God has joined together, let not man separate." They said to him, "Why then did Moses command one to give a certificate of divorce and to send her away?" He said to them, "Because of your hardness of heart Moses allowed you to divorce your wives, but from the beginning it was not so. And I say to you: whoever divorces his wife, except for sexual immorality, and marries another, commits adultery."

—Matthew 19:3–9

The Old Testament allowed divorce because of the *"hardness of their hearts."* (See Deut. 24:1–4.) First Corinthians 7:39 says, *"A wife is bound to her husband as long as he lives."* I don't see this statement as being conditional. Remember this is not a contract. God's Word makes it so simple. My friends, please study scripture; you will find the answers to everything you need if you do!

Scripture says that divorce was never in God's plan. Divorce is a result of the hard and selfish hearts of men:

- Deuteronomy 24:1–4 – divorce on the grounds of adultery.
- 1 Corinthians 7:13–15 – divorce on the grounds of abandonment.

Wherever scripture **allows** for divorce; understand that it is **not** a **command** for divorce.

For the man who does not love his wife but divorces her, says the Lord, the God of Israel, <u>covers his garment with violence</u>, says the Lord of hosts. So guard yourselves in your spirit, and do not be faithless."

—Mal. 2:16

Here's some strong language from the book of Malachi: This passage can be understood in two ways and often is. First, that God truly hates divorce. Second, God sees this unwarranted divorce as a gross act of sin likened to blood being splattered from a murder victim back onto the killer, leaving evidence of this evil deed on him personally.

If this is how God feels, and the Bible says He does, **then** our views on divorce and marriage **must** come from Scripture, not from the opinions or laws of men, not social change, or not even from personal or family circumstances.

> *You have wearied the Lord with your words. But you say, "How have we wearied him?" By saying, "Everyone who does evil is good in the sight of the Lord, and he delights in them." Or by asking, "Where is the God of justice?"*
>
> — Mal. 2:17

The people had become callous and lacked spiritual discernment, persisting in cynical expressions of innocence and rejecting all intention of taking right and wrong seriously. The bottom line is that God does not delight in evil, in sin—ever!

We saw in Matthew 19 that not only were the Pharisees looking for a way to trip Jesus up with the question on divorce, but they were also looking for loopholes. Christian, stop looking for loopholes; stop looking for a way out of your marriage or a way around what God created it to be. Instead, cry out to God for a way to save your marriage!

Once again, we can find some practical/biblical help. Christ must be the center or the "lynchpin" of your marriage. "The Jesus pin" is what military aviators refer to as that critical pin that holds the rotor blades of the helicopter in place. This pin is one of the first things checked preflight. You obviously would not want the rotor blades coming off in midflight! Make Jesus the "lynchpin" of your marriage!

- Don't be unequally yoked.
- Strive to be the servant in your marriage, not the served.
- Always be quick to repent and ready to forgive.
- Stay in church and get connected to a biblical community now.
- Seek out counseling help.
- Communicate with your spouse and regularly discuss the state of your marriage.
- Pray for your spouse daily.

Why Is Marriage Such a Big Deal to God?

Marriage is a covenant not a contract, and God expects us to do our part. Remember that after the fall of Adam and Eve in the Garden, God had every right to take the marriage covenant away from us, but He chose not to! Even in our sin, He wanted us to be able to experience the most unique of all relationships.

Genesis 2:18: *Then the Lord God said, "It is not good that the man should be alone; I will make him a helper fit for him."* And we know that the helper God was referring to was the woman. Each of us have a specified role to fulfill and a part to play in the marriage covenant.

Marriage is a covenant created by Jesus, and it meant to be a dim reflection of the relationship shared between the Holy Trinity (man, woman, Jesus). It is also a reflection of Jesus's covenant relationship with His bride, the church (see Ephesians 5). Genesis 2:24 says, *"Therefore a man shall leave his father and his mother and hold fast to his wife, and they shall become one flesh."*

God purposely and specifically uses marriage language to describe His love relationship with His people. This is beautifully on display in the story of Hosea. God uses the life of the Prophet Hosea and his extremely troubled marriage as a symbol of how He forgives. Even though Hosea's wife committed multiple acts of adultery against him, Hosea took her back every time. And this was the same with the people of Israel: Even though they committed multiple acts of spiritual adultery against the Living God, He graciously took them back. This is how God expects us to forgive. Remember:

- God is **always** faithful in His relationship with us.
- God will **always** fulfill His covenant promises with us.
- The gospel empowers us to love the way He does, and His love is always about reconciliation.

Chapter 40

Worry versus Burden

A friend asked me recently what the difference was between a worry and a burden. I thought it was such an excellent and timely question, especially since I regularly encounter so many people in our church family, through counseling and in our community group, who are experiencing a lot of both. So, I dug into a book I consult time and again to help me get prepared for this important conversation. The book is called, *Handle with Prayer: Unwrap the Source of God's Strength for Living* by Pastor Charles Stanley.[1]

In my mind, it's one thing to have to deal with the trials of life, which is hard in and of itself, but when we add the exhausting task of worrying, then it can become too much. I would say right out of the gate that burdens are something meant to be carried; while worries are not, but that might be too simplistic. Examine these two points of reasoning for a moment and see whether they make any sense to you:

- We can have legitimate concerns about things, with the temptation always being there to turn the concerns into worries.
- We can have good burdens and bad burdens in our lives, but when they are unmanaged or out of control, they can produce worries.

So, it's easy to see how there can be simple misconceptions between the definitions of these two words, since they can be situational. It doesn't help that we subconsciously blend them together, which isn't good either.

What if I were to tell you that God can eliminate worry from our lives completely, and at the same time keep burdens both bearable and beneficial to us? We will look more into this shortly, but right now, the best way to make sense of this is by way of scripture, so let's see what God has to say.

Definition of *Worry*

Webster's defines *worry* in the following manner: "[To] give way to anxiety or unease; allow one's mind to dwell on difficulty or troubles." As you examine this, I hope you would agree that worrying can be self-centered, which focuses too much on circumstances and emotions.

We can all surely agree that in the midst of the problems or the storms of life, the first casualties are usually the facts. This happens very quickly when we become overwhelmed with worrying about ourselves, the problem, or a combination of the two.

Remember that our faith is based on the facts from the truth of God's Word, not our feelings:

> *All Scripture is God-breathed and is useful for teaching, rebuking, correcting and training in righteousness, so that the servant of God may be thoroughly equipped for every good work.*
> —2 Tim. 3:16–17 NIV

Notice here that Paul is telling us that when scripture speaks, God speaks, and His Word is intended to perfectly instruct us and guide us. When we listen to Him speak through His Word, we receive all that we need to start and finish all that He has called us to endure or accomplish. This cannot happen when we focus only on ourselves or our feelings.

Notice also that worrying requires an alteration or assumption of fact. In doing so, it takes the situation or problem to a fictional place of torment—remember our definition: Worrying gives way to anxiety. Worry is usually grounded in or accompanied by fear, and fear is definitely not from God: "*For God gave us a spirit not of fear but of power and love and self-control.*" (2 Tim. 1:7).

Simply put, God is not the author of fear, and to accept or allow fear into your life is sin. I know that is very hard for some of you to hear, especially if fear already has a stronghold in you. Let's take a moment to share a few words about our feelings, but please don't be too sensitive:

> *Be angry [at sin—at immorality, at injustice, at ungodly behavior], yet do not sin; do not let your anger [cause you shame, nor allow it to] last until the sun goes down. And do not give the devil an opportunity [to lead you into sin by holding a grudge, or nurturing anger, or harboring resentment, or cultivating bitterness].*
>
> —Eph. 4:26–27 AMP

One of the ways we are created in God's image is that we possess many of His characteristics. Like God, we have feelings, but unlike God, we rarely if ever execute (with consistency) the expression of our feelings in a righteous manner.

Notice here that the Apostle Paul does not say that anger in and of itself is the problem—it's what we do with the anger that creates or becomes the problem! Most of the time, our emotions are expressed out of selfishness, even when emotions are expressed in a positive manner.

Here's an example: Love is a very important ingredient to a healthy heart, but we experience love as well as express it from a selfish perspective. Since love is a choice much more than it is an emotion, in order to express it we must choose to make ourselves vulnerable and lay it out there, and let's admit it—that's pretty risky most of the time.

We can easily love a pet or even child because they are both mostly dependent on us. But in a marriage, a close friendship or even between a believer and God, love is often perceived as a huge risk—I'm almost at my point here.

How many times has the fear of risk run through your mind when you are about to allow yourself to move forward and express love: "What can I get out of this? Well, if I give this, I should get that." The intent to us at the time may seem pure, but really it's not. Rarely will a human being give love knowing in advance that it will not be reciprocated. Our selfish hearts will not allow love or affection to be given away and not returned!

This creates an incredible and unnecessary burden on our hearts, because the conflict created by selfishness can and often does keep us from loving others in the manner Christ loves us—unconditionally.

So, if you honestly examine your heart, you will find the usual course of the expression of feelings comes from a "me first" mentality and left unchallenged, our flesh will see to it that we have it no other way but ours!

Our enemy is aware of this, and he is a professional at knowing just how to tempt us so as to make sure the "me button" gets pushed more times than not. Strongholds of fear that influence our feelings and their expressions do not have to exist in us. Through Christ, the selfish heart can become the serving heart, and an unhealthy love of self can be transformed into love in Christ, which can then be released from us as love for others.

And the awesome thing is, Christ will never withhold any of His perfect truth from us, and if you seek Him through His perfect Word, He will teach you to identify the unhealthy patterns that feed self and expose the lies of the enemy, thereby destroying the false strongholds within you.

And when the strongholds in us are torn down, worry has no place to live in us! So, what are burdens?

Definition of *Burden*

Our friend Webster defines *burden* as "a load, especially a heavy one." "In contrast to worry, which is self-centered, burdens are God-centered and in order to bear them, He requires all our attention to be focused on Him."[2] Yes, God divinely appointed or allows burdens in order that through them we may be drawn nearer to Him by trusting Him.

Charles Stanley says that "the intensity of the burden will be determined by two factors: the magnitude of the situation God wants to deal with, and the immediacy within which He wants to deal with it."[3]

- According to Stanley, "The difference between immediacy and magnitude is this: Magnitude can be the burden for others that we are given in order to love and serve or intercede in prayer, or It can be a great task at hand that God puts on us such as the burden given to Nehemiah to rebuild the walls around Jerusalem."[4]
- And let us never forget the heaviest and most difficult burden of all time—the burden of the sin of the world, which our Savior willingly took upon Himself. When we have a hard time accepting a heavy burden from God, we should train ourselves to quickly remember this.

- The immediacy of a burden may come because we need to change something in our lives, move immediately in the lives of others, or just learn something important really quick.[5]

The length of a burden can be determined by how much we resist it: God may delay His actions no matter how long it takes to gain our full attention. In my own life, I have seen this happen and have no doubt that trials came my way in order to teach me how to properly respond to the burden and then learn to embrace it.

Burdens are **never** bigger than God.
Burdens are not bad.
Burdens train us to endure suffering.
Burdens teach us humility.

When God places a burden on our heart, it is evidence that He is already in the process of moving on our behalf or someone else's. How can we do this?

It starts with learning to live with an expectation from Jesus. This means we expect God to do amazing things in us and through us. That is, we seriously expect God to be all that the Bible says He is; we rest on all His promises, and His Word is the only and absolute truth we believe.

We expect to be victorious in Him, and we are thankful we can overcome through His grace. Pastor Charles Spurgeon had this to say about His grace:

"Whether its work be to pardon, to cleanse, to preserve, to strengthen, to enlighten, to quicken, or to restore, is ever to be had from Him freely and without price; nor is there one form of the work of grace which He has not bestowed upon his people."[6]

Next, we learn to keep our humanity in check and from getting in the way: This means that we fight against the temptation to worry; we reject fear when offered to us and pray constantly for the strength to endure.

If we can have faith enough to live with an **expectation from Jesus**, then we can also learn to live with a **desperation for Jesus**: This means that we develop such a deep hunger to know Him that we do everything we can to learn, grow, and trust in Him in every way possible. Here's the simple secret to living with desperation for Jesus: Immerse yourself in His Word daily. You will always find Him there.

In my journey toward desperation for Jesus, I have often found it very easy to put worries in their place (in God's Hands) and gratefully accept burdens with the excitement of how they will change me!

As I bring these thoughts to a close, I feel I must stress two main points about how we can miss or delay what God is trying to do in our lives through the blessing of burdens. First, and foremost, we let life get in the way. Today's world requires us to be multitaskers, which stretches us in more ways than we can handle and in ways that are definitely not healthy—especially to our spiritual lives.

Consider this simple analogy: A professional athlete spends most of his or her time honing their particular talent, whether it be a quarterback, first baseman, or tennis pro; for many earthly reasons, their talent becomes their obsession and their idol. Since most of their time is spent preparing for the upcoming season or tournament, there will only be some small leftover periods of time. Well, that small amount of time is usually what is given to their families—basically the crumbs. All the money and fame they obtain can never replace the requirement of spiritual fellowship and mentorship that can only be expressed through the love of Christ in the family.

In 1 Corinthians 7:32–35, Paul explains that God understands that we have many things that need to be done (both for the married and the single person), but God requires that we maintain a proper order in our lives, and what He is saying is that Christ must come first: Our devotion to God is what we are supposed to build the rest of our lives around.

Are you the extreme multitasker? Think about it, the more you try to take on in your life, the more you will not only rob God of the time He wants to spend with you, but you will also most certainly create more opportunities for worry and fear to exist in your life as you struggle to handle things your way.

The second way we fail in receiving blessing from God through the blessings of burdens is our selfishness. This cold hard truth is revealed right here:

> *Very rarely will anyone die for a righteous person, though for a good person someone might possibly dare to die. But God demonstrates his own love for us in this: While we were still sinners, Christ died for us.*
>
> —Rom. 5:7–8 NIV

What the Apostle Paul is telling us here is that our human love has limitations. What he clearly explains to us is that as uncommon as this type of sacrifice is, we are neither of these persons—we care too much about ourselves to give up everything for another, even for a good man. Yet Christ so willingly sacrificed Himself for us, and we committed the sins that killed Him.

Yes, our selfish, self-centered, and self-gratifying nature is probably the most common factor in missing communion with God and not enjoying the blessings He so eagerly wants to bestow upon us. My friends, the burdens of life are gifts from Him, and remember this: He carries most of the load for us and helps us to do so for others (Psalm 55:22, Galatians 6:2, Matthew 11:30).

I hope this sheds some light on worries versus burdens, and I hope you take some time to examine your heart and see whether you are drowning in a sea of worries or seeking divine fellowship through the acceptance of His beautiful burdens.

Chapter 41

Scriptures to Combat Fear

Fear does not come from God. Fear is a choice and probably one of the strongest and most preferred weapons of the enemy. When we submit to fear, it can lead us into some very desperate places, and it can also coax us into taking some very drastic actions.

Today, we will examine the difference between a promise versus a sentence and proclamations versus assumptions when it comes to fear. What I want you to realize is that God makes promises and keeps them all, while the devil attempts to pass a sentence, which he knows he has no authority to execute. God makes proclamations, which are all true and always come to pass while the devil tries to scare us with vague assumptions. Below are scriptures to help you fight the good fight daily. I highly recommend that you strive to memorize a few from each category so that you can use them to daily renew your mind.

A Promise versus a Sentence

A promise from the Living God is irrefutable and irreversible; His promises are yes and amen and provide a hope that cannot be taken from us. In direct contrast to God's promises are the lies and accusations of the devil. The enemy will do everything he can to force a false sentence upon you with the intent to cause you to doubt God's great promises and then lead you into self-condemnation.

I brought you from the ends of the earth and called you from its farthest corners. I said to you: You are my servant; I have chosen you; I haven't rejected you. Do not fear, for I am with you; do not be afraid, for I am your God. I will strengthen you; I will help you; I will hold on to you with my righteous right hand.

—Isa. 41:9–10 CSB

Say to the cowardly: "Be strong; do not fear! Here is your God; vengeance is coming. God's retribution is coming; he will save you."

—Isa. 35:4 CSB

Do not be afraid, for you will not be put to shame; don't be humiliated, for you will not be disgraced. For you will forget the shame of your youth, and you will no longer remember the disgrace of your widowhood.

—Isa. 54:4 CSB

Be strong and courageous; don't be terrified or afraid of them. For the LORD *your God is the one who will go with you; he will not leave you or abandon you.*

—Deut. 31:6 CSB

Peace I leave with you. My peace I give to you. I do not give to you as the world gives. Don't let your heart be troubled or fearful.

—John 14:27 CSB

For you did not receive a spirit of slavery to fall back into fear. Instead, you received the Spirit of adoption, by whom we cry out, "Abba, Father!"

—Rom. 8:15 CSB

Keep your life free from the love of money. Be satisfied with what you have, for he himself has said, I will never leave you or abandon you.

—Heb. 13:5 CSB

Humble yourselves, therefore, under the mighty hand of God, so that he may exalt you at the proper time, casting all your cares on him, because he cares about you. Be sober-minded, be alert. Your adversary the devil is prowling around like a roaring lion, looking for anyone he can devour.

—1 Pet. 5:6–8 CSB

Proclamations versus Assumptions

The promises of God are proclaimed and preached throughout scripture. What God has proclaimed is the purest form of truth ever spoken or written down. We can have full confidence in His holy proclamations and expect God to fulfill every one of them in His time. In direct contrast to this, we find lies and assumptions of the enemy. He is a professional at twisting and perverting the proclamations of God with the sole intent of building doubt in our hearts about them.

There is no fear in love; instead, perfect love drives out fear, because fear involves punishment. So the one who fears is not complete in love.

—1 John 4:18 CSB

The LORD is my light and my salvation— whom shall I fear? The LORD is the stronghold of my life— whom should I dread?

—Ps.27:1 CSB

I sought the LORD, and he answered me and rescued me from all my fears.

—Ps.34:4 CSB

When I am afraid, I will trust in you. In God, whose word I praise, in God I trust; I will not be afraid. What can mere mortals do to me?

—Ps. 56:3–4 CSB

When I am filled with cares, your comfort brings me joy.

—Ps. 94:19 CSB

The LORD is for me; I will not be afraid. What can a mere mortal do to me?

—Ps. 18:6 CSB

Therefore, we may boldly say, The LORD is my helper; I will not be afraid. What can man do to me?

—Heb. 13:6 CSB

For God has not given us a spirit of fear, but one of power, love, and sound judgment.

—2 Tim. 1:7 CSB

A Note to the Reader

I saved this last page in the book for a very specific reason.

Most people who don't come to Christ stay away because they are mad at God for something, or the way He is portrayed by other believers pushes them away.

What I have shared with you below is something I wrote when I was asked to speak at an event for victims of violent crimes.

I believe that if anyone has a right to be mad at God or see Him as distant or unappealing, it would be these folks. But I have seen God comfort even the most broken and beat-up hearts.

Here's what I said:

> *As a pastor I have often found myself given to thought as to why bad things happen in this world.*
>
> *What I have seen on display at least in my life is the existence of a strange duality: life can be both complex and at the same time relatively simple.*
>
> *And I believe it's in this duality where evil and chaos can and do find opportunity to spill over into our lives.*
>
> *I believe that our trying to figure this out comes from wanting to be able to understand the nature of human beings better and also to try to gather some hope and clarity into our own hearts.*
>
> *So, as a man who has deep faith in God and truly believes in His sovereignty, I have often asked myself this very question: Why do bad things happen?*
>
> *Where is God in the midst of tragedy?*
>
> *Is this a mystery we just can't know right now?*

As I do for all things when I want answers, I look to the Bible for truth.

In the Gospel of John, chapter 9, Jesus is approached by His disciples, and they are once again needing an answer to a very important question:

They have encountered a man who had been born blind.

Now, the theology of the day said that the reason he was born blind was due to the sins of his parents or his own sin.

But Jesus replied, "It was neither that this man sinned, nor His parents; but it was in order that the works of God might be displayed in him" (John 9:3).

What Jesus said was this: This man's blindness had a purpose!

The Apostle Paul wrote in his second letter to the Corinthian church about his own personal infirmity: He had what he called, a "thorn in his flesh."

Paul said it had been given to him to keep him from exalting himself.

And even though Paul had asked God three times to remove it, God said, no.

So, wait a minute here: God allowed this man to be born blind so that God's power in his healing could be revealed, and God used suffering in order to keep the Apostle Paul humble?

Yes.

Can it be that God uses suffering?

My friends, I am 100 percent convinced that God is not the author of suffering.

Let me say very clearly that God never intended for us to experience the suffering and adversity that has resulted from man's fallen condition.

But I have been able to understand through instruction from scripture, that bad things happen for at least three reasons:

- *Bad things happen when we make bad choices.*
- *Bad things happen because we live in a fallen and sinful world.*
- *God allows bad things to happen for His glory to be revealed.*

"But Pastor Mike, that doesn't help me!"

There are times when we may say to ourselves: Where is the hope? Why does it always seem to be so far away?

Or for some even, the hope is there, but always just a bit out of reach.

We might even reason, if I can't reach the hope, then how far away is love?

Well, I'm here to tell you that hope has come near.

And I am here to tell you that love is within your reach.

They both are near, because the cross is near!

Because God sent His Son to suffer, so we would know He understands what suffering is like.

But it's not just the cross that we need to reach out to—it's whose hands that bore the nails that pierced Him to that cross!

Those hands which were attached to those arms that were stretched out as far as they could go.

Stretched as far as they could go for you and me!

And those arms were attached to a body which had the sins of all mankind written in every language all over it.

Each one carefully carved on purpose for a purpose.

And it was in the blood that poured out of every one of those wounds that God had shouted, "I love you with an everlasting love."

My friends, because hope was there at that cross, flowing out in blood with the everlasting love of God for us, ALL who believe in Him can have that hope in right here in us!

The Bible says that love covers a multitude of sins.

And it's His incredible love that plows right through that strange duality that I spoke of a few minutes ago.

A love that transcends the complicated and the simple and has ultimately defeated the evil and the chaos.

You might be saying right now, "Where is it, Pastor Mike? Where is it? I can't feel it; I'm still hurting so bad."

I have to give you the same answer I had to give to myself: Let it in!

Stop allowing your pain to be greater than His mighty love!
Hope is right here.
Love is right here.
Let Him in.

So, what about you? We went through this entire book together. Are you ready now to make some decisions about your eternity?

My friend, there is no magic formula or special set of ceremonial words that need to be said. You don't have to walk the aisle of the church or be in any other particular type of building or place.

The Apostle Paul told us what the Lord wants to hear us say in Romans 10:9–13:

> *If you confess with your mouth, "Jesus is Lord," and believe in your heart that God raised Him from the dead, you will be saved. One believes with the heart, resulting in righteousness, and one confesses with the mouth, resulting in salvation. For the Scripture says, Everyone who believes on Him will not be put to shame, since there is no distinction between Jew and Greek, because the same Lord of all richly blesses all who call on Him. For everyone who calls on the name of the Lord will be saved.*

I urge you to confess with your mouth and believe in your heart today; for it is promised that if you call on Him, you will be saved.

May God richly bless you.

Love in Christ,
Pastor Mike Govan

About the Author

Born in sunny Anaheim, California, Mike spent the first 18 years of his life growing up in Michigan. Mike then proudly served 13 years in the US army as a combat medic; he is a veteran of the first Gulf War, Operation Desert Shield/Storm. It was in the army that he would meet and marry the love of his life, Linda. Mike and Linda are blessed with two children and one granddaughter.

Life took a drastic turn for him when he moved his family to South Texas in 2001. Thereafter, God confirmed Mike's calling into ministry, and a whole new and exciting chapter opened in his life: first as a counseling pastor and later as a church planter. Mike currently serves as the Campus Pastor of BT Church in Edinburg, Texas, and also continues his much-loved counseling ministry.

This book comes from the life experience of a man in search of a relationship with his Creator. Through the ups and downs of this short journey we call life, Mike shows how a person can discover the Living God, grow through fear and failure, and learn to live fully in the joy of the Lord no matter what may come.

Notes

Chapter 5

1. Adolph Hitler, *Mein Kampf,* published 1922.

Chapter 9

1. John MacArthur, "Did Jesus Need Perfecting?" gty.org, 2020, https://www.gty.org/library/bibleqnas-library/QA0306/did-jesus-need-perfecting.

Chapter 10

1. Donald S. Whitney, *Ten Questions to Diagnose Your Spiritual Health* (Colorado Springs, CO: NavPress, 2001).
2. Whitney, 16–22.
3. Whitney, 29.
4. Whitney, 55.
5. Whitney, 69.
6. Whitney, 101.
7. Whitney, 111.
8. Whitney, 121.

Chapter 12

1. Benjamin Franklin, "Work as if you were to live a hundred years," https://www.pinterest.com/pin/1838873597259750995/.

Chapter 15

1. Jeffery E. Miller, *Hazards of Being a Man* (Grand Rapids, MI: Baker Books, 2007).

Chapter 18

1. Greg Ogden, *Disciple Essentials* (Downers Grove, IL: InterVarsity Press, 2007).
2. Ogden, 35–37.
3. Ogden, 35.
4. Ogden, 35.
5. Ogden, 35.
6. Ogden, 57–60.

Chapter 23

1. C. H. Surgeon, "February 23rd Morning Reading," *Morning and Evening,* https://www.blueletterbible.org/devotionals/me/view.cfm?Date=02/23&Time=both&body=1.
2. Spurgeon, *February 23rd Morning Reading.*
3. Spurgeon, *February 23rd Morning Reading.*

Chapter 27

1. "Is Porn Harmful? The Evidence, the Myths and the Unknowns," September 26, 2017, *BBC Future,* https://www.bbc.com.
2. "The Ted Bundy Dilemma: Should You Be Scared of Pornography Addiction?" www.advancedpsychologyartners.com.
3. Greg Ogden, *Discipleship Essentials* (Downers Grove, IL: Intervarsity Press, 2019), 200.

Chapter 30

1. Oswald Chambers, *My Utmost for His Highest* (Grand Rapids, MI: Discovery House Publishers, 1992), December 27 Reading.

Chapter 32

1. John Calvin, *Calvin: Commentaries on the Bible, Matthew 9,* Studylight.org.
2. Wikipedia, s.v. "Goldman's dilemma," last edited on April 28, 2021, 01:50, https://en.wikipedia.org › wiki › Goldman's_dilemma.
3. "Whatever Happened to the 12 Apostles? How Did They Die?" https://www.christianity.com/church/church-history/timeline/1-300/whatever-happened-to-the-twelve-apostles-11629558.html.

Chapter 33

1. Sun Tzu, *The Art of War* (New York: Barnes and Noble Classics, 2003) 46.

Chapter 34

1. "Does Premarital Cohabitation Raise Your Risk of Divorce," *Council of Contemporary Families Report,* https://contemporaryfamilies. org/cohabitation-divorce-brief-report/.
2. *"The Majority of Children Live With Two Parents, Census Reports,"* *CISION PR Newswire,* November 17, 2016, https://www.prnewswire. com/news-releases/the-majority-of-children-live-with-two-parents-census-bureau-reports-300365509.html.

Chapter 37

1. "Sexually Transmitted Disease Surveillance 2016," https://www. cdc.gov/std/stats16/CDC_2016_STDS_Report-for508WebSep21_ 2017_1644.pdf.

Chapter 39

1. Goldberg Jones, "Fascinating Remarriage Statistics," 2017, Fascinating Remarriage Statistics | Goldberg Jones, https://www.goldbergjones-sandiego.com › Blog.
2. "Divorce Statistics: Over 115 Studies, Facts and Rates for 2020," *Wilkinson and Finkbeiner, Family Attorneys.* 2020, https://www.wf-lawyers.com › divorce-statistics-and-facts.
3. "Facebook and Divorce – Proceed with Caution," *WomansDivorce. com,* Social Media, Facebook and Divorce - WomansDivorce.com, https://www.womansdivorce.com › Divorce Basics.
4. "Divorce Statistics: Over 115 Studies, Facts and Rates for 2020," *Wilkinson and Finkbeiner, Family Attorneys.*
5. Rossana Condoleo, "Rossana Condoleo Quotes," https://www. goodreads.com/author/quotes/6964634.Rossana_Condoleo.
6. Jennifer Weiner, "Divorce Isn't Such a Tragedy," https://www. goodreads.com/quotes/283223-divorce-isn-t-such-a-tragedy-a-tragedy-s-staying-in-.

7. Robin Williams, "Hollywood funnyman on why he's gone down the aisle for the third time," *The Telegraph*, November 28, 2011, https://www.telegraph.co.uk/culture/film/starsandstories/8915998/Robin-Williams-Divorce-is-like-ripping-a-mans-genitals-out-through-his-wallet.html.

8. Jay Leno, "Jay Leno Quotes on Divorce," *AZ Quotes,* https://www.azquotes.com/author/8722-Jay_Leno/tag/divorce.

9. *If Marriage Means You Fell in Love, Does Divorce Mean to Climb Out?* Published by Funny Divorce Party Publishing, 2019.

Chapter 40

1. Charles Stanley, *Handle with Prayer: Unwrap the Source of God's Strength for Living* (Colorado Springs, CO: David C. Cook, 2011).

2. Stanley, 46–47.

3. Stanley, 46–47.

4. Stanley, 46–47.

5. Stanley, 46–47.

6. C. H. Spurgeon, *Morning by Morning* (New York: Sheldon and Company, 1866), 75.